Tulsa Sounds 2024 Edition

Contributions to American Music

Elven Lindblad

Visit the website www.booksabouttulsa.com

Follow Books About Tulsa on Facebook or on X (formerly Twitter) @BooksAboutTulsa as well as on Instagram and Threads. Contact the author/publisher by email at booksabouttulsa@gmail.com.

Book Cover and Design by Cal Sharp of Caligraphics, Inc. (www.caligraphics.net)

Cover artwork by Marek Kulhavy

First edition 2024

This book is dedicated to...

My father, Elven "Swede" Lindblad, and my mother, Ada Lindblad.
Despite often limited resources, they provided my younger brother,
Ed Lindblad, and I with a love and appreciation for the performing
arts in the city of Tulsa.
Most of all, this book is dedicated to the past, present and future
residents of the metropolitan Tulsa area who have a passion for the
performing arts along with the joys found in music and life.

Acknowledgements

This book would not have been possible without contributions from many people, so a heartfelt thank you goes to...

John Wooley, a renowned Oklahoma historian and author, a member of the Oklahoma Music and Jazz Halls of Fame and long-time writer for the *Tulsa World*. John provided invaluable contributions related to Tulsa's musical heritage in the genres of rock, blues, country and Western Swing.

Cal Sharp, the Creative Director of Caligraphics Design in Daykin, Nebraska who has designed covers for all of my electronic and print books for nearly a decade. More of Cal's amazing work can be found at www.caligraphics.net.

The staff at Draft2Digital publishing based in metro Tulsa and metro Oklahoma City. They have empowered self-publishing authors for over a decade and more information is available at www.draft2digital.com.

Debbie Brown of Jenks, Oklahoma for volunteering to provide editorial assistance for the Tulsa Sound chapter of this book.

Tulsa World pop culture writer Jimmie Trammel along with the late John Montgomery and the late Shannon Phillips, each of whom have provided unique inspirations for this book.

My wife, Denise Townsend Lindblad, for her encouragement and support throughout this project.

Contents

Introduction

In its own unique way, Tulsa, Oklahoma proudly stands shoulder to shoulder alongside some of America's largest cities when it comes to a broad influence on multiple genres of music.

This book not only documents the depth and breadth of those influences but, most importantly, celebrates their contributions to the mosaic that is American music.

Stories about the musical genius of Leon Russell and his influence on the rock and roll version of the Tulsa Sound are well known. Likewise for Bob Wills and how Tulsa became the place where Western Swing music grew up. Many other individuals and significant events are covered in this book. Such as how...

A guitar-picking graduate of Tulsa's Central High School became a musical mentor for international guitar hero Eric Clapton.

A young man wailing on a saxophone became part of Tulsa's music scene prior to becoming a seminal member of the musical entourage of the Rolling Stones.

A young member of the United States Navy rode a tidal wave of social media popularity to become one of the brightest stars in the modern galaxy of country music.

A chance encounter outside of a downtown Tulsa hotel became a turning point in the evolution of Bill Basie into jazz legend Count Basie.

The Sapulpa-based cousin of an iconic folk singer tweaked one of the former's songs and made it a top-selling country music hit of his own...and how that song led to a conflict between the two cousins.

Three brothers from Booker T. Washington High School became international stars with their infections and danceable blend of funk music.

The Will Rogers High School alumnus known back then as Hank would use a different first name and become one of the world's most talented performers of flamenco music.

The Oral Roberts University graduate who became a highly sought producer for superstars such as Maroon 5, Carrie Underwood and Beyonce while being the lead singer of his own band.

The spirited and diminutive cheerleader from Broken Arrow High School that used her soaring soprano voice to become a Broadway star.

The trio of brothers that went from singing on a Tulsa radio station to being the backup band for the first recording session by country music icon Hank Williams.

One of the biggest stars of contemporary Christian music chose to make Tulsa his home instead of seeking the bright lights in bigger cities.

The youngest boy in a family of 13 children near Owasso was part of Buddy Holly's rise to fame and how a coin flip kept that young man from dying alongside Holly in the plane crash that changed rock and roll history.

The legendary rhythm and blues singer that took time after performing at a nightclub in predominantly black north Tulsa to visit a teenage white girl who later changed the face of rock and roll.

So as the legendary Tulsa disc jockey Johnny Martin would say on his big-band themed weeknight radio program, "Those are the words...here is the music."

Chapter One

The Tulsa Sound

"*Leon (Russell) had always been my hero. I absolutely loved his piano playing; it was so distinctive.*"

Elton John

"*In my humble opinion, (JJ Cale) is one of the most important people artists in the history of rock, quietly representing the greatest asset his country has ever had, and a lot of people in Europe have never even heard of him.*"

Eric Clapton

"*All you have to do to hear the Tulsa guys' influence on Eric Clapton is listen to his records just before the time he came to Tulsa, put together his Tulsa band and directly after on his 461 Ocean Boulevard album from 1974.*"

John Wooley

"*(Leon Russell) was Modern Americana personified, carrying a deep understanding of rock, blues, gospel, country, bluegrass, R&B, soul, funk, the Great American Songbook...Genius is not a word that should be thrown around lightly but anyone who knew Leon or worked with him described him as such.*"

Jesse Lauter

***

John Wooley is the award-winning author of the book *From the Blue Devils to Red Dirt: The Colors of Oklahoma Music* and served for more than two decades as the music and pop culture beat writer for Tulsa *World*. Wooley is also a member of the Oklahoma Music Hall of Fame.

Wooley said that the origins of the Tulsa Sound could be traced to the 1950s when Oklahoma had a law for bars and night clubs known as "liquor by the wink." Back then, the only alcoholic beverage to legally be found in any Tulsa night club was beer that contained an alcohol concentration of only 3.2 per cent.

Many club owners found unique ways to circumvent that require-ment. Other club owners chose to rely on favorable connections with members of Tulsa's police department or members of the county sheriff's office.

More than one musician linked to the Tulsa Sound has said in so many words that they were just a bunch of guys trying to play the blues while performing in those nightclubs.

"It helps to explain the certain deep-groove, repetitive R&B-based style that many call the Tulsa Sound," Wooley said. "To paraphrase Leon Russell, since they were breaking the law anyway, they pretty much did what they wanted to and sometimes these places would be open with live music throughout much of the night and well into the morning,"

"That laid back sound, to me, reflects guys stretching songs out as much as they can to cover the hours and hours that they have to play.

"It's that whole thing about space between notes, which is often cited as one of the characteristics of the sound."

"And I think it specifically refers to the guys who made the migration to Southern California in the early 1960s—Leon Russell, David Gates, J.J. Cale, Jim Karstein, Chuck Blackwell, Tom Tripplehorn, Dave Teegarden and many more–who stayed out there with one another, helped each other get gigs and ended up making a big mark on the American rock and roll scene as studio cats, band members and, occasionally, headliners."

Tulsa Sound musicians also had a profound influence on the career path of rock and roll legend Eric Clapton. On more than one occasion, Clapton has said that two musicians had the most profound influence on his musical career. One was the Mississippi Delta blues legend Robert Johnson. The other was Tulsa Sound legend J.J. Cale.

"All you have to do to hear the Tulsa guys' influence on him is listen to his records just before the time he came to Tulsa, put together his Tulsa band and directly after on his *461 Ocean Boulevard* album from 1974," Wooley said of Clapton.

"His band then was pretty much all Tulsans: Jamie Oldaker on drums, Carl Radle on bass and Dick Sims on keyboard. And, of course, he heard J.J. Cale's 'After Midnight' on the radio and recorded it.

"I'm also told he listened a lot to the album from the Tulsa band Rockin' Jimmy Byfield and the Brothers of the Night and in particular, guitarist Steve Hickerson. He covered their tune "Little Rachel" on his 1975 album *There's One in Every Crowd*."

But is there more to the Tulsa Sound than just a type of music?

"I've spent a lot of my life trying to pin down the Tulsa Sound and sometimes I don't think I'm any closer to it than when I started,"

Wooley responded. "Some of the linchpins of the sound, including Karstein, don't think there's really one at all.

"More and more, I'm thinking that the Tulsa Sound refers as much to a brotherhood of musicians as it does to a particular music style."

***

Leon Russell

If there was such a title of godfather, missionary or pied piper for the Tulsa Sound, it was Leon Russell.

In a career that spanned over 50 years, Russell performed on or participated in the arrangement, production or writing of some of the best-selling records in contemporary music. The crowning moment came in 2011 with his induction into the Rock and Roll Hall of Fame and the Songwriters Hall of Fame.

Born as Claude Russell Bridges, he played piano at the age of four. That was remarkable considering Russell once said that his second and third vertebrae were damaged by a physician during his birth. The result was spastic paralysis; an affliction that would impair his balance, movement and posture.

Russell said it also forced him to change his piano playing style into something with more involvement by his left hand in order to compensate for the problems with his right hand.

While attending Tulsa's Will Rogers High School, he performed at local nightclubs with club owners winking at the fact that he was too young to legally be there. His band back then, the Starlighters, spent two months as the opening act for rock and roll legend Jerry Lee Lewis.

Russell moved from Tulsa to Los Angeles and quickly established himself in that local nightclub scene. Subsequently, he became part of a group of studio musicians known locally as The Wrecking Crew that performed on many of the popular songs of the 1960s.

Wrecking Crew members performed with famous singers and groups such as Frank Sinatra, The Beach Boys, The Mamas and Papas, The Ronettes, Doris Day, Sam Cooke, Elvis Presley, Nancy Sinatra, Sonny and Cher, The Righteous Brothers, Darlene Love, Simon and Garfunkel, Ike and Tina Turner, The Monkees, Jan and Dean, The Carpenters, Johnny Rivers, The Byrds, Ricky Nelson, Gary Lewis and the Playboys and Herb Alpert and The Tijuana Brass.

While the Wrecking Crew members never got proper credit on the final albums by those performers and were never paid the life-changing royalties from the sales of those singles and albums due to deceptive practices by record label managers, Russell and the other musicians took great pride in their work.

In 1964, Russell was the piano player for the house band on *Shindig!* the ABC Television musical variety show that featured live performances by big-name singing acts.

Russell's other early works included playing piano on the Beach Boys' classic "California Girls," the Halloween novelty hit by Bobby (Boris) Pickett, "Monster Mash" and on Glen Campbell's country album *Gentle on My Mind*. He also participated in writing two hits for Gary Lewis and the Playboys, "Everybody Loves a Clown" and "This Diamond Ring."

Among other songs written by Russell that became hits for other artists are "A Song for You" by Ray Charles, "Superstar" by the Carpenters and "Hummingbird" by B.B. King.

George Benson's rendition of Russell's "This Masquerade" was the first song to reach number one on the R&B, jazz and pop music charts.

Russell's song "Delta Lady" was a 1969 hit for English rocker Joe Cocker and that led to participation in Cocker's Mad Dogs and Englishmen Tour. His piano accompaniment is heard on Cocker's live hits "Cry Me a River," "Feelin' Alright" and "The Letter."

The 1970s would not only see the launching of Russell's solo career but a trip to the highest levels of rock and roll stardom. His self-titled debut album in 1970 not only led off with what would be one of his signature songs, "A Song for You," but the roster of supporting singers and musicians read like a Dream Team of Rock and Roll.

Vocalists were Bonnie Bramlett and Joe Cocker. George Harrison and Ringo Starr from the Beatles contributed as well. Representing the Rolling Stones were Mick Jagger, Charlie Watts and Bill Wyman with Keith Richards co-writing a song. Steve Winwood (Spencer Davis Group, Traffic and Blind Faith) played keyboards. Eric Clapton rounded out the roster with alternating blistering and bluesy guitar playing.

Russell's second album, *Leon Russell and the Shelter People*, was released in 1971 and became a gold record with sales of more than 500,000 copies. His follow-up album, *Carney*, topped those numbers and the novelty song "Slipping into Christmas" was the fourth-highest selling Christmas song of 1972.

In 1971 former Beatle George Harrison and musician Ravi Shankar organized a concert at New York City's Madison Square Garden to provide financial assistance for refugees from the wartime atrocities in Bangladesh (formerly East Pakistan).

Russell was joined by Bob Dylan, Ringo Starr, Eric Clapton and other musicians in forming an all-star band. That event turned into a live album and documentary, *George Harrison and Friends: The Concert for Bangladesh*.

One of the concert's highlights was Russell's rousing nine-minutes-plus medley of The Rolling Stones' "Jumpin' Jack Flash" and The Coasters' "Youngblood."

Many elements of the Tulsa Sound were showcased in Russell's performance, and it was further demonstrated in his subsequent performances with Dylan and Harrison.

"Tight Rope" became Russell's biggest selling single, peaking at number 11 in the 1972 Billboard rock charts. Among his other hits during the 1970s were "Roll Away the Stone," "A Hard Rain's a-Gonna Fall," "Lady Blue," "Good Time Charlie's Got the Blues" and "Back to the Island."

During that time, Russell moved back to Tulsa and partnered with internationally respected music producer Denny Cordell to convert a former church just east of downtown Tulsa into a top-flight recording facility. What was once the First Evangelical United Brethren Church at the southwest corner of East Third Street and South Trenton Avenue became The Church Studio. They also relocated Shelter Records from Los Angeles to Tulsa.

Russell moved into a mansion at the intersection of East 24th Street and Woodward Boulevard in the historic Maple Ridge addition of midtown Tulsa. He also owned a small home at Grand Lake, one of Oklahoma's largest lakes and located about an hour's drive northeast of Tulsa.

While Russell was known for building an eight-foot wall around that Tulsa mansion and occasionally riding around town in one of his two Rolls Royce limousines, he also opened his home for local residents to organize protests against a proposed expressway coming through their neighborhood. Those protests were successful, and that highway was built elsewhere.

Between 1972 and 1976, international superstars such as George Harrison, Bob Dylan, Freddie King, Phoebe Snow and Eric Clapton came to Tulsa to visit Russell at The Church Studio.

A rock band from Gainesville, Florida named Mudcrutch featured a lead singer named Tom Petty and their first recording contract was signed at a restaurant across the street from Church Studio. That band would become the forerunner of Tom Petty and the Heartbreakers.

Russell and Cordell eventually parted ways with Cordell keeping Shelter Records and Russell going back to California and creating Paradise Records.

Russell switched gears later in the 1970s with a focus on country music. A duet album with Willie Nelson, *One for the Road*, reached number three on the *Billboard* country album charts in 1979 and their version of the Elvis Presley classic "Heartbreak Hotel" reached the top spot on the country singles chart. Russell also released a couple of country albums under the pseudonym Hank Wilson.

Nelson has frequently told a story about Russell being the first musician to autograph his Martin N-20 classical guitar, albeit in a unique manner. Nelson signed Russell's guitar with an ink marker then Russell asked Nelson if it would be okay to use something else to scratch his name into the guitar, saying it would make Nelson's guitar more valuable.

In subsequent years, countless other musicians and celebrities followed Russell's precedent and scratched their names into Nelson's guitar; a practice that music historians have claimed further enhanced the unique sound of Nelson's guitar.

After battling pneumonia, heart-related problems and a leaking of brain fluid during 2010, Russell was brought back into the musical spotlight by Rock and Roll Hall of Famer and long-time fan Elton John. Their collaboration album, *The Union*, peaked at number three on the 2010 *Billboard* album charts.

Prior to passing away on November 13, 2016 shortly after undergoing heart surgery, Russell released newer music on his own label, Leon Russell Records.

Three of his children, son Teddy Jack Bridges and daughters Sugaree Bridges and Tina Rose Bridges have their own musical careers and occasionally toured with Russell. Tina Rose was among 18 female singers invited by Willie Nelson to sing on his 2013 duets album *To All the Girls*.

Leon Russell was posthumously inducted into the Oklahoma Hall of Fame in 2022. Teresa Knox, owner of The Church Studio in Tulsa, was present for the award. None of Russell's six children attended the event.

J.J. Cale

John Wesley Cale's music never fit into a single genre but has drawn a following from many musicians down through the years. As previously stated, Eric Clapton counts Cale as one of the two musicians with the greatest influence in his career. Another current singer-songwriter, John Mayer, is also a major fan of his work.

It could also be said that Cale thought that being under the radar or out of the spotlight was his preferred way of life.

Cale drew upon influences from folk, rock, country and blues while honing his craft in Tulsa night clubs. His style could best be described as minimalist with an emphasis on spacing between notes and being sung just above a whisper.

He said in the past that guitarists Les Paul, Chuck Berry and Chet Atkins were among his earliest influences. "But in trying to imitate them, I missed it and came up with my own kinda thing."

Cale's biggest individual single "Crazy Mama" reached number 22 on the *Billboard* rock charts in 1972. Other artists had big hits with Cale's songs. These include Poco in 1973 with "Magnolia," Lynard Skynyrd in 1974 with "They Call Me the Breeze" and Waylon Jennings in 1980 with "Clyde.".

His songs would also be recorded by such diverse artists as Johnny Cash, Kansas, Widespread Panic, Deep Purple, The Allman Brothers Band, Santana, Bryan Ferry and Captain Beefheart.

Cale grew up in Tulsa and was a 1956 graduate of Central High School. He was part of the large group of Tulsa musicians who followed Leon Russell to Los Angeles in the 1960s. Back then, Cale would often be his own session player, engineer and producer.

While in Los Angeles, a nightclub owner persuaded him to change his name from John or Johnny Cale to J.J. Cale to avoid being confused with John Cale from the rock group Velvet Underground. Success in Los Angeles was elusive so Cale returned to Tulsa and seriously considered quitting music.

That is, until 1970 when Clapton released his version of Cale's 1966 song "After Midnight." It became a top 20 hit for Clapton, Cale's career was revived, and success and appreciation of his works soon followed.

It increased in 1977 when Clapton's version of Cale's anti-drug song "Cocaine" became an international hit and appeared on one of Clapton's most popular albums, *Slowhand*.

Cale only recorded 15 albums in a 40-year career prior to his death from heart failure in July 2013 at the age of 74. His collaboration with Clapton on *The Road to Escondido* won a Grammy Award in 2008 for Best Contemporary Blues Album. Cale's widow, Christine Lakeland Cale, teamed with Cale's manager Mike Kappus in 2019 to release a

CD with 15 tracks of previously unreleased songs Cale recorded in his California home.

Wooley has said on several occasions that the Tulsa Sound influence on Clapton is still profound, as evidenced by Clapton's 2014 tribute CD *Eric Clapton & Friends: The Breeze (An Appreciation of JJ Cale).* Clapton took five Tulsa-based musicians to California for the recording sessions: Don White on guitar and vocals, Walt Richmond on keyboards, Jimmy "Junior" Markham on harmonica and drummers Dave Teegarden and Jim Karstein.

Clapton expressed his professional and personal admiration for Cale in his 2007 self-titled autobiography. He described Cale as enjoying his own company yet having a sharp sense of humor and very sociable. This description sharply contrasts with long-held opinions from others that Cale was a recluse.

Clapton went on to say that in his opinion, J.J. Cale was one of rock music's most important artists ever but a lot of people that he would meet in Europe would say they'd never heard of the Tulsa native.

Other prominent guest artists on the J.J. Cale tribute CD were Tom Petty, Willie Nelson, Mark Knopfler, John Mayer and Cale's widow, Christine Lakeland.

Ann Bell

If Leon Russell was the king of the Tulsa Sound, then the powerful and soulful singing of Ann Bell crowned her as the Tulsa Sound's queen.

Her global musical journey was capped by a 2021 induction into the Oklahoma Music Hall of Fame and returning home to mentor aspiring local musicians.

As a 16-year-old student at Edison High School, Ann Bishop burst onto Tulsa's music scene as the lead singer of a local band named Rubbery Cargoe. Her powerhouse vocals, much in the manner of a younger Grace Slick or Janis Joplin or Patti LaBelle, caught the ears and eyes of local club goers.

Among the captive fans was Larry Bell, then the keyboardist for the Sunday Servants band. The two soon became music partners in Larry's band and soon afterwards, husband and wife.

Then one day in 1968, Larry brought home one album by Aretha Franklin and one by Tina Turner. He told Ann to choose six songs from each album and learn them. She said that was when she chose R&B music to elevate her to the next level.

"Those girls were the ones that were really moving me," she said in a 2022 interview for *Oklahoma Magazine*. "That pain of heartbreak. That's what drew me in."

Leon Russell stayed with the Bells while his home was remodeled, and Ann was pregnant with twin girls. He also bought the Bells a new Cadillac because he knew they would need a better car and went to the hospital when Ann went into labor.

In Ann's opinion, Russell provided personal validation for her music style and urged her to not be so concerned about what others might say or think.

"That's when I started getting my boldness," she added. "That's when I said, OK, that's what I'm going to do."

Ann later toured for four years with Russell's musical entourage followed by five years with Joe Cocker's Mad Dogs and Englishmen Tour.

After leaving Cocker's group, she was based out of Woodstock, New York and worked with rock singers such as Robbie Dupree, Richie Havens and Todd Rundgren plus the pop group Orleans.

Bell walked away from rock and roll in 1998 and spent the next 15 years focusing on black-flavored gospel and contemporary Christian genres. She and husband Tom Nicholson, a keyboardist and music producer in his own right, became ordained gospel ministers.

That connection isn't surprising because prior to the Bishop family moving into the wealthier Edison district, they lived in a neighborhood northwest of downtown Tulsa. There was a predominantly black church located close to their home and when that family opened their windows and doors during the summertime, the power and joy from that type of music captivated Ann.

Bell has become an ambassador for the Tulsa Sound and doesn't hesitate to sing the praises of the movement's founding fathers, as evidenced in a 2021 interview with the *Greater Tulsa Reporter* newspaper.

"They didn't crave the spotlight," she added. "They didn't crave it for their own self gain. What they craved was the music...They didn't get intoxicated with their own celebrity. They actually had their priorities right."

"When Eric Clapton came to Tulsa, it was to hire players because they were the greatest players in the world. When Ringo (Starr), when Elton (John) when Peter Frampton, when any artist came to Tulsa, they wanted the Tulsa players because the Tulsa players played the blues better than anybody."

Chuck Blackwell

A graduate of Tulsa's Central High School, Chuck "Brother" Blackwell was a drummer for The Everly Brothers and legendary bluesman Taj Mahal. He also performed with Joe Cocker, Jerry Lee Lewis and Little Richard.

Blackwell was also part of the Tulsa musician migration to Los Angeles led by Leon Russell in the late 1950s. He began playing in local night clubs at the age of 13, always carrying a note signed by his mother and father that told the club owners that Chuck had their permission to perform there.

He has said in numerous interviews that Bill Doggett's 1956 instrumental hit "Honky Tonk" was the inspiration for the shuffle rhythm that became his signature drumming technique and was also a foundation of the Tulsa Sound.

Blackwell became a highly sought session musician. He became the drummer on the ABC-TV musical variety show *Shindig!* with Russell being the piano player for the Shindogs.

Other musical legends in the Shindogs included Rock and Roll Hall of Fame guitar player James Burton (Ricky Nelson and Elvis Presley), keyboardist Billy Preston (The Beatles) and singer Delaney Bramlett (Bonnie and Delaney and Friends).

Later in life, Blackwell wanted out of rock and roll's fast lifestyle and returned to the Tulsa area and played in some local night spots. He got a job as an errand boy at a business that made stained glass windows and within a year, moved up the corporate ladder to own that same business. Then he contacted a high school sweetheart, they got married and she became co-owner of that business.

Blackwell passed away in 2017 at the age of 77.

Jack Dunham

Known back then as "Jumpin' Jackie" Dunham for his on-stage antics, Dunham was greatly influenced by Little Richard and formed two bands as a youth. The first one featured J.J. Cale as a guitar player and Leon Russell was the piano player in the second one.

Dunham and his family moved to Tulsa when he was one year old, and he later attended Tulsa's Central High School and the University of Tulsa. He and Russell were among the first of those aforementioned Tulsa musicians migrating to Los Angeles in search of musical fame and fortune.

Dunham later joined Fats Domino on the Imperial Records roster, released a couple of records and began a national concert tour. He also wrote several songs for Conway Twitty's country-pop albums, highlighted by the 1979 number one song "Your Love Had Taken Me That High."

Scott Ellison

While he never had a breakout single, this veteran guitarist has been a highly sought musician by national and international record acts for nearly 40 years.

Like many other American youth, Ellison was spellbound watching The Beatles and other British Invasion bands during their frequent appearances on Ed Sullivan's TV show and he quickly learned how to play the guitar. Then blues legend Clarence "Gatemouth" Brown, a friend of Tulsa country musician Roy Clark, chose Ellison to join his touring band.

He later moved to Los Angeles and was either a backup musician or opening act for performers like B.B. King, Leon Russell, The Shirelles, Buddy Guy, Roy Orbison, The Box Tops and Joe Cocker.

His songs would later appear in the cult TV show *Buffy The Vampire Slayer* along with *Sister, Sister* and *Santa Barbara, Reindeer Games* and *Joan of Arcadia*.

Ellison later returned to Tulsa and was inducted into the Oklahoma Music Hall of Fame in 2013 but is still actively touring on the national and international levels.

Richard Feldman

This Grammy winning songwriter and producer worked at Leon Russell's Church Studio in Tulsa before moving to Los Angeles with Leon to launch Shelter Records.

Feldman teamed with Roger Linn in 1978 to write "Promises" for Eric Clapton; a song described by some as having a swaying beat with elements of the original Tulsa Sound.

Ironically, the gentle backing vocals on that song came from another Tulsa Sound vocalist, Marcy Levy.

As a music producer, composer and arranger, Feldman expanded his musical horizons to include jazz, country and rhythm and blues. He won a Grammy Award in 2004 for his production of the 2004 jazz album True Love by Toots & The Maytals.

Some of the big-name artists who utilized Feldman's production skills are Pat Benatar, Al Jarreau, Tom Jones, Willie Nelson, The Pointer Sisters, Ringo Starr, The Commodores, Etta James and Hank Williams Jr.

Feldman served as president of the Association of Independent Music Publishers (AIMP) from 2009 through 2012 and was active in the fight to prevent music piracy.

Rocky Frisco

The Tulsa Central High School graduate was the long-time pianist-keyboardist for J.J. Cale and was one of many musicians credited as having influenced the evolution of the Tulsa Sound. His keyboard wizardry was long admired by Eric Clapton, who asked him to appear on stage at the 2004 Crossroads Guitar Festival in Dallas, Texas.

Born as Don Roscoe Joseph Frisco III in St. Louis, Missouri, he was playing the ukulele and accordion at the age of eight. At 15, he played mellophone in the Central High School band. Frisco got a record contract with Mercury Records in 1958 and recorded under the pseudonym Rocky Curtiss. While working for a radio station, he took part in a publicity stunt where he rode a bicycle across Texas for seven days to meet Elvis Presley. The two men met, and Presley's mother provided cookies.

Shortly thereafter, he soured on the music industry after learning unscrupulous agents were taking money that he had earned performing. He returned to Tulsa in 1969 and maintained a busy schedule at local entertainment establishments until his death. Frisco was also an eccentric personality, known for driving a bright blue roadster around Tulsa and even running for mayor of the city. He was inducted into the Oklahoma Music Hall of Fame in 2009 and died in 2015.

Ron Getman

A guitarist with the country-rock band the Tractors during the mid-1990s, Getman was a co-owner and co-producer of The Church Studio founded by Leon Russell. Roy Clark and Freddie Fender were two of the many artists that Getman worked with as an album co-producer.

A graduate of Oklahoma State University, Getman started a band with some of his college fraternity brothers before moving to New York City. While in the Big Apple, Getman sang on numerous commercials as well as recording with Janis Ian, Loudon Wainwright III and the iconic Leonard Cohen.

When not involved in Tulsa's music scene, Getman was an avid golf fan and worked for a local non-profit agency helping individuals with development disabilities achieve independent living. He passed away in 2021 after a brief illness.

Jim Karstein

One of two renowned drummers associated with the Tulsa Sound, Karstein spent nearly 40 years as the drummer for fellow Tulsa singer/songwriter J.J. Cale.

Prior to moving to Los Angeles, Karstein and Leon Russell were long-time friends from their days performing in Tulsa night clubs. Karstein was the drummer for the Accents, which featured David Gates as the lead singer.

When Gary Lewis, the son of comedy legend Jerry Lewis, was putting together a band, Russell was handling the song arrangements and recommended Karstein to Lewis. That led to Karstein being the drummer for the 1960s pop group Gary Lewis and the Playboys.

Other acts Karstein collaborated with through the years were Eric Clapton, Buffalo Springfield, Joe Cocker and Delaney and Bonnie and Friends.

One of Karstein's most unusual performances was on a top 20 comedy-style single by Cheech & Chong called "Basketball Jones featuring Tyrone Shoelaces." Other notable musicians performing on that novelty number were ex-Beatle George Harrison, Michelle Phillips, Carole King, Darlene Love and Billy Preston.

After returning to Oklahoma, Karstein spent nearly a dozen years as the drummer for the Red Dirt Rangers, one of the best-known bands in the Red Dirt musical genre popular in Oklahoma and Texas.

Karstein passed away in 2022 after a long illness.

Jim Keltner

Born and raised in Tulsa, drummer Jim Keltner has collaborated with every Beatle except for Paul McCartney as well as a veritable Who's Who in numerous music genres.

His technique has been described as highly precise while using simple patterns along with a casual feel. Some of the best examples of his technique are heard on Gary Wright's "Dream Weaver", Steely Dan's "Josie" and Bob Dylan's "Knocking on Heaven's Door."

Keltner's original interest was in jazz, but he capitalized on pop/rock in the early 1960s and relocated to Los Angeles to become a highly sought session performer.

His first LA studio session was on a song by Gary Lewis and The Playboys, "She's Just My Style" that reached number three on the 1965 *Billboard* pop charts. His association with Leon Russell led to subsequent work with Joe Cocker's Mad Dogs and Englishmen band along with J.J. Cale.

His work with former Beatles is heard on Ringo Starr's debut album, *Ringo*, George Harrison's *Living in the Material World* and John Lennon's *Walls and Bridges*. Harrison later hired Keltner as the drummer for his supergroup called The Traveling Wilburys. The other bandmates were Bob Dylan, Tom Petty, Jeff Lynne and Roy Orbison.

From the 1970s through the present time, Keltner has collaborated with such diverse artists as Barbara Streisand, the Bee Gees, Celine Dion, Crosby, Stills and Nash, Neil Young, Manhattan Transfer, Simon and Garfunkel, Ry Cooder, John Mayer, Michael Buble, Lana Del Rey, Lucinda Williams and Elton John.

Keltner performed with the London Metropolitan Orchestra on the song "An American Symphony" for the soundtrack of the 1995 dramatic movie, *Mr. Holland's Opus*. He also co-produced Jerry Lee Lewis' 2010 all-star duets CD, *Mean Old Man*.

Marcy Levy (aka Marcella Detroit)

Musical partnerships formed in Tulsa with Leon Russell and Eric Clapton were the launching pad for the 50-plus year career of this talented singer and songwriter. Levy co-wrote and sang backup vocals for Clapton's 1977 hit song "Lay Down Sally" which peaked at number three on the Billboard Hot 100 chart.

Levy was part of Clapton's touring acts, along with several other Tulsa Sound musicians, from 1974 through 1978 and again in 1984 and 1985. She also sang on Johnny Lee's 1980 country hit "Looking for Love" which was featured in the 1980 movie *Urban Cowboy* starring John Travolta.

She also recorded duets with international stars such as Sir Elton John, Jimmy Ruffin, Robin Gibb and Alice Cooper. Levy worked as a session singer alongside Bette Midler, Al Jarreau, Belinda Carlisle, Burt Bacharach, Philip Bailey and Aretha Franklin.

Born in Detroit, Michigan, Levy came from a musical family and the heyday of Motown soul music during her teenage years struck a chord with her. Singing also provided a release for her following the end of what she described as a physically abusive relationship.

Her first solo album was entitled *Marcella*, It was released in 1982 between her tenures with Clapton. But after very little commercial success, she returned to backup singing. During the 1980s she re-branded herself as Marcella Detroit and made connections in the British music world which led to another professional breakthrough. Ironically, a member of the Tulsa Sound entourage would have a hand in that process.

Songwriter Richard Feldman, another Leon Russell protégé, introduced her to Siobhan Fahey, formerly with the British pop group Bananarama and they formed a duo named Shakespeares Sisters. Their 1991 song "Stay" made history by staying a number one on the British record charts for eight weeks: the longest such tenure by a British female duo. The song also reached number one in numerous other countries and peaked at number five in the USA.

In later years, Levy ventured into electronic dance music in addition to a Motown-style sound. She currently lives in Los Angeles where she is part of a trio named The Nasty Housewives. Levy is also involved in composing music for movies and TV shows and has dabbled in designing clothes.

Jimmy "Junior" Markham

The blues grabbed hold of this harmonica player back in 1957 and took him on a ride that led to recording with some of the biggest names in rock and country for nearly 60 years. He was among the many Tulsans who accompanied Leon Russell, Cale and others to the Los Angeles rock and roll scene in the early 1960s.

Markham said in several interviews that seeing Elvis Presley in 1956 at the Tulsa Fairgrounds Pavilion first got him interested in music. Then he and a friend named J.J. Cale ventured to the predominantly black section of north Tulsa to hear local blues legend Flash Terry. Markham had listened to blues music on the radio but was captivated by hearing it live and watching the performers.

During his lengthy career, Markham recorded songs with blues legends Muddy Waters, John Lee Hooker and Taj Mahal, rockabilly legend Jerry Lee Lewis, country stars Waylon Jennings and Willie Nelson and Rolling Stones tenor saxophone player Bobby Keyes. In 2014, Eric Clapton invited Markham and three other Tulsa musicians to join him in recording the J.J. Cale tribute album, *The Breeze*. Markham was inducted into the Oklahoma Music Hall of Fame in 2017 and passed away in 2018 after a brief illness.

Jamie Oldaker

While best known for his drum work with Eric Clapton, Peter Frampton and the country-rock group The Tractors, Oldaker collaborated with musicians in the fields of blues, country and rock for nearly 40 years.

As a 13-year-old, Oldaker's first band was a Beatles-wannabe group called the Rogues Five. He said that in grade school, his first musical love was the violin but that class was full. There was an opening in percussion and Oldaker took playing drums like a duck takes to water. Drumming ran in his family since his father was a drummer and was an early fan of Gene Krupa, the famed percussionist in Benny Goodman's band.

After a brief tenure in St. Louis, Oldaker returned to Tulsa and worked with a popular local band named Tulsa County. He also performed with Leon Russell and J.J. Cale.

Oldaker's first mainstream work was with Bob Seger on the album *Back in '72* and on the top 10 hit "Turn the Page." In the years following this hit, he had numerous collaborations with Clapton including "I Shot the Sheriff" and "Lay Down Sally." He later worked with such diverse artists as Peter Frampton, Ronnie Dunn, Phil Driscoll, Buddy Guy, The Bee Gees, Willie Nelson, Ace Frehley, Phil Collins and Vince Gill.

During 2005, Oldaker released a CD saluting the lives and music of Oklahoma-based musicians entitled *Mad Dogs & Okies*. He passed away in 2020 at the age of 68.

Carl Radle

Radle was the bass player for many of the top rock and blues-rock recording acts during the 1960s and 1970s. He was best known for his collaborations with Eric Clapton and George Harrison and is one of several Tulsa-based musicians that Clapton has credited with being major influences in his musical career.

Radle's bass playing is heard on legendary Clapton albums such as *Layla and Other Assorted Love Songs* ("Layla" and "Bell Bottom Blues"), *Eric Clapton* ("After Midnight" and "Let It Rain"), *461 Ocean Boulevard* ("I Shot the Sheriff" and "Motherless Children"), *No Reason to Cry* ("Hello Old Friend"), *Slowhand* ("Wonderful Tonight" and "Lay Down Sally") and *Backless* ("Promises" and "Tulsa Time.")

His connection with George Harrison started with playing on the 1970 album *All Things Must Pass* ("My Sweet Lord" and "What is Life") and taking part in The Concert for Bangladesh at New York City's Madison Square Garden.

A graduate of Tulsa's Edison High School, Radle studied the clarinet and piano as a youngster but became fascinated with the bass guitar and taught himself how to play it. He had a knack for keeping the bass lines simple and repetitive while enhancing the song without calling attention to him. That led to gigs with Leon Russell, J.J. Cale and David Gates in local nightclubs.

After failing in his first bid for fortune and fame in California, Radle returned to Tulsa and joined the Air National Guard. One day, Russell offered him the role of bass player for Gary Lewis and the Playboys and his music career took off from there. Later in his career he performed alongside Buddy Guy, John Lee Hooker, Freddie King, Duane Allman, Donovan, Rita Coolidge, Joe Cocker, The Band and Delaney and Bonnie Bramlett.

Radle was a 2006 posthumous inductee into the Oklahoma Music Hall of Fame. He passed away in 1980 at the age of 37 from a kidney illness that was complicated by a long history of substance abuse.

Walt Richmond

This Tulsa pianist, producer and songwriter has played on 10 of Eric Clapton's albums and has toured with the Rock and Roll Hall of Famer throughout the United States and around the world. That partnership began after another Clapton musical colleague, Tulsa native JJ Cale, introduced them to each other. One of those recent collaborations was on Clapton's 2018 holiday album *Happy Xmas*. He played piano on "Have Yourself a Merry Little Christmas," a song written by Broken Arrow resident Ralph Blaine.

Richmond began playing piano during his teenage years and when not touring, performs frequently at Tulsa-area nightclubs with several of his musical friends. He was a co-founder of the country-rock band The Tractors and has recorded with stars such as Bonnie Raitt, The Bellamy Brothers, Michael Bolton and The Doobie Brothers.

Gordon Shryock

This Holland Hall graduate spent nearly 25 years in southern California as a Grammy Award-winning music producer for numerous nationally known singers and bands. Two of his three Grammy Awards were for his work with Christian music legend Andre Crouch and the third was for a Christian-music ensemble's rendition of The Lord's Prayer.

Shryock was part of the Leon Russell-led migration of Tulsa musicians to southern California in the 1960s. Prior to that, he and some his friends formed a group called The Band and had a local hit with "Mr. Guitar Man." The song, with vocals by legendary Tulsa singer Larry Bell, reached the top spot on the KELI-AM Radio survey and number two on the KAKC-AM Radio Survey. After moving to Los Angeles, Shryock became friends with Elvis Presley and landed a spot as an extra in Presley's 1965 movie *Girl Happy*, which co-starred Shelly Fabares. Shryock returned to Tulsa in later years and worked at the University of Tulsa's public radio station KWGS-FM.

Other artists that he worked with include R&B stars Natalie Cole and Peabo Bryson, country music stars Dwight Yoakum, Roy Clark and Barbara Mandrell, rock acts Three Dog Night and Delaney Bramlett, jazz musicians Stan Kenton, Weather Report and Taj Mahal and Tulsa Sound artists JJ Cale and The Tractors.

Dick Sims

This keyboardist spent 10 years touring with Eric Clapton. His work on the Hammond B-3 organ stood out on two of Clapton's best-known songs, "Wonderful Tonight" and "I Shot the Sheriff."

Sims joined Carl Radle and Jamie Oldaker to form the local supergroup Tulsa County in their younger years. Several music historians credited these three men as being primary influences on Clapton's musical career. Their debut came on Clapton's *461 Ocean Boulevard* album. Sims, who also collaborated with Bob Seger and Vince Gill, released the solo CD *Within Arm's Reach* prior to his death in 2011 from cancer at the age of 60.

Dave Teegarden

The Grammy-winning drummer performed with Bob Seger and The Silver Bullet Band during the 1970s and 1980s and played on some of Seger's biggest hits.

Teegarden's Grammy came for his work on *Against the Wind*, the 1980 album that spent six weeks atop the Billboard charts and knocked Pink Floyd's legendary album, *The Wall*, from the top spot. In addition to playing on the album's title song, he performed on Seger's "You'll Accompany Me" and "Betty Lou's Gettin' Out Tonight." On Seger's 1978 album *Stranger in Town*, he played on "Still the Same" and "Hollywood Nights."

His singing career began in 1970 when he and singer-organist Skip Knape formed a psychedelic rock duo called Teegarden & Van Winkle. Their only national hit was "God, Love and Rock & Roll," a song that peaked at number 22 on the *Billboard* pop charts.

After leaving Seger's group, he returned home to operate a recording studio just east of downtown Tulsa and not far from The Church Studio where Russell recorded. Among the pop and rock artists that have recorded in Teegarden's Tulsa studio are Hanson and Eric Clapton. Teegarden was inducted into the Oklahoma Music Hall of Fame in 2017.

Tommy Tripplehorn

This guitarist spent 18 months with the pop group Gary Lewis and the Playboys during the 1960s after playing in Tulsa's music scene and attending the University of Tulsa.

Tripplehorn went to Los Angeles at the invitation of Leon Russell and Carl Radle to work as a studio musician. Russell later told him that a band with the son of legendary comedian Jerry Lewis as its singer/drummer was looking for a guitar player.

The TV debut of Gary Lewis and the Playboys came in 1965 on *The Ed Sullivan Show*. It helped their debut single "This Diamond Ring" ascend to the top spot on the *Billboard* pop chart.

Their next four singles that year peaked in the *Billboard* top five rankings and their first two songs of 1967 reached the *Billboard* top 10. But the band's success essentially ended later that year when Lewis was drafted into military service.

A little-known fact is that had things gone differently, Tripplehorn could have become one of the founding members of one of the greatest bands in rock and roll history.

In November of 1966 when Tripplehorn and his bandmates played at Tulsa's Assembly Center as part of the Dick Clark Caravan of Stars tour, one of the acts on that show was The Yardbirds. That band once had Eric Clapton as a guitarist along with Jeff Beck and Jimmy Page.

Beck had quit the Yardbirds after no-showing at several prior concerts and Page was very impressed with Tripplehorn's guitar mastery and asked if he could take Beck's spot. Tripplehorn replied that he was interested but wanted to get the approval of Lewis first. Lewis flatly rejected the request, so Tripplehorn stayed where he was. Beck's spot with the Yardbirds was never filled.

Two years later when the Yardbirds broke up, Page teamed with guitarist/keyboardist John Paul Jones, drummer John Bonham and singer Robert Plant to form Led Zeppelin.

Tripplehorn, who passed away in 2019, returned to Tulsa and played in one of Tulsa's most popular rock and blues groups, The Bill Davis Band. His daughter is the famous movie actress, Jeannie Tripplehorn. Some of her noteworthy movies are *Basic Instinct* (with

Michael Douglas and Sharon Stone), *The Firm* (with Tom Cruise) and *Waterworld* (with Kevin Costner).

Dwight Twilley

The Tulsa Edison High School alumnus was a power pop singer who had two singles that reached the *Billboard* Top 20 charts: "I'm On Fire" in 1975 and "Girls" in 1984. The latter song and video featured then-label mate Tom Petty on alternating vocals.

Music critics described Twilley's style as a blend of Beatles-style pop and the rockabilly-style echo. His ballad "Why You Wanna Break My Heart" was part of the soundtrack for 1992 movie *Wayne's World*.

Twilley was part of a local band in the early 1970s with lead guitarist Bill Pitcock IV and bassist-drummer Phil Seymour. The Beatles' movie *A Hard Day's Night* was the inspiration for Seymour and Twilley to begin writing songs and singing together.

After being rejected by record labels in Memphis and Nashville, the duo landed a record deal in 1974 with Leon Russell's Los Angeles-based Shelter Records. But when Shelter co-owner Denny Cordell changed the band's name to the Dwight Twilley Band, that was a small crack that would lead the band's eventual crumbling due to internal strife.

"I'm on Fire" received very little promotional support from the recording company but strong word-of-mouth support from fans boosted the song to number 16 on the *Billboard* charts in 1975.

Dismal sales of the next two albums were the catalyst for Seymour leaving the band in 1977 to pursue a solo career. Following Seymour's cancer-related death in 1993, Twilley didn't perform songs that featured Seymour as the lead singer.

Twilley then formed a musical partnership with Tom Petty whose band Mudcrutch signed its first recording contract with Shelter Records. Petty sang backing vocals on "Girls" and played on "Looking for the Magic" which was a track on the Dwight Twilley Band's second album. Seymour sang backing vocals on Petty's "American Girl."

When "Breakdown" was originally recorded for Tom Petty and the Heartbreakers' debut album in 1976, Petty planned to use a catchy guitar lick by Mike Campbell only near the end of the song. After Twilley suggested using that distinctive guitar lick throughout the song, Petty re-recorded "Breakdown" and that catchy melody was literally instrumental in becoming one of the album's featured tracks.

Twilley later began a solo career along with joining musical forces with Susan Cowsill, a member of the 1960s pop group The Cowsills.

The advent of digital music gave Twilley's musical catalog a second lease on life in recent years. He was voted into the Oklahoma Music Hall of Fame just before he died on October 18, 2023. While driving by himself in Tulsa, Twilley suffered a stroke and his car crashed into a tree.

Martha Quinn, one of the original veejays on MTV, said after Twilley's death that he was a key part of the original group of artists that put MTV on the map for American music.

Casey Van Beek

This bass guitarist became part of the Tulsa Sound with a musical journey from Los Angeles to Tulsa; the opposite path that Leon Russell and other Tulsa Sound members had taken.

Casey Van Beek and the Tulsa Groove, which includes former Tractors and Tulsa Sound keyboardist Walt Richmond, released a 2020 album *Heaven Forever* that received wide critical acclaim and reached the top 40 charts in the blues, Americana, bluegrass and rock genres.

Van Beek's most successful Tulsa venture was being part of the Tractors, who in 1994 had the fastest-selling debut album by a country group in music history.

Born in Holland and raised near Los Angeles, Van Beek has performed with Ike and Tina Turner, Jerry Lee Lewis, Glen Campbell, the Coasters and Linda Ronstadt. He was part of an LA-based based called The Vibrants; a group promoted by TV game show host Bob Eubanks which opened for the Dave Clark Five, Peter and Gordon and the Rolling Stones.

Van Beek was one of three members of Ronstadt's backup band: two others being drummer Don Henley and guitarist/vocalist Glenn Frey. One day, Frey said he and Henley were leaving to start a new project. He was emphatic about wanting Van Beek to be part of that new band called the Eagles.

However, Van Beek had a separate deal working with a new band called Moccasin; a country-rock band musically influenced by Gram Parsons and Duane Hillman of the Flying Burrito Brothers. But Moccasin had a brief life due to conflicts with the record label's promoters.

Van Beek moved to Tulsa in 1975 to work with Don Preston, who was part of Leon Russell's Shelter Records and he never left.

Chapter Two

Pop and Rock

"*It used to be called boogie-woogie, it used to be called blues, used to be called rhythm and blues...it's called rock now.*"

Chuck Berry

"*If you tried to give rock and roll another name, you might call it 'Chuck Berry.'*"

John Lennon

"*You see, rock and roll isn't a career or hobby – it's a life force. It's something very essential.*"

The Edge

"*Rock and roll music: if you like it, if you feel it, you can't help but move to it. That's what happens to me. I can't help it.*"

Elvis Presley

"*Stay with rock and roll...and you'll stay young forever.*"

"Rockin' John" Henry

***

Agony Scene

This Tulsa-based five-man band was arguably Oklahoma's most successful performer in the "metal core" genre, which blended heavy metal and hardcore anchored by overpowering guitar work and rhythm sections.

While most of Agony Scene's concerts were in Oklahoma and the Midwestern United States, they also toured Europe as an opening act for European metal bands.

Core members of the group were vocalist Mike Williams, guitarists Brian Hodges and Chris Emmons, bassist Chris Rye and drummer Brent Masters

The band released three albums between 2001 and 2008: *The Agony Scene* in 2003, *The Darkest Red* in 2005 and *Get Damned* in 2007.

Agony Scene announced in 2008 that it had broken up but it resurfaced in 2018 with the CD *Tormentor*, a dark-themed project that addressed bloodshed, religion and psychosis.

Tommy Allsup

This Owasso native was the lead guitarist for rock and roll pioneers Buddy Holly and the Crickets. His guitar work is heard on two of that group's biggest hits: "It's So Easy" and "Heartbeat." The other members of the band were future country music superstar Waylon Jennings on bass guitar and drummer Carl Bunch.

Later in Allsup's career, he joined the surviving members of the legendary Western swing band Bob Wills and the Texas Playboys for special concert dates. He also produced records for such diverse artists as Bobby Vee, Julie London and Willie Nelson.

Allsup's career started in 1949 as a senior at Claremore High School with a band called the Oklahoma Swingbillies. A stint with Johnnie Lee Wills' Tulsa-based band and performances at Cain's Ballroom was sandwiched between performances with other Western Swing outfits in Lawton and Miami, Oklahoma and Wichita, Kansas.

Allsup met Holly in 1958 during a recording session in Clovis, New Mexico and accepted an invitation to join The Crickets. The following year, Allsup was involved in a pivotal moment in the history of rock and roll.

On February 2, 1959, Holly and other top rock-and-roll stars performed a concert in Clear Lake, Iowa as part of the Winter Dance Party. That package show featured Dion and the Belmonts ("Runaround Sue" and "The Wanderer"), Ritchie Valens ("La Bamba" and "Donna") and J.P. "The Big Bopper" Richardson ("Chantilly Lace.")

Holly chartered a three-passenger plane to fly to the next performance in Moorhead, Minnesota. Holly, Richardson and pilot Roger Peterson were already on the plane but one vacant seat remained.

Allsup and Richardson flipped a coin to see who would take the flight. Richardson won and got the seat. The plane took off shortly after midnight but soon crashed in a snowstorm and all four men were killed.

After Holly's death, Allsup became a driving force for the country music division of Liberty Records as well as a highly-sought session musician. Among the performers who personally asked Allsup to play on their albums were The Everly Brothers, Jerry Lee Lewis, Reba McEntire, Ernest Tubb and Kenny Rogers.

Following the death of Bob Wills in 1973, Allsup reunited several of Bob's original band members and with the blessing of the Wills family, toured for nearly 20 years as Bob Wills' Original Texas Playboys.

Tommy's son, Austin Allsup, is a musician based in Austin, Texas who advanced to the final 10 performers in the fall 2016 version of the NBC-TV reality show, *The Voice.*

Allsup passed away in 2017 at the age of 85. Sir Paul McCartney sent flowers to the funeral home that handled Allsup's memorial service.

Aqueduct

Founded by Tulsan Dave Terry, this indie pop band was based in Seattle, Washington, and played alongside Seattle's legendary bands Death Cab for Cutie and Modest Mouse. The quintet released five albums between 2003 and 2015. Terry, whose musical composition style in lo-fi sound has been likened to Beach Boys legend Brian Wilson, played in local bands with singer Tony Romanello and fronted an indie pop group called Epperly.

Elvin Bishop

One of the top blues-rock guitarists for nearly half a century, Elvin Bishop graduated from Tulsa's Will Rogers High School before moving to Chicago to find his musical home.

Bishop's family moved to Tulsa when he was 10 years old and he was a National Merit Scholar finalist during his high school years. He studied physics while attending the University of Chicago but was drawn as a teenager to the guitar and harmonica playing of Jimmy Reed, the legendary bluesman that the Rolling Stones frequently cite as one of their major influences.

Bishop befriended Paul Butterfield, who was greatly influenced by Muddy Waters, and they formed the nucleus of the Paul Butterfield Blues Band. Bill Graham, owner of the Fillmore music halls on the eastern and western coasts, signed them to a record contract. That led to performances with B.B. King, The Allman Brothers Band, Eric Clapton, Jimi Hendrix and The Grateful Dead.

By his own admission, Bishop had singing limitations and was content to let others take the spotlight so his guitar work could shine through. That resulted in his biggest-selling song with Mickey Thomas handling the vocals. "Fooled Around and Fell in Love" peaked at number three on the *Billboard* rock charts in 1976. Thomas and Bishop's drummer, Donny Baldwin, later left the band to join Jefferson Starship.

Bishop's respect among other musicians resulted in his being name-checked in two songs during the 1970s. Charlie Daniels did so in 1975 with "The South's Gonna Do It" and Molly Hatchet did likewise in 1978 in "Gator Country."

His most recent project is with a band called The Big Fun Trio with former Fleetwood Mac band member Bob Welsh playing piano and guitar and Willy Jordan on vocals and a drum box.

Bishop was inducted into the Rock and Roll Hall of Fame in 2015 as an original member of the Paul Butterfield Blues Band. He was inducted into the Blues Hall of Fame in 2016.

Bob Bogle

This bass guitarist was a member of The Ventures, the band that brought electric guitar groups to the forefront of rock and roll during the 1950s and 1960s. Bogle and fellow Oklahoman Nokie Edwards comprised half of The Ventures' four-man roster.

The Ventures were inducted into the Rock and Roll Hall of Fame in 2008. Two of the group's best-known songs were "Walk Don't Run" and the theme from the CBS-TV detective show "Hawaii Five-O."

The Ventures ranked sixth among all artists during the 1960s in album sales. The only acts ahead of them were The Beatles, Frank Sinatra, Elvis Presley, Ray Conniff and Ray Charles.

Edwards was one of 12 children fond was born in the tiny western Oklahoma town of Lahoma during the peak of the Dust Bowl era.

In a 2003 interview, Bogle recalled days when his family listened to the radio for entertainment after working on the family's farm. He specifically recalled listening to radio broadcasts of Bob Wills and the Texas Playboys and the Grand Ole Opry.

Bogle's family moved to California when he was six years old and after encountering hard times there, relocated to Portland, Oregon. His older brother, Dennis, gave him his guitar prior to being inducted into the Air Force. Bob relocated to Seattle, Washington, and later teamed with Edwards to lay the foundation for The Ventures.

Buddy Bruce

Originally a Tulsa-based jazz guitarist, he became the lead guitarist for a quartet that became one of the biggest "one-hit wonders" in rock and roll history.

Bruce was part of a band called The Champs and their instrumental song "Tequila" spent five weeks atop the *Billboard* pop charts in 1958. The song had a Latin melody and earned the first Grammy Award presented in the rhythm and blues category.

Saxophonist Danny Flores provided Bruce with his first taste of that adult beverage the day before a recording session. Bruce thought a song title based on that beverage would work since there were already songs about beer, whiskey and champagne. On the song, Flores twice says the word "Tequila" before the song ends with the entire band shouting that word.

"Tequila" was actually the B-side of the single "Train to Nowhere." A disc jockey in Cleveland, Ohio flipped the record over one day and played it on a whim, leading to a deluge of listener requests. Other radio DJs started playing "Tequila" and more music fans bought the record and the rest is musical history.

Born as Buddy Bruce Stoops, he was playing the guitar, banjo, stand-up bass and mandolin at the age of eight and was part of a family band that played for fairs and parties, mostly in Missouri. Later in

Bruce's career, he performed with legendary guitar players Les Paul, Roy Clark and Chet Atkins before returning to Tulsa.

He passed away in 2014 at the age of 84.

Anita Bryant

This Tulsa Will Rogers High School alumnus was a singer, celebrity spokesperson and social activist whose entertainment career was overshadowed by a passionate opposition to the gay rights movement.

Vocal music was Bryant's forte in high school and shortly after her graduation; she won the Miss Oklahoma beauty-scholarship pageant and was second runner-up in the 1959 Miss America pageant. That led to appearances on television variety shows, performing as part of Bob Hope's USO entourage that entertained military servicemen overseas and a career that placed three songs in the *Billboard* Top 20 pop charts during the 1960s.

Bryant had a pair of Top 10 singles in the 1960s with "Paper Roses" peaking at number five and "My Little Corner of the World" reaching number 10. Marie Osmond covered those two songs in the 1970s, taking "Paper Roses" to the top spot in 1973 and "My Little Corner of the World" to number 33 in 1974.

Her family-friendly reputation grew stronger in the 1970s, highlighted by an emotional rendition of "The Battle Hymn of the Republic" at President Lyndon Johnson's 1973 funeral and by doing commercials for products such as soft drinks, kitchenware, the Florida Citrus Commission in general and orange juice in particular.

A devout Christian, Bryant became an outspoken opponent of the gay rights movement during that time. A pivotal moment came at a press conference in Des Moines, Iowa, when a gay rights activist planted a pie in Bryant's face while cameras were rolling.

The combination of a backlash from the gay community and elsewhere resulted in lost commercial endorsements for Bryant. When much of the conservative Christian community turned against her after divorcing first husband Bob Green along with financial and personal struggles, her career would never reach the heights that it once attained.

Then in 2021 a granddaughter, Sarah Green, announced she would marry another woman, much to Bryant's dismay.

Bryant and her husband, former NASA astronaut Charlie Dry, later operated a non-denominational Christian organization, Anita Bryant Ministries, and also participated in charitable programs. Bryant returned to Will Rogers High School in 2007 as a guest performer in the school's yearly musical revue.

Caroline's Spine

Despite actually being formed in 1993 in San Diego, California, this pop-metal band called Oklahoma its home for nearly 14 years and was anchored by two graduates of Tulsa's Bishop Kelley High School. Mark Haugh (Class of 1988) and bass guitarist Scott Jones (Class of 1995),

Haugh and Jones met the other band members while attending Loyola Marymount University in Los Angeles. .

The band quickly became popular with college students for its blend of meditative and moody music that drew comparisons to Pearl Jam.

Despite relatively little airplay on radio stations, the band's popularity grew quickly through word-of-mouth and a virtual non-stop touring schedule from 1999 through 2000. That subsequently landed opening act engagements with superstar rock bands KISS, Queensryche and Aerosmith.

Caroline's Spine released 12 albums and two of its songs appeared on movie soundtracks. One of its earliest hits was "Turned Blue" which music critics hailed as one of the best songs from the soundtrack of the 1997 comedy-horror movie *An American Werewolf* in Paris, which was directed by John Landis. Then

The band's biggest songs were "Sullivan" in 1997 and "Nothing to Prove" in 1999, each of which peaked at number 23 on mainstream rock charts. The band put out a greatest hits compilation, *The Collection*, in 2006. Haugh and Jones left in 2007 when Caroline's Spine announced on its website that they had broken up.

Lorrie and Larry Collins

"The Rockin' Rollin' Collins Kids" were the brother-sister vocal duo of Lorrie and Larry Collins. During the 1950s, these residents of the southwestern Tulsa suburb of Sapulpa appeared on the *Ed Sullivan Show* and other TV variety programs and performed as an opening act for Johnny Cash and Carl Perkins during their rockabilly heydays. Lorrie and Larry were later inducted into the Rockabilly Music Hall of Fame.

Their big break came with an appearance on the Los Angeles-based show *Town Hall Party* during the 1950s. One of that show's stars was teenage heartthrob Ricky Nelson, who later became Lorrie's boyfriend and that led to an appearance on *The Adventures of Ozzie and Harriett*.

By the age of 10, Larry became a highly skilled guitar player and used a double-necked Mosrite guitar; following in the footsteps of his musical mentor, flashy country music performer Joe Maphis.

Some music critics have said Larry's guitar playing, especially use of the *staccato* style of playing one note with countless quick picking strokes, was influential in the evolution of surf music (think The Ventures or Dick Dale) and punk rock (think The Sex Pistols).

Larry co-wrote two songs which reached the top spot on the *Billboard* music charts. "Delta Dawn" became Helen Reddy's first number one pop single in 1973 after being a top 10 country hit for Tanya

Tucker one year earlier. "You're the Reason God Made Oklahoma" was a 1981 number one country hit for David Frizzell and Shelly West after being featured in a Clint Eastwood movie.

Lorrie stood shoulder to shoulder with rockabilly singers Brenda Lee and Wanda Jackson as one of that genre's top female singers during the 1950s. Her romance with Ricky Nelson was a brief one and she would marry Stu Carnall, the road manager for Johnny Cash, and have two daughters.

She performed in local clubs and casinos in California and Nevada before reuniting with Larry in 1993 at a rockabilly music festival in England. That reunion lasted until 2012 when health issues ended her singing career.

Lorrie passed away in 2018. Larry passed away in 2024.

John Convertino

Since 1990, this Tulsa Edison graduate has been the drummer for Calexico, a band that can best be described as blending Latin and Tejano rhythms with jazz, country and post-rock for a highly popular and danceable sound.

He moved from Tulsa to Irvine, California to play for a heavy rock band called Giant Sand. Then he and future bandmate Joey Burns moved to Tucson, Arizona in 1994 to join another band but that group disbanded two years later. Convertino and Burns spent a couple of years as a freelance rhythm section before forming Calexico.

In a 2015 interview with *Modern Drummer Magazine*, Convertino spoke of the band's long-lasting success by saying, "Fans who were in their 30s and 40s when we started out are still coming to the shows; but now they're in the 50s and 60s and bringing their kids."

Convertino's drum work was also featured in three movie soundtracks; the 1991 action comedy *Bill & Ted's Bogus Journey*, the 2004

Tom Cruise crime drama *Collateral* (2004) and a 2007 documentary about Bob Dylan's music *I'm Not There*.

Crooked X

Between 2007 and 2011, six teenagers from Coweta, a small town southeast of Tulsa, formed a heavy metal rock band that went from playing in a garage to being the opening act for KISS in Sweden and then breaking up.

Crooked X placed second in a national talent segment on the CBS Television's *The Early Show*. Their work caught the eyes and ears of two men who managed KISS as well as Bon Jovi and Motley Crue. That led to a 2009 album, *Crooked X*, and gigs with KISS, Alice Cooper, Ted Nugent, Skid Row and Black Stone Cherry as well as being part of the *Rock Band* video game.

Original band members were Forrest French (lead vocals and rhythm guitar), Boomer Simpson (drummer and backing vocals), Jesse Cooper (lead guitar and back-up vocals) and bass guitarists Josh McDowell. French and McDowell left the band in 2010 and were respectively replaced by Kevin Currie and Brad Johnson prior to the band's breakup in 2011.

Simon Curtis

This singer, songwriter and actor attended Jenks High School and the University of Tulsa prior to making his mark in dance and electronic pop music.

The most successful of his three studio albums was RA which was released in 2011 and peaked at number 20 on the *Billboard* Dance/Electronic Albums chart,

Curtis made his acting debut in 2009 in a made-for-TV music show Spectacular which aired on the Nickelodeon cable/satellite channel. His character, Royce DuLac, was the lead singer in a show choir. Also that year, he appeared in an episode of the Disney Channel sitcom *Hannah Montana*, opposite Miley Cyrus.

He was also part of a national touring production of the hit Broadway musical *Joseph and the Amazing Technicolor Dreamcoat*.

Ester Drang

Formed in 1995 in Broken Arrow by vocalist and multi-instrumentalist Bryce Chambers along with bassist Kyle Winner, this alternative rock band had a trademark of layered vocal harmony, alternating percussion styles and looping guitar melodies.

Band members cited My Bloody Valentine and The Beatles as major musical influences. Some music critics, however, have said the band has a subtle way of expressing religious beliefs but the appeal goes beyond the typical Christian contemporary format.

After releasing four CDs along with one EP, the band took a hiatus in 2007. Chambers and Winner brought the band back in 2012, added two new members and toured with Echo and the Bunnymen and Pedro the Lion.

Sarah Fimm

Born in Tulsa as Sarah Laurel Friedman, she was featured on the MTV reality show *Real World/Road Rules* and has been likened to Tori Armos for her breathy, yet passionate singing style.

Fimm lives in Woodstock, New York and has also been a session musician and sells paintings and poetry online.

David Gates

A graduate of Tulsa's Will Rogers High School, this singer-songwriter became one of the most popular soft rock artists of the 1970s as the lead singer of the group Bread and later as a solo artist.

During the 1970s, Bread had six songs that peaked in the *Billboard* Top 10 and four others that peaked in the Top 20. "Make It with You" was their debut single and their only number one hit. Gates' biggest hit as a solo artist was "Goodbye Girl", the theme song from the 1978 romantic comedy movie, *The Goodbye Girl* and that song reached number 15 on the *Billboard* pop charts.

While attending Rogers in the late 1950s, Gates formed a band called The Accents with Leon Russell playing the piano and that band backed Chuck Berry during his 1957 Tulsa concert. Gates once said his band kept busy by focusing on pop tunes while other bands back then were absorbed with copying Elvis Presley. He also said they made more money playing for high school and college events than they did as part of Tulsa's nightclub scene.

Gates moved to Los Angeles in the early 1960s and became a successful songwriter, arranger and studio musician while having modest success as a solo artist. He wrote The Murmaids' 1964 number three *Billboard* hit "Popsicles and Icicles" and collaborated with singers such as Pat Boone, Elvis Presley, The Monkees, Merle Haggard and Brian Wilson. Later in that decade, he teamed with Robb Royer, Jimmy Griffin and Mike Botts to create the band that would become Bread.

Gates and his wife left Tulsa several years ago and currently live in Mount Vernon, Washington.

Barrick Jonathan "J.B." Griffiths

This graduate of Broken Arrow High School and Oklahoma State University has become of the music industry's most sought-after musical arrangers.

Artists that have used Griffith's expertise are a Who's Who of musical heavyweights with names such as Dionne Warwick, Stevie Wonder, Barry Manilow, Amy Grant, George Strait, Amy Grant, Mariah Carey, Bette Midler, Garth Brooks, Frank Sinatra, Liza Minnelli and Sammy Davis, Jr., to name but just a few.

Griffiths was the chief music arranger for Michael Jackson's 30th Anniversary Celebration, broadcast on CBS in 1991 and the Marc Anthony 2001 Madison Square Garden concert aired in 2001 on HBO.

The Jackson concert was particularly challenging because he scored and arranged music for all performances not involving Jackson. That meant creating the best possible sounds for diverse genres such as rock, disco, gospel, quiet storm soul, hip-hop, reggae and lush-sounding ballads.

He also proofread and assisted with music for movies such as *Blackhawk Down, Bridget Jones' Diary, The Notebook, Rise of the Planet of the Apes, Mr. Deeds* and *50 First Dates.*

Hanson

After hitting the big time in 1997 as a brotherly trio of bubble gum heartthrobs, Hanson gained international recognition for their achievements in the indie pop field as well as their commitment to humanitarian causes. They have sold over 17 million records and in 2003 founded their own label, 3CG Records; a title derived from their childhood home having a three-car garage.

Taylor Hanson handles lead vocals and plays keyboards, older brother Isaac plays guitar and piano while Zac Hanson plays drums.

The three brothers were homeschooled and caught the music bug after coming across their father's collection of classic rock and roll albums. Their professional debut came at the 1992 Mayfest International Arts Festival in downtown Tulsa when they performed a cappella and gave their own renditions of 1950s classics such as "Johnny B. Goode," "Splish Splash" and "Rockin' Robin."

"MMMBop" was originally recorded in Tulsa in 1996 and released independently but didn't cause much of a stir. But when it was added In May 1997 to Hanson's debut album, *Middle of Nowhere,* it sold four million copies in the United States and reached the top spot on music charts in America, Australia, Germany and the United Kingdom.

A couple of months later, Hanson's management quickly released an album of Christmas songs called *Snowed In*. That featured versions of traditional Christmas carols and pop-flavored Christmas songs along with holiday songs the group had written. *Snowed In* peaked at number seven in the United States and number three in Australia.

Since 2001, Hanson has been at the forefront of artists pursuing careers independent from entanglements with major record companies and formed their own record label, 3CG to support up-and-coming musicians. The 3CG stands for three-car garage, something that was in their childhood home.

As their career evolved, one of their passions was supporting research related to preventing the spread of AIDS-related poverty through African nations. Some of their other efforts involved providing shoes for needy families, building school and providing clean drinking water.

The group went through a challenging time in 2007 when Isaac Hanson underwent life-saving surgery after a blood clot went from his arm into both lungs. Doctors said the clot developed because a severe compression of blood vessels in his arm that resulted from his repetitive motion of playing guitar.

The Hanson brothers created their own craft beer company in 2013 then the following year founded a craft beer and music festival known as Hop Jam. That event has drawn crowds approaching 40,000 to the downtown Tulsa Arts District.

In early 2019, Hanson delved into the orchestral world with an international tour called Hanson String Theory Project. They performed at iconic musical venues throughout North America, Australia and Europe.

Those three brothers today have families of their own and are equally passionate about philanthropic work both in the Tulsa metropolitan area and globally.

Lee Hazlewood

Hazlewood was born in the western Tulsa suburb of Mannford and is best known for his musical collaborations with rock guitar legend Duane Eddy plus singers Dean Martin and Nancy Sinatra.

In a 2015 article, *Rolling Stone* magazine ranked the Sinatra-Hazlewood duets ninth on its list of 20 Greatest Duos; above notable acts such as The Carpenters, Sonny and Cher, Steely Dan and The Righteous Brothers.

He wrote "The Fool" for Tulsa-born rockabilly singer Sanford Clark while working in Arizona as a radio station disc jockey. That song reached number five on the *Billboard* R&B chart and number seven on its pop chart.

Hazlewood used a silo as an echo chamber during the recording process to create a big reverb twang that would be the trademark on Eddy's early hits "Rebel Rouser," "Dance with the Guitar Man" and "Cannon Ball." Eddy's frequent TV appearances on *American Bandstand* also boosted his popularity.

After writing and producing Dean Martin's hit song "Houston" and "I'm A Fool" for Dino, Desi and Billy, Hazlewood and Nancy Sinatra would become international stars for their collaborations.

"These Boots Are Made for Walkin'" became an international number one hit in 1965. That was quickly followed by "Sugar Town" and "How Does That Grab You?" in 1966 and then "Jackson" and "Some Velvet Morning" in 1967.

That partnership ended in the early 1970s because of Sinatra's disenchantment with Hazlewood's songs and his frequent drug use.

Hazlewood later moved to Sweden and expressed disillusionment with the music industry. He recorded a number of little-heard songs prior to his death in 2007.

Stacy Jones

Jones is an accomplished drummer and music producer who has performed with pop/rock acts Matchbox Twenty, The Chainsmokers, Veruca Salt, Letters to Cleo and Miley Cyrus, among others. He is also the lead singer for American Hi-Fi, an alternative pop rock band.

Jones was born in Tulsa but his family moved when he was one year old. During his collegiate years, he returned to the USA and attended Boston's legendary Berkeley College of Music.

American Hi-Fi was formed in Los Angeles in 2001 and its biggest hit was the 2001 song "Flavor of the Weak." The song peaked at number five on the *Billboard* Modern Rock Tracks, number 15 on the Pop Songs chart and number 41 on the Top 100 songs list. "Flavor of the Weak" would later be used in several movie soundtracks.

Jones later worked as a producer and songwriter and also worked as a vice president for artists and repertoire for Epic Records; a job that entailed artistic development of singers and songwriters.

He has also been a studio and touring musician for such top acts as Ariana Grande, Joan Jett, the Jonas Brothers, Sheryl Crow, Avril Lavigne and Madonna.

Jerry Keller

A 1955 graduate of Will Rogers High School and a University of Tulsa alumnus, Keller was a "one-hit wonder" in 1959 with the self-penned pop hit "Here Comes Summer."

That song topped the record charts in Great Britain and peaked at number 14 on the *Billboard* Hot 100 chart in the USA.

Keller worked as a disc jockey at Tulsa's KAKC-AM radio station and sang in a local quartet as well as the Tulsa Boy Singers prior to moving to New York in 1956. One day while attending church in the Big Apple, Pat Boone heard Keller singing and introduced him to Marty Mills, who became Keller's manager.

In later years, Keller wrote songs recorded by Andy Williams, Matt Monro, Johnny Mathis, Engelbert Humperdinck, Brenda Lee, Ricky Nelson, Jose Feliciano and The Cyrkle.

Keller also dabbled in movie sound tracks with the 1965 thriller *I Saw What You Did* and the 1965 western *The Legend of Shenandoah*. He also had a cameo role as an orchestra conductor in the 1977 TV romantic movie *You Light Up My Life*.

Bobby Keys

This tenor saxophonist spent four decades touring with The Rolling Stones and his wailing solo made "Brown Sugar" one of that band's biggest hits. He also began his rock and roll career with Buddy Holly and the Crickets and also played alongside some of the biggest names in music. But Tulsa played a role in the development of Keys' career.

After working with Holly and other musicians affiliated with Dick Clark's *American Bandstand* TV show and related tours, Keys moved to Tulsa and played in local night clubs alongside bluesman Jimmy "Junior" Markham. That led to working with Charlie Daniels and Tommy Tripplehorn and other Tulsa-based musicians. Keys later joined the musical migration from Tulsa to Los Angeles at the bequest of Leon Russell to gain additional work as studio musicians.

Keys and J.J. Cale were part of the earliest version of the rock supergroup Delaney and Bonnie and Friends. Shortly afterwards, Cale chose to return to Tulsa while Keys teamed up with the Rolling Stones. When not touring with The Rolling Stones, Keys contributed to performances by a wide variety of internationally-known musicians.

Paul Klein

This lead singer of the indie pop group LANY (short for Los Angeles and New York) graduated from Tulsa's Victory Christian School and Oral Roberts University and spent 13 years as a classically trained piano player.

After Klein met Les Priest and Jake Goss in Nashville, the group LANY was formed in 2014. The group's musical style has been described as blend of alternative rock and synthetic pop.

Their self-titled 2017 debut album peaked at number 32 on the *Billboard* U.S. rock albums chart, thanks to word-of-mouth recommendations through various social media platforms. In 2018, they shared the main stage at the Lollapalooza music festival with rap stars Cardi B and Eminem plus pop superstars Nile Rodgers and Chic and Beyonce.

Following the 2022 departure of keyboard player Les Priest, Klein and Goss have performed as a duo.

Ivy Levan

This Tulsa-born singer, actress and model has become popular in the LGBTQ+ community for a singing style not unlike that of Christina Aguilera: a powerful voice blended with a sassy attitude. She has collaborated musically with Sting, Diplo and Fitz and the Tantrums while making numerous solo releases via digital downloads.

After spending time in Tulsa and being raised in a Pentecostal church, Levan's family moved to Bentonville, Arkansas. Then at the age of 16, she relocated to Los Angeles to advance her musical career. Growing up, Levan was influenced by such diverse singers as Whitney Houston, Depeche Mode, Nine Inch Nails and Chaka Khan.

A member of the Ford Models Agency, Levan has modeled for major retailers such as JC Penney and Payless Shoe Source. As an actress, she has appeared in minor roles in numerous TV shows and movies.

John D. Levan

Born in the rural community of Beggs just south of Tulsa, John D. Levan was a 2004 inductee into the Rockabilly Music Hall of Fame.

Levan was part of Clyde Stacy and the Nightcaps, one of Oklahoma's earliest rockabilly bands. Their regional success led to a 1957 appearance on a TV show in Philadelphia, Pennsylvania that evolved into *American Bandstand*. When Levan and his family moved to New Mexico in the late 1950s, he joined a band led by Sonny West; the man who wrote "Rave On" and "Oh Boy" for Buddy Holly.

Following that was a six-year stretch when Levan returned to Tulsa and played lead guitar for Charlie Daniels and the Jaguars, the rock-and-roll house band at the Fondalite Night Club just south of downtown Tulsa at the corner of West 11th Street and South Denver Avenue. During those days, band members were nattily attired in gold blazers with white shirt and thin back ties.

Daniels left for Nashville in 1965 and became a country music superstar with the Charlie Daniels Band as well as a member of the Grand Ole Opry.

Levan returned to Tulsa in the 1970s and played alongside Leon Russell and J.J. Cale along with being part of local bands. He later relocated to northwestern Arkansas and is still active in the music industry.

Los Reactors (a/k/a The Adaptors)

This is one of only two bands from Tulsa to achieve any degree of national recognition in the world of punk rock music. Los Reactors independently released two EPs: *Dead in the Suburbs* in 1980 and *Be a Zombie/Laboratory Baby* in 1981.

In addition to the often stinging and bitter social commentary that is punk rock, the band's signature sound came from the keyboard wizardry of Joe Danger (aka Joseph Linhart). He also managed a local night club called the Blue Grotto that brought regional punk rock bands to Tulsa.

The band's name was changed to The Adaptors after Linhart's death in 1989 and released new music through online services.

J.D. McPherson

A former art and technology teacher in Broken Arrow's public school system, roots rocker J.D. McPherson blends early rock influences such as Buddy Holly, Chuck Berry and Little Richard with the high energy of indie rock bands such as Talking Heads and the Pixies.

McPherson grew up in the southeastern Oklahoma town of Talihina then earned a Masters of Fine Arts degree from the University of Tulsa.

He was a fan of punk rock music as a youth. His interest in roots rock was piqued when a local record store was going out a business and an employee gave him a two-record set of Buddy Holly's earliest songs.

Two of his first four albums cracked the Top 20 rankings on the *Billboard* U.S. Rock chart.

Signs and Signifiers was recorded in 2012 with old-time equipment such as a reel-to-reel tape recorder, guitar amplifiers and 1960s-style microphones. It was released by an independent label then quickly acquired for international distribution by roots music specialists Rounder Records. It reached the top spot on the *Billboard* Heatseekers Music chart for new artists and 47th on its Rock Music chart.

His second album, *Let the Good Times Roll*, was released in 2015 after McPherson and his family moved to metro Nashville. That CD featured what some critics described as a blend of rockabilly, soul and attitude. It also hit the top spot on the *Billboard* Heatseekers chart and 17th on the U.S. Rock Chart.

Undivided Heart and Soul came out in 2017 and explored the past and future of roots music but definitely had more rock than rockabilly. It peaked at 19th on the U.S. Rock Chart.

In November of 2018, McPherson released a Christmas-themed CD entitled *Socks*. McPherson told *Rolling Stone* magazine *Socks* was recorded with a mission to have "no jingle bells, no cover songs and no schmaltz."

The CD had growling guitar riffs in "Bad Kid," a jolly and sassy vibe in "Hey Skinny Santa," nostalgia and warmth in "All the Gifts I Need" and a shuffle groove in "Ugly Sweater Blues." Socks peaked at number five on the Heatseekers Music chart.

In recent years, McPherson's songs were featured on SiriusXM's Outlaw Country music channel and he toured with Alison Kraus and Robert Plant before relocating to Tulsa in late 2023.

Russ McKinnon

What began as a career in classical music with studies at the University of Tulsa took drummer Russ McKinnon on a six-year trip with the funk-rock group Tower of Power and 17 years as the drummer for legendary singer Barry Manilow.

He was chosen by readers of *Modern Drummer* magazine as the best rock drummer for five consecutive years.

McKinnon made his professional music debut with the Tulsa Philharmonic Orchestra and later joined the Fort Worth Symphony. He is currently based in Los Angeles but conducts drum set clinics around the world.

He was also the drummer for a host of music legends, including Joe Cocker, Engelbert Humperdinck, Marie Osmond, Michelle Shocked, Billy Vera and Bette Midler.

While attending Broken Arrow's public school system, McKinnon became band president at Sequoyah Middle School and became a student "director" when his band instructor was sidelined by heart surgery. Many of the drum cadences McKinnon created are still used today by Broken Arrow High School's nationally renowned marching band, The Pride of Broken Arrow.

Scott Musick

This Edison High School graduate was the drummer and a vocalist for the Santa Cruz, California-based alternative rock band The Call from 1980 through 2000. The band's musical reputation was one of ringing guitars and lyrics with a spiritual-like awareness and social consciousness

The Call's breakout song was the 1983 hit "The Walls Came Down" and received frequent airplay on MTV. Their 1989 song "Let the Day Begin" reached the top spot on the Billboard U.S. Mainstream Rock chart and was used as Al Gore's campaign theme song during the Democrat's presidential campaign in 2000. While Gore liked the lyrics that he felt resonated with working-class Americans, he never bothered to ask The Call for permission to use the song.

Their 1986 album *Reconciled* was regarded as their best group project with many songs from that release becoming hits on the Mainstream Rock Chart. Guest artists on that album included Peter Gabriel (Genesis), Jim Kerr (Simple Minds) and Robbie Robertson (The Band).

The Call's final album, *Red Moon*, was released in 1990 and featured U2 lead singer Bono on background vocals for "What's Happed to You?" *Red Moon* was actually the band's taking a turn into the relative new genre of Americana music.

After leaving The Call, Musick performed or recorded with Kris Kristofferson, Delbert McClinton, Smokey Robinson, Johnny Cash, David Cassidy and Barry McGuire. Musick still performs in local night clubs through the Tulsa area as well as in northeastern Oklahoma.

N.O.T.A (a/k/a None of the Above)

This band, along with Los Reactors, used its success in local clubs as a launching pad for opening act gigs with punk rock legends The Dead Kennedy, Husker Du, Black Flag and The Minutemen in 1984 and 1985. A frequently bootlegged tape from a 1983 concert at a local predominantly country music club called The Crystal Pistol boosted N.O.T.A. into cult status.

Their best known CD was *Give 'Em Enough Dope* and contained an incredible 26 tracks when released in 1996.

Frequent conflicts, both within the band's members and with increasing numbers of skinhead audience members, led to the band's demise.

Leo Okeke

This versatile Tulsa-born musician is best known for his work during the heyday of the 1980s boy bands New Kids on the Block and Marky Mark and the Funky Bunch.

Okeke played bass guitar and keyboards back then and is currently working as a producer and engineer for a number of up and coming acts.

Outline in Color

This self-described hardcore metal quintet was formed in 2009 and recorded four albums and a dozen singles and EPs. Their 2016 album

Struggle peaked at number 10 on the *Billboard* Heatseekers music chart.

Patti Page

A graduate of Tulsa's Webster High School, Patti Page's blend of pop, jazz and country music resulted in a career that spanned five decades and placed 110 songs on the *Billboard* music charts. She had four number one hits, 19 songs that reached the Top 10 and had 14 singles that sold a million copies apiece between 1950 and 1965.

Page's signature song was the 1950 ballad "Tennessee Waltz" which spent nine consecutive weeks atop the *Billboard* charts. Her other number one singles were "All My Love (Bolero)" in 1950, "I Went to Your Wedding" in 1952 and "(How Much Is That) Doggie in the Window" in 1953. Some of her other top 10 songs were "Allegheny Moon," "Mockin' Bird Hill" and "Old Cape Cod."

She was born as Clara Ann Fowler in Claremore, Oklahoma and her family later moved to Tulsa. When she was 18 years old, she was hired as the lead singer for a 15-minute show on Tulsa's KTUL Radio. With the Page Milk Company being the show's sponsor, her stage name was changed to Patti Page.

Music producer Mitch Miller had a hand in Page's success by overdubbing her vocals to make it sound like she was singing along with herself, putting Page decades ahead of a technique used by many modern singers. Miller also felt that the simple storylines and melodies found in country music could successfully cross over to pop music.

Her recording success led to appearances on several TV variety shows as well as a part in the 1960 movie *Elmer Gantry*. From the mid-1960s through the mid-1980s, Page shifted her focus towards country music and had additional songs that reached the country Top 20 rankings. The biggest seller was a 1973 duet with Tom T. Hall, "Hello, We're Lonely."

Page was inducted into the Oklahoma Music Hall of Fame prior to her death in 2013.

An off-Broadway musical show about her life, *Flipside: The Patti Page Story*, was developed by writer/director Greg White after meeting Page during the Oklahoma Centennial Celebration in 2007. The show premiered in 2011, features 28 of Page's songs and won 18 awards at the 2011 Kennedy Center National Theatre Festival. It has been presented by an ever-increasing number of local theatre production companies.

Steve Pryor

This blues-rock performer toured with the Paul Butterfield Blues Band, was the opening act for blues-rockers The Fabulous Thunderbirds and collaborated with Buddy Guy, John Lee Hooker, Johnny Winter, Greg Allman and Bonnie Raitt.

Playing a classic 1964 Fender Stratocaster, Pryor's music blended his passionate guitar playing with traditional blues. While Pryor had numerous additional chances to perform at higher levels, he chose to stay in Tulsa and performed frequently at area nightclubs.

He is member of the Oklahoma Blues Hall of Fame and countless members of what local music followers have dubbed as the New Tulsa Sound have cited Pryor's vocal and instrumental stylings as being major influences on their career.

Pryor died from injuries sustained in a motorcycle accident in north Tulsa in 2016.

Rafael (a/k/a Rafael F. Sharpe)

This Tulsa-born New Age music practitioner had a 1988 album *Music to Disappear In* that sold a half-million copies. Music from that album is frequently used in hospitals along with yoga and massage classes. From 1972 through 1984, he was one of the leaders of the New Age movement in the United States.

His father was a ragtime piano player while his mother studied the psychic world. He studied piano at the San Francisco Conservatory then spent 10 years as a music instructor and performer at the Esalen Institute at Big Sur.

Rafael and his wife, Kutira Decosterd, currently live in Hawaii where they founded the Kahua Hawaiian Institute and the Maui Eco Retreat.

Ben Rector

The 2003 graduate of Tulsa's Metro Christian Academy is a poster boy of sorts for how independent musicians can achieve success through digital music distribution and social media. This musical style of this indie pop singer-songwriter has been described as a blend of pop, folk and rock with influences from diverse artists such as Sam Cooke, Paul McCartney, Randy Newman and James Taylor.

Rector is one of the highest-ranking musicians on TuneCore, which is the world's leading digital music aggregator. His albums have been downloaded nearly a half-million times while his single tracks have been downloaded over five million times.

Three of his albums reached the top five of the *Billboard* U.S. Folk, U.S. Indie and U.S. Rock charts solely through digital downloads and word-of-mouth praise for his live performances. Rector's 2013 album, *The Walking in Between,* reached number two on U.S. Folk chart, number four on the U.S. Indie chart and number five on the U.S. Rock chart. Then his 2015 album, *Brand New,* and his 2018 album Magic, each reached the top spot on U.S. Folk chart and number two on the U.S. Indie chart. Videos from his 2022 album *The Joy of Music* featured Dave Koz and Snoop Dog.

Ayn Robbins

She and songwriting partner Carol Connors wrote the lyrics to "Gonna Fly Now (*Theme From Rocky*)" for the 1976 boxing movie that starred Sylvester Stallone and won an Oscar for Best Motion Picture. Not only would that song be included in eight subsequent movies connected with *Rocky* but it would become a staple in pop culture music history.

In a 2018 Tulsa World interview, Ayn (pronounced like Ann) Robbins said "Gonna Fly Now" was originally written as a full-length song. But when the film's producers said the song was slowing the pace, she and Connors shortened the song to just 29 words.

"Gonna Fly Now," was one of two Robbins-Collins songs that was nominated for an Oscar for Best Original Song. The other was "Someone's Waiting for You" by Shelby Flint from the 1977 Disney movie *The Rescuers*.

Robbins, who has written over 200 songs, still lives in Tulsa and has written lyrics for commercials and promotional ventures from national brands such as Mattel Toys to Tulsa-based businesses.

Tony Romanello

A graduate of Bishop Kelley High School and the University of Tulsa, Romanello is known for music that features a multitude of effects-laden vocals, sampling of other songs and overdubbing, not unlike the Oklahoma City-based band The Flaming Lips.

Romanello began playing the guitar at the age of six and formed his first band, YSY, at the age of 14. Much of his fame has come from being played on college radio stations throughout the United States.

These days, Romanello and The Black Jackets performed in venues throughout Oklahoma and have their music sold through online retailers.

SafetySuit

This pop rock band comprised of former Oral Roberts University students quickly achieved national recognition with their first two albums in addition to touring with artists like Daughtry, 3 Doors Down and The Goo Goo Dolls.

SafetySuit's 2008 debut album *Life Left to Go* peaked at number five on the Billboard Heatseekers Album chart and the video for the song "Stay" reached the top of the TV network VH1's *Top 20 Video Countdown.*

A 2012 album, *These Times,* reached number three on the *Billboard* Rock Music chart. One of the songs from that album, "Never Stop" was remixed in 2015 and quickly became popular as a wedding song with over 20 million plays and the song's video became a YouTube sensation.

Led by vocalist Doug Brown, the band was originally known as Crew but changed its name to SafetySuit to avoid legal troubles and relocated to Nashville in 2005.

Larry Shaeffer

This University of Tulsa graduate and concert promoter revived Cain's Ballroom in 1977 and for nearly 20 years it would become Tulsa's rock music mecca. He was a musical visionary who brought up-and-coming acts to play at Cain's just before they would hit the big time.

Among those aspiring rockers were Van Halen, Huey Lewis and the News, Pat Benatar, Talking Heads, INXS, Marilyn Manson, the Police and Metallica as well as pioneers in the New Wave, punk rock and techno fields.

But the most infamous event during Shaeffer's ownership of Cain's was the January 11, 1978 performance by the British punk rock legends The Sex Pistols. Lead singer Sid Vicious became so frustrated that he punched a massive hole in one wall.

That hole is still there and numerous musicians have paid tribute, of sorts, by placing their fist through that gaping hole whenever they've played at Cain's.

Shaeffer and his Little Wing Productions also promoted Tulsa concerts by Chuck Berry, Frank Sinatra, JJ Cale, Merle Haggard, BB King and Bon Jovi.

For many years, Shaeffer staged an event known as The Freaker's Ball which became Tulsa's most outrageous Halloween party for its envelope-pushing costumes and loud music. During the Christmas holidays, he also used Cain's as a distribution point for toys and food for needy children and their families.

Mike Settle

This former member of the Tulsa Boy Singers ensemble was the musical director for The New Christy Minstrels folk group and a songwriting co-founder, along with Kenny Rogers, of the pop rock band The First Edition.

Settle was born in Tulsa and lived there until the ninth grade when his family moved to Muskogee, Oklahoma. He was a member of the Tulsa Boy Singers from the fifth through seventh grades.

The Oklahoma City University graduate sang in Oklahoma coffee houses and appeared on the ABC musical variety show *Hootenanny*. Then Settle moved to California and spent 1966 and 1967 as the musical director for the New Christy Minstrels where he and Rogers began their musical partnership prior to leaving and forming The First Edition.

After Rogers and Settle had the 1967 psychedelic-themed hit "Just Dropped In (To See What Condition My Condition Was In), Settle wrote a wistful song about a man who couldn't maintain a romantic relationship with a woman due to job-related travel requirements. It would become Settle's biggest hit and was covered by 21 artists.

"But You Know I Love You" would become a major hit for Rogers as well as country music singers Bill Anderson and Dolly Parton. Rogers' version reached number 19 on the *Billboard* Hot 100 chart. Anderson's 1969 version climbed to number two on the *Billboard* Country Music chart while Parton's 1981 version reached the top spot on the Country Music chart.

Settle left The First Edition in 1970 and joined Running Bear and Goldstein. That group's original version of "Rings" would become a major hit for Cymarron in 1971 and for Lobo in 1974. In later years, he worked as a music producer for Kim Carnes and The Kingston Trio and worked as a Nashville-based music journalist.

Steve Smith

Best known as the drummer during the heyday of the Journey, Steve Smith was inducted into the Rock and Roll Hall of Fame in 2017 and has a connection to Tulsa, albeit a brief one.

Smith served as Journey's drummer in 1978-85, 1995-98 and 2015-20. His drum work was heard on icon Journey hits such as "Open Arms", "Don't Stop Believin'", "Who's Crying Now?" and "Separate Ways."

While attending the Berklee College of Music in Boston in the early 1970s, he learned that the University of Tulsa's stage band needed a drummer and Smith accepted a scholarship offer.

But for whatever reasons, Smith thought Tulsa's music scene was not to his liking and he walked away from the scholarship after one semester to return Berklee.

Smith grew up in Massachusetts and received his first drum kit at the age of two. After taking drumming lessons from a Boston-based musician, Smith would be heavily influenced by big band and jazz groups.

Modern Drummer magazine put Smith in its list of the Top 25 drummers of all time in all genres of music. He has also performed with pop superstars Bryan Adams and Mariah Carey along with jazz violinist Jean-Luc Ponty.

St. Vincent

This Tulsa-born artist has been called "the female David Bowie" by music critics for songs feature challenging arrangements, use of numerous musical instruments and lyrics that veer wildly from joy to anxicty and anything else in between.

Born Anne Erin Clark, she took up guitar playing at the age of 12 and worked as the tour manager for an uncle and aunt who performed as a jazz duo. She later moved to the Dallas-Fort Worth metroplex as a youth and spent three years at the Berklee College of Music.

The moniker of St. Vincent was adopted in 2006 and refers to the middle name of a great-grandmother as well as a song that describes the hospital where poet Dylan Thomas died.

Four of her albums reached the top 20 of the *Billboard* album charts. The most successful was her 2017 semi-biographical and glam rock album *Masseduction* which peaked at number 10 in the USA and number six in Great Britain. The title track won a 2017 Grammy Award for Best Rock Song.

St. Vincent's 2021 album *Daddy's Home* won a Grammy for Best Alternative Music album. The title track was about her father's conviction and release from prison for crimes related to financial fraud and money laundering.

Her songs have been featured in soundtracks for *The Twilight Saga* vampire movies as well as the HBO drama series *Boardwalk Empire*.

St. Vincent starred in and co-wrote the script for a 2020 thriller movie The Nowhere Inn. The film was described as a fictional attempt to create a documentary about St. Vincent's life.

She currently splits her time living in Dallas, Los Angeles and New York City.

Clyde Stacy

This man was one of Tulsa's earliest rock and roll hit makers but he learned his musical lessons well by hanging out and jamming with Buddy Holly when they were high school students in Lubbock, Texas.

Stacy and Holly each had their own bands but often sat in on each other's gigs at a local root beer stand. Waylon Jennings, who was part of Holly's band and a future country music star, performed on occasion with Stacy.

Stacy's family moved back to Tulsa and he soon caught the ear of a local disc jockey, Don Wallace. That led to a record contract with his first two songs being "So Young" and "Hoy Hoy." "So Young" had an overdubbing of a sultry female's voice that led to it being banned by some American radio stations but Stacy's songs generally fared better in Canada.

While Stacy's songs did modestly on the record charts, it resulted in some tours and a few appearances on *American Bandstand*. After a short time in Pennsylvania and being the opening act for Elvis Presley and Patsy Cline, he returned to Oklahoma in 1975 to operate a fence company and play occasional gigs with Leon Russell. Stacy was killed in a 2013 auto accident near Muskogee, Oklahoma.

Ryan Tedder

This Oral Roberts University graduate is the lead singer of the pop group OneRepublic as well as being a songwriter-producer that has worked with the likes of Leona Lewis, Maroon 5, Adele, Demi Lovato, Kelly Clarkson, Leona Lewis, Carrie Underwood, Gavin DeGraw, Jennifer Lopez, Taylor Swift and Beyonce.

Tedder was a self-taught singer who took piano lessons at the tender age of three from family members who served as church pastors or missionaries.

With OneRepublic, Tedder switches between lead vocals, piano, rhythm or bass guitar, tambourine and drums. The group's breakthrough came when they collaborated with hip-hop producer Timbaland on the song "Apologize."

That song, written by Tedder, was the most-played tune on American pop radio for the first five months of 2008 and peaked at number two on the *Billboard* U.S. singles chart and was an international top-selling single.

OneRepublic's other top 10 songs are "Good Life" which reached number eight on the *Billboard* U.S. singles chart in 2010 and "Counting Stars" which peaked at number two on that chart in 2013. Ten of the group's albums achieved platinum sales (more than one million copies sold) and three others reached gold (more than 500,000 copies sold) status.

Tedder co-wrote and produced Lewis' song "Bleeding Love," a tune that stayed atop the United Kingdom's pop charts for seven weeks in 2007 as well as hitting number one in 35 other countries. "Bleeding Love" also received a 2009 Grammy nomination for Record of the Year.

He wrote Beyonce's hit song "Halo" and helped produce the top-selling album, *I Am...Sasha Fierce*. His work with Adele on "Rumour Has It" and "Turning Tables" won Grammy for Album of the Year in 2012.

Tedder was one of the producers for two songs on Swift's best-selling CD, *1989*. That CD was best known for the wildly popular song "Shake It Off" which debuted in the top spot on the *Billboard Magazine* Hot 100 singles chart in September of 2014.

Once of Tedder's most popular hits was "I Lived" which was actually written for his young son. The song's video became a source of inspiration for many people because of a moving narrative from a teenager named Bryan Warnecke about all aspects of his life as a victim of cystic fibrosis.

In a 2019 interview with *Forbes* magazine, Tedder said he is still committed to OneRepublic's recording career but has also chosen to branch out into projects for the online media service Netflix along with musical contributions to movies and television shows.

Tyler Trepp

Trepp is one of the tenors and vocal percussionists for *a capella* group Straight No Chaser. Born in Iowa, Trepp and Lauryn Bohls were married in Tulsa in May of 2016 and make their home near Tulsa.

Known as SNC for short, the 10-man group started out performing for small student groups at the University of Indiana. Aided by positive reviews, strong social networking and having concerts aired on public television, SNC blossomed into an international sensation.

Music critics have described Straight No Chaser as having a vibe not unlike that from the "Rat Pack" era of Frank Sinatra, Dean Martin, Joey Bishop and Sammy Davis Jr. Their presentation and showmanship of songs from the 1950s through modern times are done very seriously, but also blended with doses of humor.

Their first appearance in the national spotlight came in 2006 when a video of their version of "Twelve Days of Christmas" appeared on YouTube and quickly went viral. That led to a recording contract with Atlantic Records and performances around the world.

20/20

Nathan Hale High School and Oklahoma State University graduates Ron Flynt and Steve Allen formed this power pop band in 1977 and followed Tulsa natives Dwight Twilley and Phil Seymour to Los Angeles, seeking their own musical fame and fortune.

The band existed from 1977 through 1983 and from 1995 through 2005. Of the eight albums recorded by the band, only their first two achieved most commercial success: the self-titled debut album in 1979 and *Look Out!* in 1981.

Following the band's breakup, Flynt moved to Austin, Texas and operated a recording studio while Allen did likewise in Nashville. Drummer Bill Belknap returned to Tulsa and worked at Long Branch Studio.

Jack White

This co-founder of the 2000s alternative rock band The White Stripes revealed in 2018 that he has a home in Tulsa along with a home in Nashville, Tennessee.

In a Tulsa World interview prior to his September 17, 2018 at the ONEOK Field baseball stadium, White confirmed the internet rumors about him having a home in Tulsa but refused to mention its location or how long he has been a Tulsa resident. He did confirm making a $30,000 donation to The Outsiders House Museum in Tulsa to help with its restoration and preservation.

Born as John Anthony Gillis in Detroit, Michigan, he married (and later divorced) Meg White and created an alternative rock duo named The White Stripes.

That band released six studio albums from 1999 through 2007 with three albums and six singles reaching the top 10 of the Billboard U.S. Alternative Rock music chart along with winning three Grammy Awards for Best Alternative Rock music album.

The 2003 album *Elephant* featured a song called "Seven Nation Army," a number that would become White's signature song as well as the go-to song for young people wanting to learn how to play the guitar.

White is also a record producer and played key roles in reviving the careers of country music legend Loretta Lynn (*Van Lear Rose* in 2005) and rockabilly queen Wanda Jackson (*The Party Ain't Over* in 2011).

In a 2010 article, *Rolling Stone* magazine ranked White at number 70 on its list of "The 100 Greatest Guitarists of All Time."

Chapter Three

Western Swing

"Where I grew up, Bob Wills and his Western Swing was very popular. And Western Swing is not that far from jazz and the blues."

Willie Nelson

"Swing is my favorite kind of music."

George Strait

"Rock and Roll? Why, man, that's the same kind of music we've been playin' since 1928! ...The rhythm is what's important."

Bob Wills

"(Bob Wills) was not the father of Western Swing but he was the Elvis Presley of Western Swing. He was the most popular, charismatic ambassador that Western Swing could ever have..."

Ray Benson

***

John Wooley opens *Swing on This!* his weekly one-hour radio show about Western Swing music, with a proclamation about Tulsa being "The town where Western Swing grew up." The man that was instrumental in Tulsa's influence on that music genre was Bob Wills.

What is the definition of Western Swing music, according to Wooley?

"It's a dance beat, often in two-four time, with jazz improvisation on top that relies more on stringed than brass instruments," Wooley said. "The lyrics are usually 'hillbilly' or country, but not necessarily."

Bob Wills

Jim Rob Wills hailed from Turkey, Texas and came from a musical family but began his professional life as a barber. Over time, he began performing in the Dallas-Fort Worth area and changed his name to Bob Wills. While his father's fiddle band was a great influence in his musical heritage, so were the blues and up-tempo songs from African American laborers that he worked alongside while picking cotton in fields near his childhood home.

Wills teamed with Herman Arnsparger and two brothers, Milton and Durwood Brown, to form the Wills Fiddle Band in 1930. That outfit was renamed as the Aladdin Laddies and then the Light Crust Doughboys because Light Crust Flour sponsored their radio show. Wills drove one of the company's delivery trucks as his day job then played with the band at night.

Milton Brown was the Wills band's lead vocalist until 1932 when he left to form another seminal Western Swing band, Milton Brown and the Musical Brownies. That group enjoyed great success until Brown died in a 1936 auto accident. Wills' band filled that musical void and enjoyed increased popularity, but it came with a price.

W. Lee "Pappy" O'Daniel was the radio show's master of ceremonies and the clash of their strong personalities led to Wills parting ways in 1933. O'Daniel would be elected as the governor of Texas in 1938 and three years later, he would defeat future United States President Lyndon B. Johnson in a U.S. Senate campaign.

After short tenures in Waco, Texas and Oklahoma City, Wills took his band to Tulsa and renamed them the Texas Playboys. Good fortune soon followed when they secured Cain's Ballroom in the northern part of downtown Tulsa as their musical headquarters.

A major step forward was in the form of a live weekday lunch-hour radio broadcast on KVOO Radio, a 50,000-watt station with a signal stretching from the Canadian Rocky Mountains to the Rio Grande River valley in Texas.

Wills' band also hosted a gospel radio show on the weekend, supposedly to provide a balance to the often-unsavory reputation of dance halls. They played for dances at Cain's every Thursday and Saturday night along with weeknight concerts throughout Texas and nearby states, but they never missed their daily radio show.

That time in Tulsa from 1934 to 1942 proved to be the golden era for Bob Wills and his band. Nothing brought more joy to Wills' heart, as well as to the owners of Cain's and other dance halls, than to see a jam-packed dance floor, people having a grand old time and experiencing the electric atmosphere that Wills' band created.

Vocalist Tommy Duncan had an unflappable appearance plus a smooth singing style much like Bing Crosby. Wills had a charismatic smile and stage presence and his interaction with band members was magical. Equally important was when one of Wills' trademark exclamations provided the opportunity for a band member to take the spotlight and display his own musical talent.

There were female vocalists reminiscent of the Andrews Sisters along with trumpets, saxophones, multiple fiddles, electric steel guitars, electric mandolins and drums.

It was during those Tulsa years that Wills' innovation and foresight not only took his band and Western Swing music to new heights but arguably provided a precursor for rock and roll with the horn section being replaced over time by electric guitars.

Over four decades, Wills had countless songs that reached either the top 10 or top spot on the country music charts. Some of his most memorable hits were "Spanish Two-Step" (1935), "Right or Wrong" (1936), "Maiden's Prayer" and "San Antonio Rose" (1938), "Corrine, Corrina" and "New San Antonio Rose" and "Time Changes Everything" (1939), "Take Me Back to Tulsa" and "Cherokee Maiden" (1941), "Home in San Antone" (1943), "Hang Your Head in Shame" and "Stars and Stripes on Iwo Jima" (1945), "Roly Poly" and "Stay a Little Longer" (1946), "Sugar Moon" (1947), "Bubbles in My Beer" (1948), "Ida Red Likes the Boogie" and "Faded Love" (1950) and "Heart to Heart Talk" (1960).

Two of his biggest hits played on opposite ends of the spectrum of emotions. "San Antonio Rose" was poetic in describing a lost love but had a very catchy melody. "Faded Love" was a fiddle song once played by Wills' father but Bob and his brother, Billy Jack, wrote the heartfelt lyrics for the song that has been recorded by over 300 performers. Bob also provided financial security for his mother by signing over to her all of his royalties from "Faded Love."

After a brief time of military service during World War II, Wills and his band moved to California and became a big hit thanks to many transplanted Oklahomans and others who moved there during the Great Depression.

Shortly after moving to California, Willis invited an aspiring 13-year-singer to perform with him. That teenager from Abbott, Texas named Willie Nelson later gained fame for his own unique style of music, would be inducted into the Country Music Hall of Fame and was once name-checked in a song about Bob Wills. Ironically, one of the fiddle players in the later years of Bob Wills' band, Johnny Gimble, made several records with Nelson.

But Wills' presence, both in the dances at Cain's and the live radio broadcasts on KVOO, continued for several years because younger brother Johnnie Lee Wills took over those responsibilities. It was not uncommon, though, to have members of Bob's band come back to Tulsa to play for a while in Johnnie Lee's band and vice versa.

Despite his happy-go-lucky demeanor, Wills had his issues. He was married five times (twice to Milton Brown's widow), could be temperamental and moody and got in trouble with bandmates and dance hall owners when drinking binges kept him from appearing before sellout crowds.

Wills got in trouble with the federal government after he turned over the operation of a Dallas-area nightclub with his name on it to individuals whose shady dealings resulted in non-payment of taxes to the Internal Revenue Service.

"Time Changes Everything" also described what happened to his musical career during the 1950s. Country music was changing, and rock and roll was the hot new sound for young people. Radio station managers felt Wills' music didn't fit into the format of standards or the new sounds of country or rock and roll. The results were his songs got less and less airplay and crowds for his dances grew smaller.

Wills was inducted into the Country Music Hall of Fame in 1968 but suffered two heart attacks in previous years and was partially paralyzed after a 1969 stroke. While in Texas in 1973 for a recording session which reunited him with many of the original Texas Playboys, Wills suffered a massive stroke, lapsed into a coma and passed away on May 13, 1975.

His tombstone in Tulsa's Memorial Park Cemetery has a fiddle and a bow with the opening words from "San Antonio Rose" providing a fitting epitaph: "Deep within my heart lies a melody."

Countless singers and groups continue to carry the torch for Western Swing music but Ray Benson, the founder and lead singer of Asleep at the Wheel, best summarized the impact of Wills in part of an interview posted on the website, www.texasplayboys.net.

"...He was not the father of Western Swing, but he was the Elvis Presley of Western Swing. He was the most popular, charismatic ambassador that Western Swing could ever have. He put drums and electric guitars into country music. He brought a style and a stage presence that was so in-your-face. It was what the rock and roll attitude was all about..."

Benson also co-wrote and starred in a two-act musical drama, *A Ride with Bob: From Austin to Tulsa* in which Benson and Wills meet on a tour bus and what their conversation back then would have been like. The play featured 15 Bob Wills hits along with a mini concert by Asleep at the Wheel.

Johnnie Lee Wills

Bob's younger brother and played on just as many, if not more, live radio broadcasts and dances at Cain's as Bob had done. Johnnie Lee played banjo in Bob's band in 1934 before switching to playing the fiddle.

When Wills moved to California in 1940, Johnnie Lee renamed his band as Johnnie Lee Wills and All the Boys. He also continued sponsoring the Tulsa Stampede rodeo, an event that Bob had begun and evolved into a major stop on the professional rodeo tour.

His biggest hit was a 12-bar blues novelty number called "Rag Mop" which he co-wrote with Deacon Anderson in 1949. The lyrics consisted of spelling out those two words, several sessions of scatting and lots of Western Swing instrumental music. "Rag Mop" was later covered by the Ames Brothers and Lionel Hampton and even served as the basis for a skit by The Muppets.

Johnnie Lee kept the KVOO radio broadcasts alive through 1958 and also operated a clothing store in east Tulsa prior to his death in 1984. In 1996, the street directly in front of the Expo Square Pavilion, which housed the Tulsa Stampede rodeo, was renamed as Johnnie Lee Wills Lane.

Al Clauser and His Oklahoma Outlaws

The Illinois native and his band made Western Swing popular in the midwestern United States and got a career boost from Gene Autry before relocating to Oklahoma during World War II.

Clauser played in clubs around Peoria, Illinois during his high school years and his trio became a six-piece act and performed on WMBD-AM Radio and later on Des Moines powerhouse WHO-AM Radio. Despite none of the band members ever visiting the Sooner State, Clauser came up with the nickname Oklahoma Outlaws. Autry heard the band on WHO-AM and hired them to perform three songs in his 1937 Western movie *Rootin' Tootin' Rhythm*. Shortly afterwards, Clauser's band was signed to a contract with Mutual Broadcasting Network and their shows were carried by over 270 radio stations.

The band moved to Tulsa during World War II and grew to nine members, all of whom worked day jobs in air defense production. The band appeared frequently on KTUL-AM Radio and then KTUL-TV during the 1950s. An aspiring 12-year-old singer named Clara Ann Fowler got her first big break by appearing on TV with Clauser's band. That led to her recording her first songs with Clauser's band, she later became known as Patti Page and the rest is music history.

Clauser's band broke up in the late 1950s but he continued working at KTUL-TV and became a recurring character during the 1970s on the station's afternoon children's show *Uncle Zeb's Cartoon Camp*.

In 2000, a German record company created a compilation CD of Clauser's music featuring pop tunes like "Bill Bailey" and "Little Brown Jug" along with numerous country songs record by the band.

Jake Erwin

This Tulsa native spent 20 years playing the upright bass since 2001 in the hot jazz and Western Swing band Hot Club of Cowtown.

The upright bass is also known as the "slap bass" and its popularity has progressed from its birth in the New Orleans jazz community to Western Swing and to rockabilly and even rock and roll.

Erwin became interested in roots music while in elementary school and took up playing the double bass. He is a member of the Texas Western Swing Hall of Fame.

Leon McAuliffe

The steel guitar player in Bob Wills' band and had a successful career of his own in Western Swing and country music from the 1940s through the 1970s. When it was time for McAuliffe to play his signature song "Steel Guitar Rag" or any other number, Wills' introduction was a rousing declaration of "Take it away, Leon!"

McAuliffe and Robert Lee Dunn, who played for Milton Brown and His Musical Brownies, are credited by music historians as the two men who made the steel guitar popular. Some of those same experts have said that with the blues background that McAuliffe and Dunn shared, they also helped inspire an evolution of the electric guitar in rhythm and blues nearly a quarter of a century later.

Born in Houston, Texas, McAuliffe joined Willis in the Light Crust Doughboys band at the age of 16 and stayed with Wills two years later when he moved to Tulsa and created the Texas Playboys. McAuliffe also helped Wills with the composition of the Western Swing classic, "San Antonio Rose."

McAuliffe returned to Tulsa after World War II and formed his own band, Leon McAuliffe and His Cimarron Boys. The band's name was linked to their performances at the Cimarron Ballroom at the intersection of West Fourth Street and South Denver Avenue in downtown Tulsa. Today, that plot of land is the site of Tulsa's main bus terminal.

McAuliffe had two songs that reached the top 20 of the country music charts: "Panhandle Rag" (number six in 1949) and "Cozy Inn" (number 16 in 1961). He came out of semiretirement in 1971 as the narrator and featured steel guitar player on a version of "Faded Love" recorded by Tompall and the Glaser Brothers.

Laura Lee McBride

Known as the "Queen of Western Swing" for being the first female vocalist with a Western Swing band, McBride began her career with Tulsa radio station KVOO-AM when Bob Wills invited her to join the Texas Playboys. She was inducted into the Western Swing Music Society Hall of Fame in 1987.

McBride was known for a powerful singing voice that was spiced with laughter and a sassy attitude. Her trademark song was "I Betcha My Heart I Love You" which she recorded in 1943.

After joining Wills' band, she moved to California where the band frequently toured and also appeared in a number of B-grade Western-themed movies. Her second husband was Cameron Hill, a guitarist with the Texas Playboys.

McBride later performed with Hank Williams, Tex Ritter and Ernest Tubb and recorded an album of Western Swing favorites during the 1970s. She later worked as a radio station disc jockey, sold real estate and managed a dinner theater in Mountain View, Arkansas founded by Grand Old Opry star Grandpa Jones and his wife.

She was born in the tiny town (population just over 100) of Bridgeport, Oklahoma, which is just west of Oklahoma City and along historic Route 66. Her father was "Tex" Owens who wrote the country classic "Cattle Call" that was made famous by Eddy Arnold.

The family moved to Kansas City, Missouri and she made her singing debut on KMBC-AM Radio at the age of 10. She later formed her own band, married a guitarist from her father's band then moved to California where they would appear in 13 of Gene Autry's movies.

Chapter Four

Country

"If you talk bad about country music, it's like saying bad things about my momma. Them's fighting words!"

Dolly Parton

"Country music is the poetry of the American spirit."

Steve Maraboli, author

"(Europe has) this tradition of self-revelation in popular music. We have it here – it's called Country Western music...I think that's where the deeper and more complex subjects are treated."

Leonard Cohen

"Country music is three chords and the truth."

Harlan Howard

"I started writing songs after I heard Hank Williams."

Bob Dylan

***

Garth Brooks

The foundation for the Tulsa-born singer's eventual worldwide empire was laid in Oklahoma with Tulsa playing a very significant role.

Brooks and his band, Stillwater, performed at the Tulsa City Limits nightclub on August 10, 1989 shortly after the release of his self-titled debut album. John Wooley was the *Tulsa World* entertainment writer back then and predicted that Brooks would be the next big thing in country music after hearing his musical talent and his display of showmanship that night.

Looking back now, Wooley has more than ample reason to say, "I told you so."

Brooks blurred the musical boundaries of country and pop and rock, and his concerts were extravaganzas that rivaled the biggest and loudest by any rock and roll act.

He has sold over 170 million records and trails only The Beatles (183 million) for the most ever sold by any musical act. In addition, he is the first artist to have top five singles on the *Billboard* Country Music charts across five decades: charting from the 1980s through the 2020s.

Brooks is the first artist in the history of the Recording Industry Association of America (RIAA) to earn nine career Diamond Awards, which happens when an artist sells more than one million albums. And he's also the only seven-time winner of the Country Music Association's Entertainer of the Year award.

Born in 1962 as Troyal Garth Brooks, he was part of blended family whose mother, Colleen McElroy Carroll Brooks, was a country singer on Capitol Records in the 1950s and appeared on ABC-TV's *Ozark Jubilee* musical variety show. The family also held weekly talent nights where all six children had to sing or perform a short skit.

Brooks attended Oklahoma State University from 1980 through 1983 and was a javelin thrower on the OSU Cowboys' track and field team. He graduated with a degree in advertising, but his passion was for music and he performed in several restaurants and night clubs throughout the state, both as a single act and with a small band.

Brooks' self-titled debut album was released in 1989 and musical history would be made over most of the next two decades. Nineteen singles and 13 albums reached the top spot on the *Billboard* country music charts with nine of those albums peaking at number one on the *Billboard* pop music charts. Then there would be over 100 honors from national and international music associations along with a Golden Globe nomination and a pair of Grammys.

He has also been a savvy marketer, taking time to visit local radio, TV and newspaper outlets throughout his career and not carrying a holier-than-thou attitude that many entertainers have been known to do. He went against the grain by creating exclusive distribution and merchandising agreements for digital music sales through his own website and, in later years, with Walmart and Amazon.

His 15-year marriage to Sandy Mahl produced three daughters and they built a large home east of Owasso, Oklahoma, one of Tulsa's northeastern suburbs. After the couple's divorce in 2001, Brooks fulfilled promises to help his ex-wife raise their daughters and not to tour until his youngest daughter graduated from high school.

Brooks married country singer Trisha Yearwood in 2005 and in 2009 began a five-year run of weekend-only concerts at the Encore Hotel and Casino on the Las Vegas Strip. Encore owner Steve Wynn provided a private jet to take Brooks to and from Las Vegas to help fulfill family obligations.

Other concerts were held outside of his Vegas commitments, mostly as charity fundraisers in the aftermath of natural disasters or other tragic events. A 2013 concert at the University of Oklahoma's football stadium organized by country singer Toby Keith to benefit victims of the Moore, Oklahoma tornado tragedy was Brooks' first concert in his native state since 1997.

He also fulfilled his earlier promise that a homecoming concert in Tulsa would be part of a 42-month long international tour that began in 2014. That evolved into seven sellout concerts at the BOK Center, every one of which sold out in a single day.

The 2017 Garth Brooks World Tour with his wife, Trisha Yearwood, sold over 6.3 million tickets, making it the largest musical tour in North American history. The Global Stadium Tour lasted three years and drew an average attendance of 95,000 in each venue.

Brooks has been involved in the rapid growth of internet radio; first with his own channel on the SiriusXM service then in 2023 with the launch of the country music-oriented SEVENS Radio Network on TuneIn, a global streaming service. TuneIn claims to have 75 million listeners in 122 countries.

Among Brooks' other honors are being a seven-time winner of the Country Music Association (CMA) Entertainer of the Year award, the Kennedy Center Honors and membership in The Grand Ole Opry, Songwriters Hall of Fame, Nashville Songwriters Hall of Fame, Musicians Hall of Fame and the Country Music Hall of Fame.

The eldest of Garth's three children, Allie Coleen Brooks, is the only one to follow her father's music footsteps. Performing as Allie Colleen, she is a singer-songwriter whose debut album *Stones* was released in 2021.

Jim Halsey

While he never sang a single note or told a joke on stage, Jim Halsey has been one of the most influential people in the entertainment world for over 60 years and chose Tulsa to be the base for an international business that represented over 50 entertainment acts.

The Independence, Kansas native is best known for his promotion of country music artists in general and with Roy Clark, The Oak Ridge Boys and Hank Thompson in particular. Among the other country music superstars that Halsey has represented are Reba McIntyre, Merle Haggard, George Jones, Tammy Wynette, The Judds, Clint Black and Dwight Yoakum. Performers in other fields turned to Halsey in recognition of his business knowledge. Some of those included Bob Hope, James Brown, Woody Herman, Leon Russell, Ricky Nelson, Wanda Jackson, The Osmond Brothers and The Righteous Brothers.

One of Halsey's groundbreaking achievements came in 1961 by convincing Capitol Records executives to do something unheard of back then: make an album out of a live performance by a country music star. *Hank Thompson at the Golden Nugget* was recorded at the Las Vegas casino of that same name and became one of the biggest albums in Thompson's career.

Music and diplomatic history were made in 1976 when Halsey worked with the State Department to present the first country music concerts in the Soviet Union. Clark and The Oak Ridge Boys were the headlining acts. Many diplomats hailed Halsey's efforts as helping pave the way for improved relations between the two nations. Clark's return to the Soviet Union in 1988 for another concert tour was filmed for a TV documentary.

Halsey was a junior college student when he read the biography of entertainment impresario Sol Hurok and felt that Hurok's type of work was his life's calling. A Tulsa musician, Leon McAuliffe, was the first artist to sign with his agency. Then Halsey turned to promoting events in the southeastern Kansas and northeastern Oklahoma area such as ice shows, professional wrestling and circuses as well as concerts.

Halsey later owned Churchill Records along with radio stations and was active in Tulsa business and entertainment circles. He sold the booking agency division of his business to the William Morris Agency in 1990 but stayed with William Morris as a consultant for many years.

After that, he worked with Oklahoma City University to develop a curriculum towards earning a degree in music business and entertainment and wrote two books about the industry. His current effort is a program called The Starmaker with an online educational program for young people interested in pursuing a career in the performing end or the business end of the music world.

Roy Clark

A 2009 inductee into the Country Music Hall of Fame and a member of the Grand Old Opry since 1987, Roy Clark was one of country music's hottest performers in the 1970s as well as being a television star. He also recorded albums that did well in the fields of bluegrass, jazz, pop and gospel.

Clark had nine *Billboard* Top 10 country music singles in his career as well as five Top 10 vocal albums and a pair of Top 10 instrumental albums. He won a Grammy Award in 1982 for the Best Country Instrumental Performance ("Alabama Jubilee") along with seven awards from the Country Music Association. The highlight was taking home the coveted CMA Entertainer of the Year honor in 1973.

Music was part of Clark's family when they lived near Washington, D.C. and he learned at an early age to play the guitar, banjo and fiddle while also being an adroit player of classical guitar. That led to an invitation from country singer Jimmy Dean to appear on his local TV musical variety show but Dean fired Clark for being tardy too often.

He later joined rockabilly legend Wanda Jackson as one of her guitar players.

Clark eventually signed with Tulsa-based entertainment promoter Jim Halsey and his career took off shortly afterwards with expanded opportunities in music and television.

The first of his nine Top 10 country singles was a 1962 remake of the Bill Anderson ballad "Tips of My Fingers." His only number one song was the romantic ballad "Come Live with Me." The 1969 song "Yesterday When I Was Young" which lamented about the what-ifs of life reached number nine on the country charts and crossed over to number 19 on the *Billboard* pop charts.

Novelty songs were a source of success for Clark as well. His 1969 kiss-off hit "Thank God and Greyhound" reached number six on the country charts. Another notable number had one of longest song titles in music history, "The Lawrence Welk-Hee Haw-Counter Revolution Polka." Needless to say, the song was an instrumental.

Clark and Buck Owens hosted the television variety show *Hee Haw* from 1969 through 1992. Clark was also a frequent fill-in host for Johnny Carson on NBC's *The Tonight Show* as well as periodically playing various characters on the CBS situation comedy *The Beverly Hillbillies*.

When Branson, Missouri became a tourist hotspot for live entertainment during the 1980s, Clark opened a venue and performed there for several years before selling it.

The annual Roy Clark Celebrity Golf Classic, held during a nine-year span of the 1970s and 1980s at Tulsa's Cedar Ridge Country Club raised over $800,000 for Tulsa's Children's Medical Center, one of the country music superstar's most beloved charities. The weekend event was capped off with Roy Clark's Star Night concert at the ORU Mabee Center. Among the big-name celebrities who appeared at that event were Bob Hope, Danny Thomas, Chad Everett, Dale Roberts and Fred MacMurray.

Tulsa's Union Public Schools named an elementary school in his honor in 1978 in appreciation for his charitable works and commitment to childhood education programs.

While attending grade school, Clark dreamed of pursuing a baseball career and he teamed with Tulsa businessman Bill Rollings to save professional baseball in Tulsa in 1977. After the Tulsa Oilers relocated to New Orleans due to issues with an outdated and crumbling baseball stadium, Clark and Rollings purchased a Double-A franchise based in Lafayette, Louisiana and brought it to Tulsa and the new team was named the Tulsa Drillers.

His love for the Tulsa Drillers was so strong that he even wore the team's jersey on NBC's *The Tonight Show* on August 12, 1977 when he co-hosted that night with *Welcome Back, Kotter* sitcom star Gabe Kaplan. Clark was a co-owner of the Drillers from 1977 through 1982.

Clark passed away in Tulsa in 2018 at the age of 85. He and his wife, Barbara, were married for 51 years, one of the longest marriages in country music history.

Fred Rose

Prior to signing Hank Williams to his first recording contract and co-founding the Acuff-Rose Music firm that was instrumental in country music's development, Rose worked as a disc jockey at Tulsa's KVOO-AM radio during the early 1940s.

He hosted a morning show that leaned towards popular music but over time, he befriended Bob Wills and the Texas Playboys, who were the station's superstars back then and became intrigued with the pop and jazz influences found in Wills' music.

Rose moved to Nashville in 1942 and partnered with the Grand Old Opry legend singer Roy Acuff to create that city's first music publishing company. Then in 1946, Hank Williams walked into the Acuff-Rose office and signed a contract after performing a short audition for Rose.

Over the years, Rose wrote or co-wrote some of Williams' biggest hits such as "Move It on Over," "I'll Never Get Out of This World Alive," "Kaw-Liga," "Take These Chains from My Heart," and "Mansion on a Hill."

Rose and Wills kept in touch, and he wrote or co-wrote the Wills hits "Home in San Antone," "Deep Water" and "Roly Poly." Arguably, the biggest Rose hit was "Blue Eyes Crying in the Rain" which was originally recorded by Acuff and later became a megahit for Willie Nelson.

When the Country Music Hall of Fame inducted its first three members in 1961, Fred Rose and Hank Williams were two of those honorees. The other was the pioneering country music singer from the 1920s and 1930s, Jimmie Rodgers.

Gene Autry

Spending one year as a singing cowboy on Tulsa's KVOO-AM radio station helped build the career foundation for this multi-talented performer. Autry's songs sold over 100 million copies and he was inducted into the Country Music Hall of Fame and the National Cowboy Hall of Fame.

Born as Orval Grover Autry, he performed for nine months during 1928 on KVOO-AM's weekly live broadcasts with the nickname of "Oklahoma's Yodeling Cowboy." The following year, Autry moved to Chicago and would gain national attention on WLS Radio's *National Barn Dance*.

Prior to appearing on KVOO, Autry worked night shifts as a telegrapher for the St. Louis-San Francisco Railway in small towns around Tulsa and would play his guitar and sing to pass the time. While those activities eventually got him fired, an Oklahoma-born passenger heard Autry singing and encouraged him to pursue a professional career. That passenger was the legendary humorist Will Rogers.

Autry had a prolific musical career, making 640 records and writing or co-writing over 300 songs. His breakout hit was the 1932 song "That Silver-Haired Daddy of Mine" followed by the song about a cowboy's life "Back in the Saddle Again."

Autry wrote the Christmas song "Here Comes Santa Claus" in 1948 after seeing and hearing the delight of children in what is now known as the Hollywood Christmas Parade. His version of "Rudolph the Red-Nosed Reindeer" sold over 30 million copies and covers of "Frosty the Snowman" and "Santa Claus Is Coming to Town" became million-sellers as well.

From 1940 through 1956, CBS Radio carried the Sunday night broadcasts of Autry's *Melody Ranch*; a program sponsored by Doublemint chewing gum that featured music, comedy and drama sketches. *The Gene Autry Show* was a TV series airing from 1950 through 1955 with Pat Buttram as Autry's sidekick on journeys to preserve law and order throughout the Western frontier. Buttram later appeared as the farmer-turned-salesman Mr. Haney on the CBS sitcom *Green Acres*.

Autry also owned radio and television stations and a record company, but baseball was his favorite sport. He owned the American League's California Angels 1961 through 1997. That team, which reached the playoffs three times but never won a championship for Autry, was also known as the Los Angeles Angels, the Anaheim Angels and the current moniker of the Los Angeles Angels of Anaheim.

Trenna Barnes

This Jenks High school alumnus was the lead singer for the country-rock band Cowboy Crush from 2003 through 2010. Their biggest-selling single was their debut song "Nobody Ever Died of a Broken Heart" which peaked at number 56 on the Billboard country music chart in 2005.

Since the band's breakup, Barnes has worked as an actress and singer with various local and regional theatrical companies. In later years, she portrayed June Carter Cash in a touring Broadway music show based on the movie *Ring of Fire*.

Junior Brown

Best known as a staple of the alternative country and Americana music scenes based in Austin, Texas, Jamieson "Junior" Brown's time during the 1980s as a music instructor at what is now Rogers State University in nearby Claremore redefined his professional and personal life.

Brown was born in Cottonwood, Arizona and his family relocated to Indiana during his childhood years. Growing up, he learned to play the piano at a very early age, became infatuated with rock legends The Beatles and The Beach Boys along with legendary bluesmen John Lee Hooker and Lightnin' Hopkins. During the 1970s, his focus turned to country music and legendary performers Ray Price, Ernest Tubb and Merle Haggard.

He moved to the Tulsa area for a chance to be mentored by steel guitar legend and Bob Wills cohort Leon McAuliffe. It was McAuliffe who helped Brown get a job as a guitar instructor at the Hank Thompson School of Country Music at RSU's predecessor, Rogers State College.

One of Brown's students back then, Tanya Rae, would become Brown's rhythm guitarist and background vocalist as well as his wife.

During that time, Brown developed a two-necked musical instrument he called the "Guit Steel" which allowed him to switch between a regular guitar and a steel guitar while playing a song. The "traditional" guitar was on the top half of the instrument, the steel portion was on the lower half, and it would be anchored on a stand.

Brown has often said that the Guit Steel was created as a matter of convenience in his performances and not to be stereotyped as a one-man band or musical gimmick.

Two of Brown's songs reached the lower levels of the *Billboard* Top 100 country music charts. The first was his 1993 song "Highway Patrol" (peaking at 73) and "My Wife Thinks Your Dead" in 1995 (peaking at 68) with Brown heavily imitating Tubb's singing style.

The video for that latter song won the 1996 Country Music Association's Video of the Year Award. The video's plot featured the diminutive Brown being haunted by an ex-lover, portrayed by 6-foot-7 former University of North Carolina basketball player Gwendolyn Gillingham. Tanya Rae Brown portrayed the faithful wife in the video.

"Stone Walls and Steel Bars" was a 1998 musical project involving Brown and bluegrass music legend Ralph Stanley that received an award from the International Bluegrass Music Association.

The Browns relocated to Austin during the 1990s and have earned Grammy nominations while maintaining a busy regional concert schedule.

Brown re-entered the national spotlight in 2015 by recording the theme song for *Better Call Saul*, the AMC TV network spinoff from the acclaimed crime drama *Breaking Bad*.

Zach Bryan

This native of Oologah, Oklahoma (located just northeast of Tulsa) skyrocketed from the ranks of the United States Navy into one of the hottest country acts in the 2020s, thanks to his songwriting skills that connected with fans of country, Americana and rock music and drew widespread praise from music critics.

Bryan's 2022 major-label debut album *American Heartbreak* sold over one million copies and topped the *Billboard* US Rock, US Country and US Folk music charts.

In 2023, Bryan won the Academy of Country Music Award as the Best New Male Artist of the Year and was nominated for a Grammy Award for the Best Country Music Performance for his song "Something in the Orange." But the winner of that particular Grammy award was country music icon Willie Nelson.

Bryan, who began writing songs at the age of 14, was born in Okinawa, Japan while his father served in the United States Navy. He was following his father's naval footsteps and began writing songs during his spare time.

Then in 2017, one of his friends used an iPhone to record Bryan's song "Heading South" and uploaded it to YouTube. It quickly went viral and in 2021, Bryan was granted an honorable discharge from the Navy in order to pursue his singing-songwriting opportunities.

Bryan's music has been featured on the popular TV Western drama *Yellowstone,* which starred Kevin Costner and became a mega-hit on the Paramount+ streaming service.

Kaitlin Butts

This 2011 alumnus of Tulsa Union High School has become one of the fastest-rising stars in the country and Americana music fields since her 2015 debut album *Same Hell, Different Devil*.

While the auburn-haired singer loves to dress up in rhinestone-studded outfits and a cowboy hat reminiscent of the happier times of country music, her songs frequently deal with multi-faceted women who have been bruised but not broken and how they face challenging events and people.

Butts' April 2022 album *What Else Can She Do* reached the top 10 on the *Billboard* Americana Albums chart. It received widespread critical acclaim for songs about the impact of personal loss, substance abuse, family issues, infidelity and people stuck in a personal purgatory.

Rolling Stone magazine author Jon Freeman wrote of *What Else Can She Do*: "... (it) makes a strong case that she ought to be positioned somewhere between Miranda Lambert or Kacey Musgraves at country's vanguard—an Oklahoma native with a big, malleable voice and the songwriting skills to match."

Butts' mother enrolled her in a Broken Arrow theatrical arts program, and she was influenced by 1990s country artists such as Shania Twain and The Chicks as well as Taylor Swift.

She later participated in the legendary Gypsy Café Festival in Stillwater, the songwriter-driven program which honors Red Dirt Music founder Bob Childers. Then she attended the University of Central Oklahoma in Edmond and participated in the school's Academy of Contemporary Music.

That program was founded by the guitarist (Steven Drozd) and manager (Scott Booker) of alternative rock stars The Flaming Lips and provides a condensed course in developing as a music performer as well as learning about the music business.

Butts is married to Cleto Cordero, vocalist of the Texas country/Americana band Flatland Cavalry.

Jeff Carson

Known for his smooth-sounding vocals, Carson had three songs that reached the top 10 on the *Billboard* country charts in the mid-1990s. He released three albums between 1995 and 2001 then a greatest hits compilation in 2013. Carson was born in Tulsa but during his early childhood, Carson's family moved to Gravette, Arkansas, about 10 miles east of the Oklahoma border. He would later perform in Branson, Missouri before he and his wife moved to Nashville in 1989.

Carson's ballad "Not on Your Love" reached number one on the country charts in 1995 and also sneaked into the lower section of the *Billboard Hot Pop 100* rankings for a brief time. "The Car" reached number three on the country charts that year and was about a strained father-son relationship. "Holdin' Onto Something" was a love song that peaked at number six on the country charts. He would also record a Christmas novelty song "Santa Got Lost in Texas."

His career essentially ended after suffering broken vertebrae in a sledding accident in 2002 along with declining records sales. Today, Carson works as a police office in the Nashville suburb of Franklin and has recorded public service videos.

Sanford Clark

This Tulsa-born country-rockabilly singer, who moved to Phoenix, Arizona as a child, recorded the 1956 megahit "The Fool" which was co-written by Mannford native Lee Hazlewood. He would also greatly influence the early career of Rolling Stones guitarist Keith Richards.

"The Fool" featured a classic rockabilly guitar groove by Al Casey, Clark's longtime schoolmate who also played for Carl Perkins, Eddie Cochran and Duane Eddy. It peaked at number seven on the *Billboard Top 100* rock songs: number five on the Black Singles list and 14th on the country music charts. That led to Clark being the opening act for Roy Orbison and Ray Price.

In his 2010 autobiography, Rolling Stones guitarist Keith Richards said Clark's 1959 song "Son of A Gun" about a Western gunslinger was one of the first songs that he learned to play and performed on stage prior to the formation of the Rolling Stones.

The year 1964 wouldn't be a good one for Clark. His version of the country-flavored ballad "Houston" (also written by Hazlewood) would be eclipsed by Dean Martin's 1965 rendition of that record which reached number two on the *Billboard* Adult Contemporary music chart.

Then Roger Miller wrote a humorous country song called "Dang Me" and asked Clark to sing it. After Clark turned it down, it became the first of Miller's two number one country songs.

Clark eventually left the music world and took a job in the construction industry.

Charlie Daniels

Tulsa played a key role in launching the Grammy Award-winning career of this Southern rock and country music superstar. Research by the Recording Industry Association of America showed Daniels has sold nearly 14 million records in his career, placing him alongside singing icons such as John Lennon, Paul Simon, Jefferson Airplane/Starship and The Temptations

His most recent accolade came in the spring of 2016 with induction into the Country Music Hall of Fame.

During the 1950s and 1960s, Daniels played in several rock and rhythm and blues bands in Texas and Oklahoma. His longest tenure was from 1959 through 1967 with a quartet called Charlie Daniels and the Jaguars and their Tulsa "home" was at the now-defunct Fondalite Club, just south of downtown Tulsa at the southeast corner of West 11th Street and South Denver Avenue.

One night, a Tulsa girl named Hazel, who didn't really care for the bar scene, came to the Fondalite with a female friend to hear Daniels and his band. Hazel and Daniels struck up a conversation; got married shortly afterwards in Tulsa and they were together for 56 years until Daniels passed away in 2020.

Daniels reached the top of the *Billboard* country charts in 1979 with "The Devil Went Down to Georgia." It crossed over to number three on the *Billboard* pop charts and Daniels won a Grammy Award that year for Best Country Vocal. A major factor in the song's success was being included in the soundtrack of the John Travolta movie *Urban Cowboy*, in which Daniels made a brief appearance.

Two other Daniels songs peaked in the Top 10 of the *Billboard* country listings. "Drinkin' My Baby Goodbye" reached number eight in 1986 and "Boogie Woogie Fiddle Country Blues" reached number 10 in 1988.

Among his other hits were "Uneasy Rider" in 1973, "The South's Gonna Do It" and "Long-Haired Country Boy" in 1975, "In America" in 1980, "Simple Man" in 1989 and "This Ain't No Rag, It's a Flag" in 2001.

Daniels was inducted into the Grand Old Opry in 2008 and is also known for his strong beliefs in patriotism, support of America's military servicemen and women and his Christian faith. His 1995 album *The Door* won a Dove Award, which is the Christian music industry's equivalent of a Grammy.

Joe Diffie

This singer-songwriter was one of the best-selling country artists during the 1990s and was famously saluted by country superstar Jason Aldean in his 2013 top 10 single "1994."

Diffie had 12 singles that reached the top spot on the *Billboard* country charts along with 20 songs that reached the top 10 rankings during the peak of his career. Songs that Diffie wrote early in his career have been recorded by Tim McGraw, Jo Dee Messina and Conway Twitty.

His biggest single was the novelty song "Pickup Man" and spent four weeks at the top spot on the Billboard country charts between

December 1994 and January 1995. The tune was about an average man who thinks women will fall for him because he drives a pickup truck.

Some of Diffie's other catchy hits were "Prop Me Up Beside the Jukebox (If I Die)," "LeRoy the Redneck Reindeer," "Bigger Than the Beatles" and "John Deere Green." He also had hits with heart-tugging ballads "So Help Me Girl," "Is It Cold in Here," "A Night to Remember" and "Ships That Don't Come In."

Diffie was born in Tulsa and performed for the first time as a four-year-old singer in an aunt's country band. After his family relocated several times during his childhood, he returned to Oklahoma to briefly attend Cameron University in Lawton. He later moved to Nashville to further his songwriting career before hitting the big time.

Diffie became a member of the Grand Ole Opry in 1993 and was inducted into the Oklahoma Music Hall of Fame in 2002.

In 2019, Diffie's career took an interesting turn as he became a weekday afternoon radio host on KXBL-FM (99.5) in Tulsa, a station that plays classic country music. Through the magic of technology, Diffie did his show either from his tour bus or at a concert venue instead of sitting in a studio in Tulsa.

Diffie was among the first celebrities affected by the Covid-19 virus pandemic. He passed away on March 29, 2020 from complications related to the disease.

Ronnie Dunn

Dunn had limited success as a singer-songwriter in the 1980s prior to a meeting with music executive Tim DuBois, who had a local connection by his graduation from Oklahoma State University. DuBois saw Dunn's potential and was also aware of another singer in a similar predicament to Dunn's named Kix Brooks. Following the philosophy of a sum being greater than the individual parts, DuBois convinced the two men to join forces in a duo that utilized Dunn's songwriting skills and Brooks' musicianship. Thus began one of the most famous duos in country music history.

Brooks and Dunn made country music history from 1991 through 2009 by winning the most awards presented by that genre's top two organizations. They won 19 awards from the Country Music Association, 27 from the Academy of Country Music, won a pair of Grammy Awards and had 26 number one singles.

Their 1992 hit "Boot Scootin' Boogie" was written by Dunn about his experiences at a nightclub on the eastern edge of Tulsa called Duke's Country, which had a John Wayne-style western hat as its logo. The video for that song was shot at another famous (and since closed) Tulsa country music venue, Tulsa City Limits.

Brooks and Dunn amicably parted ways in 2010 to pursue individual careers. They reunited in 2015 for a series of concerts with Reba McEntire, recorded a 2019 album of duets with numerous current country stars then went on a reunion tour of sorts in 2022 and 2023.

Dunn's self-titled 2011 album peaked at number one on the *Billboard* country music charts and number five for all albums that year. His 2016 album *Tattooed Heart* peaked at number three that year.

He was inducted into the Oklahoma Music Hall of Fame in 2003. Brooks and Dunn were inducted into the Country Music Hall of Fame in 2019.

Gus Hardin

The singer born as Carolyn Ann Blankenship started out as a blues-rock singer in Tulsa night clubs then had a modestly successful career in country music during the mid-1980s.

Two of her songs on RCA Records reached the top 10 on the *Billboard* country charts: "After the Last Goodbye" peaked at number

10 in 1983 then her duet with label mate Earl Thomas Conley, "All Tangled Up in Love," peaked at number eight in 1985.

Tulsa Sound legend Leon Russell once described Hardin's sound as "a combination of Tammy Wynette, Otis Redding and a truck driver."

She earned two country music industry awards during that time: the *Billboard* Top New Country Artist of 1983 and the 1984 Academy of Country Music Best New Female Vocalist. But that did not translate into success with her other eight single releases failing to crack the *Billboard* Top 25 country rankings.

The Nathan Hale High School graduate also went through personal challenges. She dealt with vision problems from 1974 through 1984 and was legally blind for the last five years of that period. She also had what some people called an abrasive or assertive personality. Being divorced six times didn't exactly help her image.

Hardin returned to Tulsa and resumed her singing career before being killed in a 1996 auto wreck after performing at a northeastern Oklahoma night club.

Becky Hobbs

This University of Tulsa graduate recorded four songs that reached the Billboard Top 40 country music charts but was best known for her songwriting skills. Among the artists that recorded Hobbs' songs are George Jones, Alabama, Glen Campbell, Helen Reddy, Emmylou Harris and Loretta Lynn.

While attending TU in the late 1960s, Hobbs was part of an all-female group called The Sir Prize Package that performed in go-go boots and miniskirts. Then she moved to Baton Rouge, Louisiana and Los Angeles and then Nashville. Reddy heard four songs from Hobbs' self-titled 1974 debut album and strong word-of-mouth talk led other major artists to record her songs.

Hobbs' musical style was once described as a blend of electric rock-abilly and driving honky-tonk sounds. Her biggest country hit was a 1983 duet with Moe Bandy, "Let's Get Over Them Together" which peaked at number 10 on the *Billboard* country music chart. Her other major solo songs were "Hottest 'Ex' in Texas (1985), "Jones on the Jukebox" (1986) and "Do You Feel the Same Way, Too?" (1989).

Hobbs is an enrolled Cherokee Indian and in 2011 she co-wrote a musical based on the life of her fifth great-grandmother, *Nanye'hi-The Story of Nancy Ward*. Nanye'hi is Cherokee for "woman who moves about." Ward (1738-1822) could have been called a political activist or *de facto* ambassador for her advocating peaceful existence between the Cherokee Nation and white people and in later years, her stance for restoration of Cherokee Nation tribal lands.

Jana Jae

Jana Jae has lived in Tulsa and northeastern Oklahoma since the 1980s and while best known for her playing the fiddle on the country music TV variety series *Hee Haw*, she has played the violin around the world with symphony orchestras and appeared at the Montreux Jazz Festival.

Born as Jana Margaret Meyer, she played violin for the first time when she was 30 months old. Her parents studied at the Julliard School in New York while her maternal grandfather played fiddle in a country music group. After studying classical music in college, she went to Austria and attended the Vienna Academy of Music.

The turning point came when Jae noticed that she would receive soft applause after her concertos and classical performances but the applause was much louder and longer when as an encore, she did a fiddle breakdown like her grandfather did with his band.

Jae's country music career began in the mid-1970s when Buck Owens heard her playing in a bluegrass band. When Owens' lead guitarist Don Rich died a year later in a motorcycle accident, Owens tweaked his band's sound by adding Jae as a fiddle player. When a short-lived, tumultuous marriage to Owens ended, Jae contacted Tulsa-based music promoter Jim Halsey about joining his agency.

Jae has been active in programs designed to revive music programs in public schools, performs with orchestra and at music festivals and operates a camp for children wanting to come to the Tulsa area to learn how to play the fiddle. She currently lives in the northeastern Oklahoma town of Grove, which is close to the popular Grand Lake.

Corey Kent (White)

This native of Bixby went from a 2015 contestant on the NBC reality TV series *The Voice* to one of country music hottest acts in the 2020s.

Performing these days as Corey Kent, his first number one song was "Wild as Her" which drew over 250 million streams. The song's video earned a 2023 nomination for Male Breakthrough Video of the Year by the CMT Music Awards and led to his touring with country superstar Jason Aldean.

A graduate of Bixby High School and Oklahoma State University, the aspiring singer-songwriter's musical roots were based in Western swing and he debuted at the age of 11 with a local band called Oklahoma Stomp.

Kent is most successful Tulsa-area performer to appear on *The Voice*. During Season 8 which aired in 2015, he was mentored by Blake Shelton and reached the top eight finalists. His debut EP, *Making Noise,* was distributed through digital music outlets and quickly led to his sharing the stage with country music superstars such as Toby Keith, Willie Nelson, Hank Williams Jr. and Luke Bryan. But after living in Nashville and not experiencing the success he hoped for,

White and his family relocated near Dallas, Texas in order to be closer to grandparent and relatives while relaunching his career.

White has performed several concerts as part of his affiliation with the non-profit Folds of Honor Foundation. That charitable organization provides educational scholarships for spouses and children of American military members who have fallen or were physically disabled while serving their nation.

Mark McClurg

This fiddle player/vocalist has toured with Alan Jackson's band, the Strayhorns, since the 1990s. He attended Sequoyah High School, a small school district located northeast of the Tulsa suburb of Claremore.

McClurg left Jackson's group in 2003 to join another Oklahoma-based musician, Wade McHayes, as the country music duo McHayes. That pairing lasted one year with McClurg rejoining Jackson's band. .

Gordon Payne and Rance Wasson

These two veterans of Tulsa's music scene were members of Waylon Jennings' band, The Waylors, from 1980 through 2002 as guitarists and background singers. Prior to joining the Country Music Hall of Fame singer, Payne and Wasson each in played local nightclubs alongside J.J. Cale and other Tulsa Sound veterans.

Payne later performed with the remaining members of Buddy Holly's band, The Crickets, prior to pursuing a second career as an author.

Wasson returned to Tulsa and performed with a few local musicians.

Steve Ripley

While most modern country-rock fans knew Steve Ripley as the lead singer of the 1990s group The Tractors, he had over 45 years of experience in the music industry as a songwriter, studio producer, radio documentary host and builder of custom guitars.

The Tractors were comprised of five Tulsa-based musicians who were also highly sought for their work in Nashville as well. The other band members were Jamie Oldaker on drums, Walt Richmond on keyboards, Ron Getman on bass guitar and Casey Van Beek on guitar and vocals.

Their self-titled 1994 debut album blended a boogie/rhythm and blues beat with modern country. The lead single "Baby Likes to Rock It" sold over two million copies and peaked at number 11 on the *Billboard* magazine Country Music chart. The album itself reached number two on the *Billboard* Country Music chart.

The Tractors recorded seven albums and seven music videos between 1994 and 2009 before the musicians returned to Tulsa to purse individual music projects.

Ripley's custom guitars have been used by artists such as Eddie Van Halen, Jimmy Buffet, John Hiatt and J.J. Cale. He operated Tulsa's Church Studio for several years after Leon Russell sold it and moved to California.

He collaborated with Bob Dylan, Gatemouth Brown and various other artists and created a 20-part radio documentary *Oklahoma Rock and Roll with Steve Ripley* that was aired by public radio stations throughout Oklahoma.

Ripley passed away in 2019 after a long battle with cancer.

The Wills Brothers

Tulsa's KTUL-AM Radio played a role in the career of this trio of musical brothers who would have a top 10 country song about a frustrated truck driver and contributed to the early career of Hank Williams.

Their only major hit song was the 1964 truck driving themed "Give Me 40 Acres (To Turn This Rig Around)." It peaked at number nine on the *Billboard* Country Music chart in the United States and the top spot on the same survey in Canada.

Originally known as the Oklahoma Wranglers, the trio was comprised of oldest brother James "Guy" Willis, middle brother Charles "Skeeter" Willis and youngest brother John "Vic" Willis. They performed on KTUL-AM Radio in 1933 and 1934 between engagements on radio stations in Shawnee, Oklahoma and Gallup, New Mexico. The band later moved to Kansas City, Missouri and then to Nashville and joined the Grand Ole Opry radio broadcasts.

After recording four songs as the Oklahoma Wranglers one December morning, they returned from a lunch break and were told to change their name for a single recording session to the Country Boys. Then they were told about being the backup band for the first-ever recording session by an aspiring country singer named Hank Williams.

Eight songs were recorded in that session; three of them gospel songs and the remainder of them being country songs including one that would be a Williams trademark, "Honky Tonkin.'"

Vocalist Eddy Arnold hired the band in 1949 and suggested they should change their name to avoid being typecast. Thus, the Willis Brothers were born and they would appear with Arnold in the 1949 movie *Feuding Rhythm* and the 1950 film *Hoedown*.

Then the band appeared on the Ozark Jubilee radio cast in 1953 and become Grand Ole Opry regulars from 1960 through 1981.

Jon Wolfe

This Tulsa-born singer has his musical roots firmly in the honky tonk style of country music and became a rising star in the 2010 decade.

Wolfe wrote "She Won't Be Lonely Long" which became a top-five single for Clay Walker in 2010. His 2017 album *Any Night in Texas* peaked at number five on the *Billboard* Heatseekers chart, which highlights promising new singers and bands.

He was raised in Miami, Oklahoma and became interested in country music through his stepfather, who played bass guitar in a house band with future Rascal Flatts band member Joe Don Rooney.

Wolfe has opened concerts for big-name acts such as Asleep at the Wheel, Merle Haggard, Dwight Yoakam and George Strait.

Bob Wootton

This Tulsa guitar player literally came out of the crowd in 1968 to help Johnny Cash get out of a tight spot. His reward was playing for 30 years in Cash's backup band, The Tennessee Three.

Wootton was 16 years old when his family moved to Tulsa in 1958 as part of his father's job search. One of eight children, Wootton grew up in Bakersfield, California listening to Ernest Tubb and Merle Travis then got hooked on Cash's music and learned how to play guitar like Cash's bandmate Luther Perkins.

Luther Perkins was best known for his "Boom-Chicka" guitar rhythm that became the signature sound for many of Cash's biggest hits. His brother was rockabilly legend Carl Perkins who recorded the original version of "Blue Suede Shoes."

Wootton was playing at various Tulsa night spots with a band called the Comancheros and went to see Cash's 1966 performance at Cain's Ballroom. He met the singer afterwards and had his picture taken with Cash; an event that would foretell of their future musical partnership.

Luther Perkins had died in August 1968 from injuries sustained in a house fire. One month later, Cash and his band were set to perform in Fayetteville, Arkansas, a 75-minute drive east of Tulsa. Cash, his drummer and the band's equipment made it to Fayetteville, but severe thunderstorms kept the other two bandmates from getting there.

Wootton and his girlfriend were seated on the front row at that concert and they recognized that Cash was in a dire predicament. His girlfriend spotted Cash's wife, June Carter Cash, and asked her to ask Cash if Wootton might be able to fill in. Cash was pleasantly surprised to not only hear that Wootton knew every song that he wanted to sing that night but liked Wootton's style of playing Perkins' guitar parts at a faster tempo. After a six-month "temp to hire" period, Cash made Wootton part of his band.

For 30 years, Wootton performed on the historic *Johnny Cash at San Quentin* live album, on 13 songs that reached the top spot on the *Billboard* country charts, on ABC-TV's "The Johnny Cash Show" and was part of Bob Dylan's influential *Nashville Skyline* album.

Wootton was a 2006 inductee into the Rockabilly Hall of Fame and passed away in 2017.

Chapter Five

Red Dirt and Roots

"*And if I hadn't run into the Skinner Brothers, I don't think you would've heard the sound that we have. I believe with all my heart that red dirt music is the backbone of my body of music.*"

Garth Brooks

"*There just wouldn't be red dirt music if not for what Woody (Guthrie) did. God bless him.*"

Tom Skinner

"*Red dirt is a hue of funk, a shade of sound, a basic spirit embodied in music.*"

Steve Ripley

"*We used to say it was a mix between Merle Haggard and the Rolling Stones; it's truly country rock.*"

John Cooper

***

The Red Dirt musical genre, which has grown in popularity in recent years with its down to earth and thoughtful lyrics, has been likened to the indie pop movement. However, it contains sizeable musical portions of folk music *a la* Woody Guthrie, rock and roll, country, bluegrass, honky tonk, Western Swing and even gospel.

While Red Dirt music might not get the amount of national radio airtime that the current forms of country music receives around the nation, it has a faithful and rapidly growing core of fans throughout Texas, Oklahoma and the Midwestern United States thanks to satellite radio, streaming services and consistently large concert crowds,

Many of the top Red Dirt musicians developed their musical craft at the home of the late Bob Childers outside of Stillwater. That two-story five-bedroom rural residence was lovingly nicknamed The Farm and jam sessions could be found around a campfire or on the front porch, in the living room and even in the garage.

Turnpike Troubadours

If the Red Dirt music scene had a powerhouse group such as the Beatles or Rolling Stones, it would be the Turnpike Troubadours.

Their music is influenced by bluegrass, Cajun, country honkytonk, Irish melodies and rock and roll. Music fans were immediately drawn to their songs that showcased hard truths and passionate music.

The band was formed in 2005 in Tahlequah, Oklahoma (located about 65 miles southeast of Tulsa) by vocalist and lead guitarist Evan Felker and bass player R.C. Edwards. The group soon evolved into their current form as a sextet and claimed Tulsa as a musical base.

As well as touring with other Red Dirt and alt-country acts, the Turnpike Troubadours would tour with mainstream country stars such as Little Big Town and Miranda Lambert. Following their 2023 album *Cat in the Rain*, the band embarked on their first national headlining tour.

Felker's issues with alcoholism and his disillusionment with the music industry led to the band going on hiatus in 2019. After Felker completed a counseling program and the band members agreed to a less strenuous schedule, the group returned with a bang in 2023 fueled by the comeback album *A Cat in the Rain* produced by Shooter Jennings along with a nationwide concert tour.

Their highest-ranking Billboard albums are their self-titled album in 2015 and their 2017 release *A Long Way from Your Heart*. Each of them peaked at number three while *A Long Way from Your Heart* topped the American Indie and American Folk charts.

One of the group's earliest hits was *Easton & Main*, a musical ode to Tulsa's legendary Cain's Ballroom. *Gin, Smoke and Lies* was a man dealing with his girlfriend's infidelity. *The Housefire* dealt with recovering from a natural disaster in both a personal and familial sense. *Mean Old Sun* was about Felker's finding a reward from his counseling journey as well as through physical labor.

Brandon Jenkins

Freed from the shackles of being another "hat act" from Nashville's hit-making country music factory, Brandon Jenkins became one of the top singer-songwriters in the Red Dirt music scene.

In later years, he relocated to Austin, Texas to further his music career and performed throughout the United States and several European countries.

His songs dealt with real life issues and were described as being poetic and soulful while also being rowdy and frequently questioning the status quo.

Jenkins drew from a wide variety of musical inspirations, including bluesmen Freddie King and Taj Mahal, rockers ZZ Top and The Eagles, country legends Willie Nelson and Conway Twitty and folk singer Woody Guthrie.

He collaborated with artists such as Hank Williams Jr., Jerry Jeff Walker, Pat Green, Charlie Daniels, Ray Wylie Hubbard and Willie Nelson.

Jenkins attended Tulsa's Central High School and played the role of Curly in a local production of the Rogers and Hammerstein Broadway musical *Oklahoma!*

Given that Jenkins would later have a shaved head and thick beard along with multiple tattoos on a body that resembled a football lineman, his being a person called Curly was quite ironic.

Jenkins unexpectedly died in 2018 at the age of 48 due to heart-related issues.

John Moreland

Moving seamlessly between the musical genres of Americana, folk rock and alternative country, this talented singer-songwriter has gained a strong word-of-mouth following, thanks to his frequent tours throughout the United States and Europe.

Moreland's original vocal style was very loud, citing a need to be heard while performing in noisy bars. In recent years, his vocal style has become softer; as though having a conversation with either another person or himself.

He cited Steve Earle as his biggest folk-Americana influence along with Texas alt-country legends Guy Clark and Townes Van Zandt. Though Moreland's earlier songs had more of a rock flavor, he currently favors Americana and folk rock and frequently performs with only an acoustic guitar.

His mostly self-produced music has drawn critical praise from an unlikely source: MSNBC liberal political commentator and talk show host Rachel Maddow. One of her Twitter posts once read: "If the American music business made any sense, guys like John Moreland would be household names."

Three of Moreland's songs were featured on the FX cable TV network's crime drama series *Sons of Anarchy.*

Moreland's 2015 CD *High on Tulsa Heat* was a musical valentine to Tulsa and the state of Oklahoma and drew critical acclaim for its well-crafted lyrics.

His 2017 CD *Big Bad Luv* was cited by *Rolling Stone* magazine as one of the 25 best country and Americana CDs of that year.

Moreland's family moved from Kentucky to Tulsa when he was 10 years old. During his high school years, Moreland played in local punk and hardcore metal bands before pursuing his current style of music.

Red Dirt Rangers

This trio of musicians is not only a pioneering band in the Red Dirt music movement but also somewhat of a musical oddity, having stayed together and toured nationally and internationally for over 35 years while using Tulsa, along with Stillwater, as one of their home bases.

Former *Tulsa World* music critic Thomas Conner said of the Red Dirt Rangers: "(They) always have epitomized and expanded on the Oklahoma Red Dirt sound—the elusive stew of country, folk, and whatever else is lying around..."

The band's core members and vocalists are John Cooper, who also plays mandolin and percussion, and guitarists Brad Piccolo and Ben Han. Supporting musicians have included legendary fiddle player Randy Crouch, bassist Don Morris and drummer Rick Gomez.

Red Dirt legend Jimmy LaFave gave the band its first major opportunity, performing at a musician's reunion concert at the Stillwater nightclub Willie's. Back then, though, the band had a Tex-Mex musical accent with mariachi and accordion players.

Over the years, other musicians came and went, and Cooper, Piccolo and Han chose to focus more on the essence of Red Dirt music and their popularity grew rapidly. Among their highlights was being the opening act for country music legend Willie Nelson.

A helicopter crash in 2004 at a private party near Cushing, Oklahoma (roughly midway between Tulsa and Oklahoma City) seriously injured all three members of the trio while the helicopter's pilot and another passenger were killed.

But after an extended recovery and buoyed by the monetary and emotional support from fellow Red Dirt musicians, the Red Dirt Rangers returned to recording and live concerts.

Tom Skinner

Tom Skinner was regarded as one of the three founding fathers of Red Dirt music with Childers and Jimmy LaFave being the other two.

Early in his music career, Skinner played bass guitar in one of Garth Brooks' earliest bands called Santa Fe. While Brooks chose to stay in Nashville to further his career, Skinner felt that the slickness of that country music scene wasn't to his liking. With family commitments foremost in his life, he chose to return to Oklahoma.

Time hasn't diminished one bit the respect that Brooks has for Skinner's songwriting and musical skills, as evidenced by his ringing endorsement for Skinner's self-titled 2012 album. Oklahoma music historian John Wooley even makes a case for the musical roots of Garth Brooks being encased in Red Dirt.

"Like many of the Red Dirt acts, he grew up loving rock and roll as well as country and I always believe his approach had a lot to do with his playing as a single act in Stillwater clubs," Wooley said.

"Someone might request a KISS song, someone else might follow with a George Jones request, then James Taylor. He had to know it all and he put that knowledge to good use when he started doing his own stuff."

In addition to touring in Oklahoma, Texas and the Upper Midwest, Skinner hosted a Wednesday night jam session for Red Dirt musicians in the Tulsa area entitled The Tom Skinner Wednesday Night Science Project.

Skinner passed away in July 2015 after a series of heart-related illnesses.

Jared Tyler

This talented multi-instrumentalist evolved from a hopeful country singer into one of the more promising singer-songwriter-producers in the American roots music scene.

He has collaborated with country artists Emmylou Harris, Nickle Creek and Merle Haggard as well as Red Dirt acts Jimmy LaFave and Willis Alan Ramsey and the alternative rock band Wilco.

Tyler had a bright future as a country songwriter in the early 2000s, but he returned to Tulsa to care for elderly family members. During that time, he immersed himself in Tulsa's music scene then dove into music production with his soundtrack work on a few independent films drawing rave reviews at the Sundance Film Fest.

In 2021, Tyler teamed with Tulsa Sound bassist Casey Van Beek to form a band called Saugeye. Their songs were described as a blend of folk, blues, bluegrass, country, gospel and Red Dirt.

Chapter Six

Folk

"It's a folk singer's job to comfort disturbed people and to disturb comfortable people."

Woody Guthrie

"I want to turn the clock back to when people lived in small villages and took care of each other."

Pete Seeger

"One good song with a message can bring a point more deeply to more people than a thousand rallies."

Phil Ochs

"Folk music has always contained a concern for the human condition. And since it brings people into it from different points of view, that can help illuminate what a consensus might be to important issues."

Mary Travers

"People sing each other's songs, and they cultivate standards. That's the reason we have folk music and folk songs. History is told through song."

Brandi Carlisle

***

Leon "Jack" Guthrie

A cousin of the iconic folk singer/songwriter Woody Guthrie, Leon Jerry "Jack' Guthrie is credited as a co-writer of the song "Oklahoma Hills."

That became a number one folk song for Jack, a number seven country song for Hank Thompson and the Brazos Valley Boys, a signature song for Woody and a source of conflict between Jack and Woody.

Jack was born in 1915 in Olive, Oklahoma; a tiny town 36 miles south-southwest of Tulsa. After his family moved to Texas during his grade-school years, they returned to the southwestern Tulsa suburb of Sapulpa during Jack's teenage years. A sister said Jack had no interest in public education, claiming their mother took Jack to school then he'd go right through the front door and then right out the back door.

He idolized country music pioneer Jimmie Rodgers while competing in rodeos as a bronc horse rider, After becoming interested in cowboy songs and deciding that Leon or Jerry weren't good cowboy names, he chose to call himself "Jack" or "Oke" or "Oklahoma."

During the mid-1930s, the family moved to California where Jack and Woody became a musical duo and performed on KFVD Radio (AM 1020) in Los Angeles as the "Oke and Woody Show." Jack later left the show and billed himself as "Oklahoma's Yodeling Cowboy" in a nightclub variety act with his wife, Ruth Henderson.

Woody had begun writing "Oklahoma Hills" during the 1940s but set the song aside for a long time when the lyrics and melody weren't to his liking. In October of 1944, Jack was a special forces entertainer while serving at Iwo Jima in the United States Army. He rewrote the lyrics and melody and recorded a demo thinking that Capital Records would have another singer record it. To Jack's surprise, the record company's management liked his version so much that they signed him to a contract.

Jack's version, with the act billed as Jack Guthrie and His Oklahomans, stayed at the top of the country music charts for 19 weeks in 1945. The flip side "I'm Brandin' My Darlin' With My Heart" peaked at number five on the country charts.

Woody noticed Jack's success with the song and claimed that he was due a lot of money from record sales and songwriting royalties since he was the original author. Jack countered that had he not rewritten the lyrics and the melody as well as recording the song, no one would have ever heard of it.

They reached an agreement to be credited as co-writers of the song and the royalty distribution issues were resolved. In 2001, the Oklahoma Legislative passed a resolution proclaiming "Oklahoma Hills" would be the state's Official Folk Song.

Jack's subsequent song "Oakie Boogie" peaked at number three on the country music charts in 1947. But after contracting tuberculosis later that year, Jack passed away in 1948.

Sam Hinton

With the encouragement of his musically inclined mother, the Tulsa-born Hinton became one of the earliest musicians to use "folk music" to describe songs that he would write and perform. Over his 65-year musical career, he performed for audiences throughout North America and Europe.

When Hinton was five years old, his mother took him to Jenkins Music Store and purchased his first harmonica. Before leaving the store, he played "Turkey in the Straw" all the way through. Then she taught him cowboy and folk songs passed down from his great-grand-father's time in eastern Texas. Those experiences laid the foundation for a musical career.

His best-known recordings were the children's themed "Barnyard Song" and "Old Man Atom (Talking Atomic Blues" during the 1940s and 1950s. The latter song became a favorite of the legendary folk music group The Weavers and lead singer Pete Seeger. Through the years, the Weavers would influence artists such as Peter, Paul and Mary and Bob Dylan.

Hinton graduated from Texas A&M University and worked as a marine biologist and college teacher while building his musical career.

Sarah Popejoy

An up-and-coming talent in Oklahoma's folk music scene, this Broken Arrow native blends the social activism associated with Woody Guthrie with the passionate vocal stylings similar to Lucinda Williams.

Billed as "The Oklahoma Storyteller," one of Popejoy's most recent songs is "The Victims Have Names" and dealt with the 1921 Tulsa Race Massacre and the personal and social injustices associated with that tragedy.

Other songs have touched upon the 1995 Oklahoma City bombing, the plight of Oklahomans during the Dust Bowl days, hardships facing Native Americans during their journey on the Trail of Tears and the northeastern Oklahoma mining community of Picher becoming a ghost town.

Popejoy Jackson's music has also been celebratory in nature, praising the life and works of Oklahomans such as Woody Guthrie, rockabilly music legend Wanda Jackson, baseball hero Mickey Mantle, Western Swing maestro Bob Wills and Tulsa Sound icon Leon Russell.

Music has always been a tradition in her household. Her father, Brad Popejoy, played bass guitar in a Tulsa band called Front Page News and was a salesman for Tulsa's top-rated classic rock radio station. Her grandmother, Gwen Popejoy Bonnell sang in a trio that toured Oklahoma in her early years.

Popejoy has toured extensively across the USA with appearances at the iconic Club Passim folk music venue near Harvard University where Bob Dylan and Joan Baez got their start as well as the Bluebird Café in Nashville, Tennessee, a vibrant part of the country music scene through the years.

Another passion of hers is acrylic painting with influences from Pablo Picasso, Salvador Dali and Vincent Van Gogh evident in her works.

Dr. Guy Logsdon

Though he never recorded a hit record, Logsdon's contributions to the music industry via the printed word made him America's go-to resource for the legacies of folk music icon Woody Guthrie along with cataloging the history of Western Swing music and cowboy music and poetry.

Logsdon was a consultant for the 1976 movie *Bound for Glory*, which starred David Carradine as Guthrie. He was also a co-founder of the annual Woody Guthrie Folk Festival (aka Woodyfest), held each July in Guthrie's hometown of Okemah, Oklahoma.

Interviewed by the *Tulsa World*, Logsdon once said of Guthrie, "He was a great human being who had a great desire to improve the lot of all people. He was Oklahoma's most creative so and, as far as I'm concerned, this nation's most creative son."

Logsdon was the University of Tulsa's library director from 1976 through 1981 and then served as a professor of education and American folk life until his retirement in 1989. After his retirement and until his passing in February of 2018, his life was devoted to freelance writing, research and occasional performances.

In later years, Logsdon traveled throughout the United States as a performer and lecturer. When participating in presentations on Guthrie's music legacy, he performed alongside folk music icons such as Ramblin' Jack Elliott, Arlo Guthrie (Woody's son) and Pete Seeger.

Chapter Seven

Jazz

***

Tuck Andress

Renowned for a fingerpicking guitar technique that can make one guitar sound like three during soaring melodies, this Tulsa native and his wife, Patti Cathcart, comprise the jazz-oriented duo of Tuck and Patti.

They are best known for their jazz works and have toured internationally for the past 40 years but also dabble in such musical diversities as rhythm and blues, gospel, rock and pop.

Born as William Charles Andress and then going by the nickname of Tuck, his sister taught him about piano chords at the age of seven and Andress became the pianist for a garage band with two of his neighborhood buddies in Tulsa.

While rock and roll legend Chuck Berry was the childhood idol of Andress, his first guitar teacher was Tulsa music legend Tommy Crook, a virtuoso of the fingerpicking playing style.

Back then, Andress would be influenced by the laid-back, blues-oriented Tulsa Sound played by numerous local bands and adopted by superstar Eric Clapton. After attending the University of Tulsa, he moved to Los Angeles to follow in the musical footsteps of Leon Russell and other Tulsa-based musicians.

But life in LA was not to his liking so Andress moved to San Francisco to attend Stanford University. He fell in love with the music of jazz legends such as Charlie Parker, John Coltrane and Miles Davis and also played in a Bay Area combo.

One day, Patti Cathcart auditioned for his group's vocalist position. Among her musical influences were gospel legend Mahalia Jackson and jazz greats Ellla Fitzgerald, Sara Vaughn and Nina Simone. While jamming with San Francisco-area musicians, she met rock legend Jimi Hendrix who dropped by a birthday party and called her "Foxy Lady."

Andress and Cathcart hit things off, musically and romantically, and left to form the duo of Tuck and Patti in 1981. One of their passions has been to perform songs with positive and uplifting lyrics.

They have recorded 10 albums and are still touring around the world as well as paying things forwarded by being musical mentors in the Bay Area. Andress still plays a 1953 Gibson L-5 guitar because it was the instrument of choice for jazz guitar legend Wes Montgomery.

Count Basie

William Basie was a pianist who began his career in Harlem and then became fascinated by the Kansas City jazz scene. Tulsa was a stop on his 1928 tour and while staying in the Greenwood District one morning, he heard a commotion outside of his room and went to investigate.

It turned out to be a free concert of sorts by Walter Page and His Famous Blue Devils, a jazz-blues band that played mostly around Wichita, Kansas and Oklahoma City.

Basie was captivated by the Blue Devils' sound and when lead singer Jimmy Rushing invited Basie to join the band, he jumped at the opportunity to learn more about their style of music and went with them to Kansas City. Once there, Basie changed his name to "Count" Basie (mimicking Edward "Duke" Ellington) and the world of jazz would be forever changed.

Earl Bostic

What Louis Armstrong was to the trumpet in the history of jazz music, Earl Bostic was the same to the alto saxophone. Bostic's lengthy legacy of hit singles and albums showed that other sax players could climb the *Billboard* and other music charts and sell thousands of records.

Many music historians hold this Tulsa native in the same high esteem as jazz and legends Charlie "Bird" Parker, Cannonball Adderley,

Dinah Washington and John Coltrane. Bostic also wrote arrangements for legendary musicians such as Lionel Hampton, Louis Prima, Gene Krupa, Artie Shaw and Alvino Ray.

His diverse career also featured forays into big band and swing-style jazz, combos with organs and jump blues. Bostic and his improvisational style were also influential in the rhythm and blues movement after World War II.

Another major influence in Bostic's musical style was Charlie "Bird" Parker whose fast scales in bebop were part of the evolution of progressive jazz musicians such as John Coltrane, who ironically would be a member of Bostic's bands during the late 1940s.

Early in his career, Bostic's musical style featured lengthy flowing lines along with influences from blues rhythms and a keen sense of harmony. Bostic's later efforts still featured the unmistakable growling sax but shorter lines and added a backbeat that dancers loved.

It was most noticeable in "Temptation", his 1948 hit that reached the Top 10 of the rhythm and blues charts. Then his 1956 hit "Where or When" had Bostic playing in the sax's middle ranges with a loud bass and heavy backbeat.

Some of Bostic's other hit songs were "Flamingo", "Harlem Nocturne" and "Special Delivery Stomp".

Bostic began his musical career at the age of 18 with Terrance Holder and His Twelve Clouds of Joy. That Muskogee-based regional act allowed Bostic to frequently take flight on loud and long improvisational solos.

Oscar Estell

Jazz legend Ernie Fields once said of this pianist-vocalist that the only difference between Estell and the other top singers-performers during the 1940s-50s jazz era was those other people had a recording contract and Estell did not.

Estell and Fields once played in a local jazz group called The Music Masters before Estell formed his own band. He gained a reputation *a la* Leon Russell as a "musician's musician" and that led to tours with Lionel Hampton, Roy Milton, Ernie Freeman and Sam Cooke.

Estell returned to Tulsa in 1959 after getting married and chose to continue playing in local night spots.

Toni Estes

A vocal prodigy while attending Tulsa's Central and Booker T. Washington High Schools, Estes won a Grammy Award in 2000 for co-writing Whitney Houston's megahit "It's Not Right but It's OK."

It was one of three Estes songs chosen for Houston's 1998 album "My Love Is Your Love" and Houston had Estes sing background vocals on "Get It Back" and "If I Told You That."

Thanks to her father's influence as a Tulsa-area drummer, Estes appeared in local TV commercials at the age of six and then opened for concerts by Natalie Cole and Gladys Knight when she was 14 years old.

Estes has cited R&B legends Bobby Womack and Maze as major musical influences. Releases in recent years have seen her exploring smooth R&B musical styles and rap.

Ernie Fields

Ernie Fields and The Royal Entertainers got their start in Tulsa during the late 1920s and one of their biggest supporters was Western Swing bandleader Bob Wills. Fields' band was the first African-American group to perform at the home of Western Swing music, the Cain's Ballroom.

Fields, who also played the piano and trombone, moved to New York City in 1939 and then to Los Angeles in the 1950s, creating his own sound by blending elements of big band, swing and rhythm and blues during that time. Roy Milton was a drummer in Fields' orchestra and would later become an influential figure in up-tempo jump blues.

Fields had an international hit in 1959 with an R&B version of the Glenn Miller classic "In the Mood" that reached number four on the *Billboard* R&B charts and number 13 in Great Britain.

His band's first national exposure came in 1939 with the recording of "T-Town Blues" in New York City. But with a new era of African American music being led by Motown Records, Fields eventually quit touring and passed away in 1997.

His son, Ernie Fields Jr., played baritone sax and has been a highly sought session player, performing alongside B.B. King, Stevie Wonder, Rick James and Marvin Gaye. He also served as a musical director and contractor for three music-related reality TV shows: *American Idol, The X Factor* and *The Voice.*

Fields daughter and former Boston TV news anchor Carmen Fields wrote the 2023 biography *Going Back to T-Town: The Ernie Fields Territory Big Band* telling of her father's navigating the challenges of performing during the racial segregation of the Jim Crow era as well as his role in the development of jazz music.

In a June 2023 interview with *Oklahoma Magazine*, she said her father "...was impatient about making the big time and didn't stay as long as he could have or should have. He was proud of his accomplishments, but he never achieved the level of Duke Ellington, Count Basie or Cab Calloway."

Lowell Fulson

This Tulsa native, along with T-Bone Walker, was one of the founding fathers of the jazz and blues hybrid known as the West Coast blues in the 1940s and 1950s. That musical genre is known for dominant piano playing, up-tempo guitar solos and smooth-sounding vocals.

Fulson was renowned for his powerful guitar licks and an equally powerful singing voice. After moving to California, he formed a small band and hired a young blind piano player named Ray Charles.

Among Fulson's biggest hits were the legendary "Three O'clock Blues" and his rendition of the Memphis Slim classic "Every Day I Have the Blues." Fulson's version of "Reconsider Baby" was later covered by Elvis Presley and Eric Clapton.

Jacob Fred Jazz Odyssey

The Jacob Fred Jazz Odyssey is primarily a jazz group but often blends elements of rock, funk and hip hop into its sound. The band began as an octet in 1994 and has seen its membership range from three to nine members over the years.

The Jacob Fred name came from founding keyboardist Brian Haas when he was three years old. It was what he wanted for the name of his unborn brother at that time. Jazz Odyssey came from the cult comedy-documentary *This is Spinal Tap!* And for the record, the band has never had a member whose first name was Jacob or Fred.

JFJO toured internationally and received critical acclaim for its 2011 album, *Race Riot Suite*, an all-instrumental album that captured the passion, fervor and fears of the 1921 Tulsa Race Riot.

Haas went on to play piano and guitar for an instrumental rock and funk influenced band called Mike Dillon & Punkadelic.

Pat Kelley

This versatile guitar player and session musician has been part of California's music scene for 40-plus years, has been a university music instructor and performed on TV shows, at internationally known venues and with symphony orchestras through the United States and 30 other countries.

But he's the first to tell you that his musical roots are solidly located in Tulsa.

Kelley's father played guitar around their home and guitar-playing friends of his would stop by for jam sessions. He was also influenced by the Western Swing of Bob Wills as well as the popular singers and bands from the 1950s rock-and-roll era.

When the family moved to California during the 1970s, Kelley was influenced by artists such as George Benson, Miles Davis, Herbie Hancock, John Coltrane and Chick Corea.

Kelley's 1989 album *I'll Stand Up* reached the top 25 of the *Billboard* Contemporary Jazz albums. He also performed in the TV orchestras for *The Merv Griffin Show* and *The Carol Burnett Show*.

Among the superstar musicians Kelly has performed with are Dave Brubeck, B.B. King, Burt Bacharach, Al Jarreau, Jose Feliciano, Melissa Manchester and Olivia Newton-John.

Kelley has taught for two decades at the acclaimed Thornton School of Music at the University of Southern California. He also serves on the faculty for the University of Tulsa Jazz Camp and the Monterey Jazz Festival Summer Camp.

Frank Mantooth

This Edison High School alumnus was nominated for nine Grammy Awards for his jazz-flavored big-band musical arrangements. As a youngster, Mantooth took piano lessons at the age of seven and followed in the footsteps of his older sister and his mother, who was a pianist in Tulsa's public school system.

But his "wild hair" musical adventures came when he and drummer Dave Teegarden (who later played in Bob Seger's band) would sneak into the Blue Moon Ballroom in a predominantly black section of north Tulsa and learn by watching other musicians.

Mantooth later said that a performance at Edison by a jazz band from the University of North Texas was so captivating that he decided then and there to pursue a career in jazz music at UNT. Following his college graduation, Mantooth lived in Chicago before moving to Garden City, Kansas where he became a college-level music teacher.

Cecil McBee

This Tulsa native played the upright double bass for some of the biggest names in jazz history prior to becoming an author and teacher at Harvard University and Boston's New England Conservatory of Music. He won a Grammy Award in 1988 for his performance on the tribute album *Blues for Coltrane*.

During his recording career, McBee's musical talents were utilized by legendary artists such as Dinah Washington, Jackie McLean, Wayne Shorter, Chet Baker, Yusef Lateef, Pharoah Sanders, Woody Shaw, Alice Coltrane and Miles Davis.

McBee originally played the clarinet while attending schools in Tulsa but switched to the upright double bass when he was 17 years old and began playing in local night clubs. He attended Ohio Central State University and conducted the band at Fort Knox, Kentucky, during a two-year stint in the United States Army.

Howard "Maggie" McGhee

Howard McGhee was a trumpeter who teamed with Dizzy Gillespie and Fats Navarro in the 1940s to become a forerunner in the bebop style of jazz, a style best mirrored by jazz bands in the Kansas City area. Bebop was mostly known for a fast musical tempo, fast-fingered yet skillful playing of the instrument and lots of improvisation.

McGhee spent his early childhood in Tulsa before moving to Detroit and eventually to California. After playing in the bands of Count Basie and Duke Ellington, he joined Coleman Hawkins' band and embraced the West Coast style of jazz. McGhee' music had more mellow sound and he played notes that lingered around a melody instead of scorching it. In later years, McGhee performed as a trumpeter with jazz legends Duke Ellington and Miles Davis and as an arranger for Woody Herman and Billy Eckstine.

Grady Nichols

This smooth jazz saxophonist still makes Tulsa his home but has been the opening act for concerts starring Luciano Pavarotti, The Beach Boys, Huey Lewis and The New, The O'Jays, Herb Alpert and the Tijuana Brass as well as other national and international performers.

Nichols picked up his first saxophone as a sixth grader in Siloam Springs, Arkansas and became a pupil of legendary sax player Joe Davis during his high school years. He moved to Tulsa in the mid-1990s after graduating from John Brown University.

His style of playing the sax has earned critical praise from such people as Bill Champlin, a former member of the pop-rock band Chicago, Grammy Award-winning record producer Michael Omartin and Dove Award-winning contemporary Christian artist Andy Chrisman.

Marshal Royal

This Sapulpa native played alto saxophone in the Count Basie Orchestra for 20 years and also served as Basie's behind-the-scenes leader, handling the group's day-to-day operations and band rehearsals. But when Basie had to cut his band to a septet in 1951, he chose to keep Royal and two other men as the leaders of his new outfit.

Royal's family had strong musical roots; his father was a music instructor and band leader who also taught his son to play the violin while his mother was a pianist. During his high school years, Royal stopped playing the violin and picked up the clarinet and saxophone.

Prior to joining Basie's band, Royal was part of the West Coast bands led by Duke Ellington and Lionel Hampton.

Lynn Seaton

This Tulsa-born bassist is known for his work in jazz, bebop and swing music and has appeared on nearly 130 jazz albums. For several years he performed with the Count Basie Orchestra, Woody Herman's Young Thundering Heard along with vocalists Mel Torme, Diane Schuur, Nancy Wilson and Tony Bennett.

After graduating from the University of Oklahoma, Seaton moved to Cincinnati, Ohio and then earned a fellowship to study jazz in New York City. That would lead to his work with the Basie and Herman bands.

Today, Seaton is a teacher and lecturer at North Texas State University in Denton, Texas, which is world renowned for its Jazz Studies Division within the College of Music. He teaches jazz styles and fundamentals, improvisation and a rhythm section class. He and his own jazz trio frequently perform at night clubs in the Dallas-Fort Worth Metroplex.

John Simmons

An injury suffered during a youth football game forced this Tulsa resident to switch from his beloved trumpet to becoming a bassist. As fate would have it, Simmons would become one of the jazz world's most sought-after bassists during the 1940s and 1950s.

Simmons was one of the earliest members of the Nat King Cole trio and worked with the Benny Goodman, Duke Ellington and Louis Armstrong orchestras during the 1940s. He also appeared in the 1944 movie short *Jammin' the Blues*, which featured several jazz musicians in a rare, filmed jam session.

Before his death in 1979, Simmons would record with legendary musicians such as Ella Fitzgerald, Hot Lips Page, Billie Holiday, Benny Carter, Buddy Rich, John Coltrane, Andre Previn and Thelonious Monk

Simmons' family moved from Tulsa to California during his high school years and his first musical gigs were with bands in the Los Angeles and San Diego areas.

Dara Tucker

This jazz vocalist and Oral Roberts University graduate has performed professionally since 2009 and has released four albums along with being a featured vocalist for the Charlie Hunter Trio.

Her 2009 debut album *All Right Now* was a collection of standards from The Great American Songbook. Then her 2010 album *Soul Said Yes* blended R&B and jazz and reached the top 10 list on the R&B list on the Amazon.com website. It also marked the beginning of her musical work with Hunter.

The Sun Season was released in 2014 and the 2017 album *Oklahoma Rain* was about Tucker's emotional journey following the death of her parents in 2014.

Tucker was one of seven children born in Tulsa to parents Doyle and Lynda Tucker, a gospel music minister and singer, respectively, and formed a gospel singing group called The Tuckers. All of the children performed gospel music before they were four years old along with taking piano lessons before turning eight years old.

Her most recent project was the 2023 release *Dreams of Waking: Music for a Better World*. The album took songs written by Donny Hathaway, Paul Simon and Stevie Wonder and presented them as a cry for social justice while using the medium of jazz music.

In addition to her singing career, Tucker has worked as freelance documentary filmmaker and music video producer.

Washington Rucker

An alumnus of Booker T. Washington High School, Rucker flourished as a teenage drummer and that led to a diverse career as a musical performer, college educator and even a career in the movies.

Rucker began playing alongside local singer Jimmy "Cry Cry" Hawkins before going to Los Angeles and graduating from UCLA with a bachelor's degree in history. While there, he performed with local bands and made connections that led to invitations to perform with some of the biggest names in various musical genres.

Among the artists Rucker has recorded with are jazz legend Dizzy Gillespie, gospel music icons Shirley Caesar and Reverend James Cleveland and legendary singers Nancy Wilson and Stevie Wonder. He also performed on the 1976 album rendition of George Gershwin's folk opera *Porgy and Bess* which featured Cleo Laine and Ray Charles.

In addition to teaching a master class in drumming at the University of Southern California, Rucker appeared in two movies: Martin Scorsese's 1977 film *New York, New York* (a tribute to New York City's jazz heritage) and Clint Eastwood's 1988 film *Bird* (a biography of jazz saxophonist Charlie "Bird" Parker).

As a child, Rucker learned the basics of how to play drums in his childhood home by using a fork, a knife and a black skillet. He also wrote a children-oriented book about jazz music and mentored aspiring jazz musicians throughout southern California.

He was inducted into the Oklahoma Jazz Hall of Fame in 1998.

Harold "Hal" Singer

This Tulsa-born tenor saxophone player is best known for the instrumental "Corn Bread" reached the top spot on the *Billboard* rhythm and blues chart in September of 1948.

Singer started out playing the violin before switching to the clarinet and then the tenor sax. He played alongside such jazz greats as Jay McShann, Charlie Watts, Oran "Hot Lips" Page, Duke Ellington and Earl "Fatha" Hines.

Wayman Tisdale

Tisdale was a renowned basketball player on the college, professional and international levels. The 6-foot-9 power forward spent 11 seasons in the National Basketball Association, was part of the USA's 1984 Olympic gold medal basketball championship squad and was a 2009 inductee into the College Basketball Hall of Fame.

But he was equally passionate about his music, as evidenced by the first four of his nine albums reaching the top 10 of the *Billboard* contemporary jazz charts.

The 1995 debut album *Power Forward* reached number four and *Face to Face* reached the top spot in 2001. After Tisdale died from bone cancer in 2009, a tribute album was released called *Wayman Tisdale: The Absolute Greatest Hits* with guest appearances by jazz keyboardist George Duke and country singer-songwriter Toby Keith.

The foundation for Wayman's musical heritage came by playing in the choir on Sunday mornings at north Tulsa's Friendship Missionary Baptist Church, whose senior pastor was his father, Reverend Louis L. Tisdale. Wayman's older brother, Weldon, served as that congregation's senior pastor for nearly 20 years.

Wayman taught himself how to play the bass guitar. But when he could not find a bass guitar for a lefthander like himself, the solution was created by his taking a regular bass guitar, turning it upside down and playing it.

Tisdale died in 2009 at the age of 44 due to complications from bone cancer. College basketball's annual award for the Most Outstanding Male Basketball Player is named in his honor.

Lee Wiley

After running away from her Fort Gibson, Oklahoma home as a teenager and coming to Tulsa, Wiley would become one of the premier female jazz vocalists during the 1930s and 1940s.

She was best known for interpreting songs by George Gershwin, Cole Porter and Rodgers and Hart and would be accompanied by jazz legends Fats Waller and Eddie Condon. Critics said her singing style had an unusual sensitivity along with sensuous phrasing.

In addition, she was the first jazz vocalist to create a vocal project dedicated to the works of a single composer. She did that for the works of Rodgers and Hart, Porter and Gershwin as well as for Irving Berlin.

Wiley, who was part Cherokee Indian, developed a fondness for the singing styles of Ethel Waters and Mildred Bailey while living in Tulsa and also sang on a local radio station. She later moved to Chicago and eventually to New York City where she gained national attention on the CBS Radio Network's Saturday night program *Saturday Night Swing*.

She once said of her success, "I don't sing jazz, I just sing. The only vocal trick I've ever done is putting in the vibrato and taking it out. I don't believe in vocal gimmickry and never had commercial instincts."

Wiley later recorded with Bing Crosby but became disenchanted with the music world and retired in 1958 and died of cancer in 1975. She was inducted into the Oklahoma Music Hall of Fame in 2003.

Terry Woodson

This graduate of Tulsa Central High School and the University of Tulsa went from playing bass trombone in local jazz clubs and being a local music teacher to being one of the most sought-after figures by artists whose works have comprised The Great American Songbook such as Henry Mancini, Percy Faith and Frank Sinatra.

Woodson has been the musical librarian and conductor for both Frank Sinatras (Senior and Junior) for over 30 years. He played key roles in producing the electronically-enhanced *Duets* albums in the mid-1990s, which proved to be the last studio recordings by Sinatra before his death in 1998.

He was associated with the Henry Mancini Orchestra for 30 years and participated in many of the legendary Mancini's music in movies and TV shows. He also toured the world with the Percy Faith Orchestra.

In recent years, Woodson also handled musical arrangements for such artists as Rosemary Clooney, Diane Schuur, Barry Manilow, Vince Gill, Amy Grant and Bette Midler. He was inducted into the Oklahoma Jazz Hall of Fame in 2010.

Chapter Eight
Rhythm and Blues

"Everybody started calling my music rock and roll, but it wasn't anything but the same rhythm and blues I'd been playing down in New Orleans."

Fats Domino

"The Righteous Brothers were purely rhythm and blues; black music."

Bill Medley

"Rhythm and blues used to be called race music...This music was going on for years, but nobody paid any attention to it."

Ray Charles

"When you sit down and think about what rock 'n' roll music really is, then you have to change that question. Played up-tempo, you call it rock 'n' roll; at regular tempo, you call it rhythm and blues."

Little Richard

***

The Gap Band and Charlie Wilson

This was one of the top funk-rhythm and blues acts during the 1980s with 14 of their songs reaching the *Billboard* Top 10 R&B charts and four of those reaching the top spot. And over 40 years later, its lead singer is still influencing the worlds of R&B, rap and hip hop music.

The word Gap, in this instance, is a nod to Tulsa's once-thriving African American business district which was anchored by North Greenwood Avenue and bounded on the south by East Archer Street and on the north by East Pine Street.

Charlie, Ronnie and Robert Wilson attended Tulsa's Booker T. Washington High School and their father was a Pentecostal minister. Charlie was the lead vocalist and played piano and drums, Robert handled backup vocals and bass guitar and Ronnie played piano and the synthesizer. Their trademarks included brightly colored outfits and oversized hats.

Their first big break came thanks to Tulsa Sound icon Leon Russell who used the funk-flavored music by the Wilsons the backup band on Russell's 1974 album *Stop All That Jazz*.

Russell was involved in the band's next two albums but when those projects didn't produce any charting singles, Russell and the Wilsons parted ways. Los Angeles-based producer Lonnie Simmons quickly signed the band to a record deal with Mercury Records and the 1979 single "Shake" became the band's first top 10 R&B hit.

The Gap Band was equally adroit in creating danceable songs as well as slow-burning love songs. Their number one hits were "Burn Rubber (Why You Wanna Hurt Me)" in 1980, "Outstanding" and "Early in the Morning" in 1983 and "All My Love" in 1989.

Other top selling songs included "You Dropped a Bomb on Me," "I Don't Believe You Want to Get Up and Dance (Oops!)" and "Party Train."

Living in the fast lane during The Gap Band's heyday and after its breakup resulted in major health and social issues for Charlie Wilson. Among those were sleeping on the streets of Los Angeles, drug rehabilitation and a battle with prostate cancer.

After cleaning up his life, Wilson embarked on a new career as a singer-producer and has enjoyed major success in the R&B, hip-hop, rap and urban contemporary fields since 2000. As a solo artist, Wilson has topped the *Billboard* R&B charts 13 times, earned 13 Grammy nominations and was honored in 2009 and 2020 as the Billboard adult R&B Male Artist of the Year.

His 2009 CD *Uncle Charlie* debuted at the top of the *Billboard* R&B/Hip-Hop chart and his 2010 song "You Are" spent 13 weeks in the number one spot. Wilson has collaborated with rappers Kanye West and Snoop Dogg along with pop stars Justin Timberlake, Beyoncé, Rihanna, Jay-Z, Nicki Minaj, Pharrell Williams (one of Wilson's nephews), Jodeci, New Edition and Bruno Mars. Wilson was featured on 12 songs in West's 2011 CD *My Beautiful Dark Twisted Fantasy*.

His most recent project was the 2022 album *No Stoppin' Us* alongside R&B legends Johnny Gill, Babyface and K-Ci Hailey. It peaked at number one on the *Billboard* R&B Male Artist airplay chart. Another top-selling album saw Wilson joining Motown legend Smokey Robinson in 2020 for *All of My Love*.

His 2016 autobiography *I Am Charlie Wilson* reached the *New York Times* and *Washington Post* bestseller lists. In January of 2024, Wilson was honored with the 2,770th star on the Hollywood Walk of Fame.

Richard "Moon" Calhoun

Richard "Moon" Calhoun was a session drummer and songwriter who played on albums by The Gap Band, Ray Parker Jr., Chaka Khan, Elvin Bishop and other R&B-funk music acts. The Broken Arrow High School graduate was into reggae music and got his nickname from being able to draw out the reggae word for man (*mon*) into what sounded like "moon."

Calhoun later moved to Los Angeles and after getting caught up in the fast lane of alcohol and drugs, turned his life around. But a freak accident in 1994 while riding a bicycle without a helmet resulted in a fall that left him as a partial quadriplegic. Undeterred, Calhoun revived his musical career and has been a lead singer in four bands and also did background vocals for Motley Crue's album *Decade of Decadence*. His most recent project was the 2023 album *The Love Goes On* as part of the classic rock Michael Thompson Band.

Gary Gilmore

This bass guitarist and photographer was one of three Tulsa musicians to play in Taj Mahal's band in the 1960s and 1970s. His musical style featured what could be described as loping or with a light hop.

Gilmore played on Mahal's 1968 albums *Natch'l Blues* and *Taj Mahal* and *Giant Step/De Old Folks at Home* in 1969. He also appeared in the Rolling Stones' made-for-TV special *Rock and Roll Circus*.

He returned to his Tulsa roots several years later, teaming up with J.J. Cale, Jamie Oldaker and Steve Ripley's group, The Tractors. He was also part of Cale's 2006 blues-influenced *Road to Escondido* which was the 2006 Grammy for best contemporary blues album.

Gilmore's work with Cale was featured on the soundtrack for the 2003 Martin Scorsese documentary *Martin Scorsese Presents the Blues: A Musical Journey*.

Kim Manning

This 2000 University of Tulsa graduate was a featured singer with funk music legends George Clinton and the P-Funk All-Stars prior to becoming a band's lead singer, actress, model and reality TV star.

In addition to performing with Clinton plus the Red Hot Chili Peppers and rapper Snoop Dogg, Manning has released three CDs with *Space Queen* in 2015 being the most recent. Her vocal style has been described as a blend of R&B and soul and funk music.

Manning studied classical music at the age of six and earned a theatre degree from TU prior to moving to Canada, England and California. While in Los Angeles, she attended a late night jam session and after a phone call placed by her mother in Ponca City, Oklahoma to Clinton plus her opera recital tape, she landed a spot in Clinton's band.

Manning's movies are the dark comedy *Moments of Clarity* in 2016, the 2009 horror film *Room 33* and *Ghost of the Red Rose* in 2001. In 2006, she appeared in four episodes of the VH1 reality TV series *Flavor of Love* as Peaches, an aspiring suitor for hip-hop legend Flavor Flav.

Maxayn Lewis (Paulette Parker)

Born as Paulette Parker, this Tulsa native was part of The Ikettes, backup singers for Rock and Roll Hall of Famers Ike and Tina Turner. She has also performed with Bonnie Raitt, Duran Duran, Smokey Robinson, Britney Spears, Ray Charles, Jerry Lee Lewis and Celine Dion.

Growing up in Tulsa's historic Greenwood District, the music of Ella Fitzgerald, Duke Ellington, Muddy Waters and Mahalia Jackson would be the inspiration for Lewis creating an all-female vocal group, The Continentals, while in the fifth grade.

She became a conservatory-trained pianist and attended Oklahoma State University but left school after being assaulted on campus by a white male. Ensuing depression led her to consider abandoning her music career but a while male singer asked her to form a vocal duo.

Lewis sang background vocals on the soundtrack for the 1978 movie *Grease* and performed with Gino Vannelli, Rufus and Donna Summer. During the 1980s she was a backup singer on several records for the Tulsa-based R&B group The Gap Band. Promoters planned for Lewis to be the lead singer of a new group called Snap! But when the album bombed commercially, Lewis and the band's members were released.

Roy Milton

Tulsa was the launching pad for this singer-turned-drummer who achieved national fame and top 10 singles during the 1940s and 1950s in the fields of R&B and jump blues. Nineteen of his songs reached the top 10 rankings of the *Billboard* R&B charts.

Milton was born in the southern Oklahoma town of Wynnewood and spent time on an Indian reservation before moving to Tulsa to join Ernie Fields' orchestra in the late 1920s. He moved to Los Angeles in 1933 and formed a new band called The Solid Senders.

His breakout single was the 1945 hit "R.M. Blues" which peaked at number two on the *Billboard* R&B chart and at number 20 on the *Billboard* pop chart. Other big hits were "Hop, Skip and Jump" in 1948, "Information Blues" in 1950 and "Best Wishes" in 1951.

Milton was inducted into the Oklahoma Jazz Hall of Fame in 1991.

Tori Ruffin

The lead guitarist for Morris Day and The Time for over 25 years also leads the Tulsa-based band Freak Juice, a mashup of funk, rhythm and blues and riff-laden power rock and roll. Ruffin has also worked with such Grammy Award-winning musicians as Prince, Mick Jagger, Michael Jackson, Mariah Carey and Smokey Robinson.

He was born in Chicago and spent time in Detroit, Austin and Los Angeles before relocating to Tulsa to join his brother Greg in operating a midtown nightclub featuring R&B and hip-hop artists. The 17-year-old Ruffin and some friends heard Davis and his band switching from a rock-style riff into something he hadn't heard before. His friends told him it was a bebop beat that was popularized by Ella Fitzgerald and Dizzy Gillespie during the 1940s. That night, Ruffin said he wanted to play rock and bebop in a Led Zeppelin-style band.

Ruffin cited James Brown, Jimi Hendrix and the Isley Brothers along with Led Zeppelin and Rush as his early musical influences. In a 2021 interview with *Guitar World* magazine, Ruffin told of an encounter with jazz legend Miles Davis at the Hollywood Bowl and its influence on his current style of music.

As a movie actor, Ruffin appeared in Eddie Murphy's two *Coming to America* movies. Murphy portrayed the flamboyant lounge singer Randy Watson and Ruffin was part of Watson's band called Sexual Chocolate.

David Skinner

This guitarist-singer has been part of Tulsa's music scene since 1980, coming to this city after being part of the 1970s Austin music scene that featured gigs with ZZ Top, Johnny Winter and Stevie Ray Vaughn.

Skinner was born in the state of Washington and moved as a youngster with his family to Texas. Music ranging from classical to folk to Broadway musicals to jazz always played at his house, but Skinner said watching The Beatles on *The Ed Sullivan Show* changed his musical career path. Skinner was inducted into the Oklahoma Jazz Hall of Fame in 2005.

James Talley

This Tulsa-born artist is known for blending country and electric blues music and was the lead guitarist for B.B. King's first recording session in Nashville in 1976.

Talley's family moved to the state of Washington when he was a youngster then to New Mexico where he went to college. While in New Mexico, he met folk music icon Pete Seeger who encouraged Talley to write songs about the culture of the southwestern United States.

He recorded 14 albums between 1975 and 2008 and also wrote songs for country music stars Alan Jackson, Johnny Cash, Johnny Paycheck and dance music superstar Moby.

Flash Terry

A bus driver when the sun was out and a popular R&B act when the sun went down, Verbie Gene "Flash" Terry and his Uptown Blues Band enjoyed local and regional success by keeping alive the horn-driven sounds of R&B from the 1940s that later influenced R&B and rock and roll in the late 1950s.

Leon Russell and a host of Tulsa Sound musicians have credited Terry and his band that played in various north Tulsa nightclubs as being one of the prime influences in their respective musical careers.

Terry's best-known R&B song was also his first single, "Her Name is Lou" and was released in 1958. In following years, he would tour with Bobby "Blue" Bland and make recordings with Eric Clapton bassist Carl Radle and Bob Wills steel guitar legend Leon McAuliffe.

Terry was inducted into the Oklahoma Jazz Hall of Fame in 1994 and died in 2004.

David T. Walker

Another person that proudly wore the label of "a musician's musician," this Tulsa native produced and recorded 15 solo albums during a recording career than lasted from 1968 through 2010 and performed on more than 2,000 other albums, TV/radio commercials and movie soundtracks.

Walker's website described his guitar playing style as "Soul. In Light and Grace."

The list of superstar singers who utilized this Tulsa native for their recordings reads like a Who's Who of American music history. Topping that extensive and prestigious list are names like Smokey Robinson, Barbara Streisand, Lou Rawls, Solomon Burke, Little Richard, Carole King, Ray Charles, the Mamas and Papas, James Brown, Marvin Gaye, Quincy Jones, Dean Martin, the Isley Brothers, Gladys Knight and the Jackson 5.

In addition, his music was sampled by hip-hop and rap legends such as A Tribe Called Quest, Busta Rhymes, De La Soul and Tupac Shakur.

The oldest of 10 children, Walker's family moved to central California during his childhood. He began playing the saxophone in the fourth grade and became a self-taught guitarist at the age of 16.

He was inducted into the Oklahoma Jazz Hall of Fame in 2005.

Chapter Nine
Christian

"Everything that we're singing about (in contemporary Christian music) is true; and even when you take away all the glitz, it's still true in the darkest, ugliest and most hopeless places."

Steven Curtis Chapman

"Gospel music is so ingrained in my bones. I can't do a concert without singing a gospel song. It's what I was raised on."

Johnny Cash

"Remember: In the end, you're not living to impress your friends or your relatives or your coworkers. All of life is for Jesus."

Chris Tomlin

"My heart is still there in gospel music. It never left...I'm gonna make a gospel record and tell Jesus I cannot bear these burdens alone."

Aretha Franklin

"Gospel music is the purest thing there is on this earth."

Elvis Presley

***

Carman

During the 1980s and 1990s, Carman was to Christian Contemporary Music what Michael Jackson was to pop music: a one-of-a-kind superstar.

Carman Domenic Licciardello based his ministry in Tulsa during that era and his story-telling songs proclaimed the message of the gospel of Jesus Christ and the hope of salvation, much like what one heard in a Billy Graham sermon. Yet Carman's concerts in football stadiums or other large arenas contained the glitz and glamour that are trademarks of shows often presented by U2 or Metallica.

Blessed with ruggedly handsome facial appearances, he came from a musical family and spent his early days performing in night clubs; a trade that took him to Las Vegas and then California. He became a Christian after attending a concert by gospel singer Andre Crouch and then spent five years laying the foundation for his non-denominational ministry.

Some of Carman's biggest hits, many of which featured multi-level drama and a victorious Jesus Christ, were "Lazarus, Come Forth," "Revival in the Land," "Witches Invitation," "Satan, Bite the Dust" and "The Champion." He was a frequent guest host on Christian talk shows and also appeared in Christian-themed movies.

Carman sold 10 million records and in 1990 and 1992, *Billboard Magazine* named him as the Contemporary Christian Artist of the Year. And over more than 10 years, he would win seven Dove Awards, the Christian music industry's equivalent of a Grammy.

He produced a 1994 music video about the Biblical battle between David and Goliath that featured the three brothers who comprised the Tulsa-based pop music band Hanson. Lead singer Taylor Hanson was cast as David and older brother/guitarist Isaac was the event announcer. Younger brother/drummer Zac and other family members were in the audience witnessing the battle.

After a 12-year exile which included a prolonged fight with cancer-related complications, Carman resumed a national concert tour, albeit in much smaller venues than he previously utilized. He blamed his disappearance from Christian music on industry executives who disliked charismatic churches and performers such as him.

Carman's only marriage happened in 2017 at the age of 61. He passed away in 2021.

The Arnolds

This Southern Gospel trio recorded albums during the 1980s and 1990s and was featured in concerts and videos presented by Christian music icon Bill Gaither.

The trio's members were the husband-and-wife duo of Frank and Vicki Arnold along with Sheri LaFontaine. For LaFontaine, her four years with the Arnolds were the launching pad for her own highly successful singing career and collaborations with Bill Gaither and Bishop Marvin Winans.

At the age of 16, Frank Arnold began performing in a group consisting of his parents, two sisters and a brother. In later years, Frank became a prominent concert promoter in Oklahoma and Texas and the southeastern United States.

Helen Baylor

Born in Tulsa as Helen LaRue Lowe, Baylor has been one of the gospel music industry's top singers since 1990. One of her earliest gospel albums, *The Live Experience*, spent 27 weeks at the top spot on the *Billboard* gospel charts. She won two Dove Awards, four Grammy nominations and received the *Soul Train* Lady of Soul Award for her career achievements in black gospel music. Baylor also performed alongside musical superstars such as Aretha Franklin, B.B. King, the Captain and Tennile, Chaka Khan and Stevie Wonder.

After moving from Tulsa to Los Angeles, Baylor was an R&B singing sensation in her youth and during the 1970s at the age of 17, joined the cast of the Broadway musical *Hair!* But she was sexually molested as a child and a drug addiction lasting 20-plus years helped to mask the pain she dealt with.

With a grandmother being the only true friend she had, Baylor became a Christian and entered the gospel music industry. Her autobiography, *No Greater Love: The Helen Baylor Story* tells the story of those times in greater detail.

Baylor was inducted into the Oklahoma Jazz Hall of Fame in 2000.

Trinity Dawson

Once a standout football running back at Tulsa's Union High School, Dawson is a rising star in the field of urban gospel music. Critics have said his musical style is a blend of Christian and gospel artists like Mercy Me, Hillsong United, Israel Houghton and Kirk Franklin and R&B stars like Stevie Wonder, Jill Scott and John Legend.

After leaving Tulsa for Detroit, Michigan, Dawson was in route to being a coveted pro football prospect while playing at the University of Toledo when a serious hip injury during his junior season dashed those dreams and hastened his pursuit of gospel music.

Dawson released a hip-hop flavored gospel album in 2014, *With All I Am,* which peaked at number four on the *Billboard* Top Gospel Albums chart.

Phil Driscoll

Grammy Award-winning trumpeter Phil Driscoll is primarily known for his work in the rock and roll, rhythm and blues and Christian music fields.

Driscoll was 12 years old when his family moved from Texas to Tulsa in 1959. Driscoll's father had pastored several small churches and his mother played piano and organ. He quickly became a featured soloist in the Tulsa Youth Symphony and proceeded to win national and international awards for his music.

He attended Baylor University and won a CBS-TV talent program called *The All-American Talent Show.* The runner-up act on that show was a brother-sister duo that would leave its own mark in pop music history, the Carpenters.

Driscoll's success led to appearances on TV variety shows and collaborating with rock icons such as Blood Sweat and Tears, Steven Stills, Joe Cocker, .38 Special, Billy Preston and Leon Russell.

Driscoll and his future wife became Christians in 1979 and he returned to his religious roots by focusing on Christian music. That resulted in winning multiple Dove Awards.

His career was hampered by a 2006 conviction on federal felony charges of using his Christian music ministry to avoid paying income taxes. Driscoll insisted that mistakes may have been made but he never intentionally tried to avoid paying taxes. Nevertheless, he was sentenced to one year in a federal prison. After leaving prison, Driscoll resumed his career by focusing heavily on Christian and patriotic music.

In recent years, Driscoll hosted a 30-minute show on the Christian Television Network called *Divine Awakening.* The show's format, according to Driscoll's website, aimed to transform Bible passages into songs.

Dennis Jernigan

Born in the southwest Tulsa suburb of Sapulpa, Dennis Jernigan has been one of the top singer-songwriters in contemporary Christian music since the 1990s. He was a 2018 inductee into the Oklahoma Music Hall of Fame.

Jernigan's songs have sold over one million copies and have been recorded by leading singers in the CCM industry such as Rebecca St. James, Ron Kenoly, Twila Paris and Natalie Grant.

A 1981 graduate of Oklahoma Baptist University, he has also written several books, magazine articles, produced a documentary and operates a music-based ministry with his wife, Melinda, and other family members in Muskogee, Oklahoma.

Among his biggest-selling songs that are used in contemporary praise and worship services are "You Are My All in All," "We Will Worship the Lamb of Glory," "Who Can Satisfy My Soul," "Thank You, Lord" and "Nobody Fills My Heart Like Jesus."

Even with that considerably body of work, Jernigan has been a lightning rod for controversy over his declaration that God divinely healed him of homosexuality.

Jernigan has said in written works and speeches to religious and youth groups that despite his church upbringing and a grandmother who nurtured his early love for music, his feelings were bottled up about being accosted in a public restroom by a male adult attempting to perform a sex act on him when he was five years old.

He said his long-term involvement in same-sex physical activity evolved from a search for affirmation and acceptance among men. Those activities were kept secret from family members, friends and the woman who became his wife.

Jernigan also said he was miserable about same-sex relationships, even trying once to commit suicide, as well as living a double life with church members, college classmates and when he and Melinda started dating

During an Oklahoma City-area Christian music concert, Jernigan said he realized that homosexuality was one of the many sins that Jesus Christ died to redeem people from.

Jernigan said God forgave him, healed him immediately of his homosexuality and then brought other people into his life to help him in his journey.

In 2014, Jernigan and family members released a self-funded documentary about his life called *Sing Over Me*. The film features Jernigan's testimony and used an Old Testament passage (Zephaniah 3:17) as a focal point for his life's story. That passage says that God rejoices over His children and loves them and won't accuse them.

Kari Jobe

This Oral Roberts University alumnus has been one of the brightest stars in Contemporary Christian music for over two decades.

Jobe has won six Dove Awards along with one Grammy nomination. Two of her Dove Awards came in 2012 for Special Events Album of the Year (*Glory Revealed II: The Word of God in Worship*) and Spanish Language Album of the Year (*Le Canto*). She won the 2017 Dove Award for Contemporary Christian Artist of the Year.

Her biggest selling single was the 2020 song *The Blessing* which was recorded with Elevation Worship and her husband, Cody Carnes. It peaked at number two on the *Billboard* US Christian Music chart and sold over 500,000 copies.

Two of her singles from the 2014 CD *Majestic* reached the top 10 rankings of the *Billboard* Contemporary Christian Music chart. "Forever" peaked at number six and "I Am Not Alone" reached number nine.

Four of her CDs reached the Christian Contemporary Music top five rankings with *Majestic* and *Where I Find You* in 2012 each reaching the top spot.

While Jobe has served as an associate worship pastor at churches in Texas and Nashville, Tennessee, she's also toured with internationally known Contemporary Christian artists such as Chris Tomlin and Hillsong.

Mourning September

This Tulsa-based trio whose sound could also have been considered as alternative Christian rock or emo lasted from 2001 through 2007.

The band released a 2004 CD entitled *A Man Can Change His Stars*, which featured a typical format for Christian music of softer verses and much louder choruses along with asking questions essential to the Christian life.

Pillar

Renowned for their hard rock-rap style of Christian music, Pillar was one of the top Christian music groups in the 2000s and released a comeback album in August 2014.

The group won three Dove Awards, was a finalist for three other Dove Awards and earned a 2008 Grammy nomination for Best Rock or Rap Gospel Album.

Vocalist Rob Beckley and bass guitarist Michael "Kalel" Wittig were among five students at Fort Hays State University in Kansas who got together in 1998 to form the band. After two independent albums were released and tours of Kansas failed to generate success, the band relocated to Tulsa with the hope of finding more fans.

Their big break came in 2002 with the album *Fireproof*, which won a Dove Award and sold over 300,000 copies. Subsequent singles "Frontline" and "Bring Me Down" crossed over to be frequently played on secular hard rock radio stations.

When the band went on hiatus, Beckley became a pastor for the Owasso campus of the non-denominational LifeChurch.

Billy Sprague

Born in Tulsa, Sprague wrote songs for artists such as CeCe Winans, Sandi Patty, Gary Chapman and Debby Boone. He also played in Amy Grant's backup band.

He co-wrote "Via Dolorosa" for Sandi Patti, a moving ballad about the crucifixion of Jesus Christ. It won a 1986 Dove Award as Song of the Year and the album earned a Grammy nomination for Best Gospel Performance by a Female Vocalist.

In his childhood days, Sprague's family moved from Tulsa to Borger, Texas and he would earn degrees from Texas Christian University and the University of Texas before launching his music career.

In later years, Sprague wrote several books. *Ice Cream as a Clue to the Meaning of the Universe* is about lessons learned in life. *Letter to a Grieving Heart* deals with the loss of a loved one and originated from the death of his fiancée.

His 2023 mystery novel *Music City Mayhymn: The Hits Just Keep Coming* is a detective story set in Nashville.

Sprague later served as a worship leader at churches in Colorado and Florida and recently wrote a music-related mystery.

Stars Go Dim

Originally a Christian pop quartet, this is now the moniker for singer-songwriter Chris Cleveland. Stars Go Dim had four songs reach the top 15 on the *Billboard* Christian Adult Contemporary music chart.

The band started out as a side project for three Pillar band members. Cleveland was a worship leader at Tulsa's Asbury Methodist Church, one of America's largest congregations, before taking the band into the national spotlight.

Because of their musicianship, Stars Go Dim opened for such diverse artists as The Fray, Daughtry, The All-American Rejects and The

Roots; the latter being the house band for NBC-TV's *The Tonight Show Starring Jimmy Fallon*.

"You Are Loved" was on the band's self-titled 2015 album and peaked at number two on the *Billboard* Christian Adult Contemporary music chart in 2016. "How Glorious the Love of Heaven" from their *Christmas is Here* album later that year, reached number four on that same music chart.

In 2018, the songs "Heaven on Earth" and "Christmas Is Here" reached the top 15 of that chart. The 2022 song "Yes He Does" became a number one single on Christian music charts around the world.

Cleveland has written songs for and performed alongside international pop music stars such as Justin Bieber, Billy Joel, Elton John and Jason Derulo. He has done likewise with Contemporary Christian stars For King & Country, Bethel Music, Maverick City and Lauren Daigle.

Tim Storms

This Tulsa native achieved two music feats that landed him in the Guinness Book of World Records: the world's widest vocal range (10 octaves) and the world's lowest recorded vocal note.

Storms' vocal range was measured at 10 octaves. For comparison, singer Mariah Carey's vocal range is five octaves and a piano's range are seven octaves.

In an interview, Storms told of an ear, nose and throat specialist who examined Storms after a concert. The doctor found that Storms' vocal cords were nearly double the average length and the muscles around the vocal cords had more movement than normal.

The lowest vocal note was measured at G-7 or 0.189 Hz. For comparison, another former holder of that record was J.D. Sumner, the legendary Southern Gospel bass singer who was also featured on Elvis Presley's song "Way Down."

Storms has recorded Christian music since 2001 and performed in musical shows in Branson, Missouri. He was inducted into the Branson Entertainers Hall of Fame in 2006.

Chapter Ten

Classical and Opera

"I know that the most joy in my life has come to me from my violin."

Albert Einstein

"Of course, we didn't have any sewers or street paving, but these were luxuries that could wait; whereas an opera house loomed as an immediate necessity."

L.J. Martin, Mayor of Tulsa, 1910-12

"In an opera, the poetry must be the obedient daughter of music."

Wolfgang Amadeus Mozart

"I think a life in music is a life beautifully spent, and this is what I have devoted my life to."

Luciano Pavarotti

"I know this will blow your mind but most people would never get it; but I listen to classical music when no one else is around..."

Vanilla Ice

***

Mark Baker

While his family's time in Tulsa was short-lived, Mark Baker established a lengthy career as one of the premier American-born tenors in
the operatic world.

Nicknamed "The Tulsa Tenor," Baker sang nearly 250 times for
New York City's prestigious Metropolitan Opera between 1986 and
2005 and was also cast in major roles in renowned international opera
houses in Canada, Germany, France, Argentina and Chile.

The Baker family moved from Tulsa to Florida during Mark's
childhood. He earned an Associate of Arts degree from Brevard Community College in Cocoa, Florida along with bachelor's and master's
degrees from the University of Indiana.

Baker currently serves as a vocal music instructor at the Performing
and Visual Arts department at Eastern Florida State College in Cocoa,
Florida.

Tosca Kramer

Dr. Tosca Berger Kramer was a violinist whose family brought
classical music to Tulsa and also founded the city's first symphony
orchestra, the Tulsa Philharmonic.

She was born in New Zealand to a family with a rich appreciation
for the fine arts. Her father, Kurt Berger, was an orchestra conductor
and her mother, Lucy, was an impressionist painter. While the family
was living in Germany, Tosca studied at the Royal Conservatory at
Sondershausen in Thuringia.

The family was touring American in the 1920s when Kurt became seriously ill and was hospitalized in Tulsa. During his extended recovery, civic leaders convinced the family to stay and help expand the city's cultural offerings.

That led to the creating of the Tulsa Philharmonic, the beginning of Tosca's teaching career and her marriage to Adolph Kramer, a local violinist who also made stringed musical instruments. The couple later adopted four children.

Tosca also served on the school of music faculty at four universities: the University of Tulsa, the University of Oklahoma, Oklahoma City University and the University of North Texas in Denton, Texas. She was the first chair violinist for the Oklahoma City Symphony Orchestra and performed numerous charity concerts along with solo and chamber recitals.

She could have rested on her laurels during her sixties but chose to return to the Eastman School of Music in Rochester, New York and earned degrees as a Master of Music and Doctor of Musical Arts.

Fredell Lack

This Tulsa-born musician took violin lessons from Tosca Berger then went on to become a renowned soloist and fine arts educator at the University of Houston. She taught violin for 50 years at that university as well as performing with symphony orchestras around the world.

During the peak of her performing career, Lack played a violin made in 1727 by Antonio Stradivarius, the "Baron Deurbrouco" with a bow made by Francois Tourte. She was praised by patrons of classical music for both the warmth of tone and intensity that she used in performing sonatas and concertos written by Joseph Haydn, Felix Mendelssohn, Johannes Brahms and Ludwig von Beethoven.

Luck was six years old when she took violin lessons from Berger. As an 11-year-old girl, she performed her first solo with the Tulsa Philharmonic. A little over a year later, she was accepted into the New York City violin program taught by Louis Persinger, an accomplished instructor who also taught Isaac Stern and Yehudi Menuhin.

She made over 20 concert tours in Europe during her career and performed with London's famous Royal Philharmonic Orchestra, the BBC Symphony and the Halle Orchestra in Manchester, England. In 1947, she was a featured performer on weekly classical music broadcasts carried by the Mutual Radio Network.

Lack moved to Houston in 1951 when her husband, Ralph Eichhorn, accepted an offer by the University of Houston to serve as a professor. Her career suffered a setback in 1952 when a dog bit off the tip of her left little finger but she kept performing after extensive rehabilitation and adjusting her playing technique.

Lack passed away in 2017 at the age of 85.

Reed Mathis

The eclectic career of this bass guitarist and Booker T. Washington High School graduate came full circle in 2016 when he created a quartet called Electric Beethoven. Promotional material described the band's musical style using the works of Ludwig von Beethoven as "a launching point for a heavily improvisational sound described as Classical Dance Music (CDM)." The band's other members came from the worlds of jam rock, folk, blues and funk.

The band's first release was a double album entitled *Beathoven* with Beethoven's third and sixth symphonies performed in their entirety. Some guest musicians with that "orchestra" included members of Pearl Jam and Phish. The band released six albums between 2017 and 2019.

Mathis and his family frequently performed classical music in their home and at the age of 15, he performed with the Tulsa Philharmonic on a piece written by Antonio Vivaldi.

Mathis also spent 15 years with the Tulsa jazz band Jacob Fred Jazz Odyssey before switching careers to perform as a solo guitarist.

Barbara McAlister

This internationally acclaimed mezzo-soprano is a University of Tulsa graduate and an enrolled member of the Cherokee Nation of Oklahoma. She is also an accomplished painter whose works have been displayed in art museums throughout the United States. And her advocacy for promoting and preserving the Cherokee language resulted in her receiving the Native American tribe's Medal of Honor.

After attending TU and Oklahoma City University's prestigious music school, McAlister's operatic career was launched in Los Angeles by winning the Loren L. Zachary Society's vocal music competition in 1974 and 1975. Then she spent 10 years living and performing at Carnegie Hall in New York City as well as performing in opera houses from Germany to Hong Kong.

She later returned to Oklahoma to work as a fine arts instructor at Northeastern State University in Tahlequah along with teaching vocal music to aspiring Cherokee singers.

Edgar Meyer

A five-time Grammy Award winning instrumentalist, the Tulsa-born Meyer is widely regarded as one of the most versatile double bassists (better known as the stand-up bass) in the world as well as being an accomplished composer of classical music.

Meyer and his family moved from Tulsa to Tennessee when he was four years old. His musical versatility is evidenced by performances with classical bassist legend Yo-Yo Ma, Contemporary Christian vocalist Sandi Patty, guitarist Leo Kottke and country superstars Garth Brooks and Reba McEntire.

Since 2003, Meyer has been on the faculty of the Curtis School of Music in Philadelphia.

John Elwood Price

This University of Tulsa alumnus became one of the most prolific African-American composers in music history. He has written over 600 works for a wide variety of performances, including orchestra, opera, bands, piano solos, theatrical performances, churches and choirs as well as chamber music.

Price was a music prodigy; studying piano at the age of five then performing a self-composed piano piece at his sixth-grade graduation. One of his earliest works was a salute to his hometown. *Serenade for Tulsa* was a 1950 composition for piano and orchestra.

After earning a Master of Music degree from TU in 1963, Price taught music at several universities including Tuskegee University where he was named as an artist-in-residence.

Ronald Radford

One of the world's preeminent flamenco guitarists spent his teenage years in Tulsa and has toured around the world, bringing to life the flair and passion found in the classical guitar and the gypsy music of Spain.

Radford played the ukulele at the age of seven and was known as "Hank" Radford while attending Will Rogers High School and the University of Tulsa. As a teenager, Radford played in a rock and roll band before hearing an album by flamenco guitarist Carlos Montoya.

What the Beatles or Rolling Stones were to rock and roll, Montoya was their equivalent in the flamenco music world. A backstage meeting with Montoya after a Tulsa concert led to an invitation to become one of Montoya's few flamenco students in New York City.

Fast forward a couple of years and the young Tulsan drew a standing ovation in Carnegie Hall.

Radford has performed in 15 countries and served as a music ambassador on behalf of the U.S. State Department. He currently lives in the St. Louis area where he teaches music and records new albums. He was inducted into the Will Rogers High School Hall of Fame in 1992.

Chapter Eleven

Orchestras

"Music is meaningless noise unless it touches a receiving mind."

Paul Hindemith

"I grew up in an era where an orchestra was like a treasure chest."

Arturo Toscanini

"I'm not interested in having an orchestra sound like itself. I want it to sound like the composer."

Leonard Bernstein

"All a conductor has to do is stand back and try not to get in the way. Mozart is doing all the work."

Sir Colin David

"The sound of the orchestra is one of the most magnificent musical sounds that has ever existed."

Chick Corea

Tulsa is one of the few American cities that successfully support two orchestras. The origins of the Tulsa Symphony Orchestra date back to the 1920s while the Signature Symphony was founded in 1978.

TSO holds its concerts at the downtown Performing Arts Center while the Signature Symphony concerts are at the Van Trease Performing Arts Center at Tulsa Community College's southeastern campus.

In addition to regularly scheduled concerts, both orchestras offer educational and mentoring programs for local public schools and sections of the community that would not normally have opportunities to engage in the performing arts.

Tulsa Symphony Orchestra

Tulsa's first orchestra was the Civic Symphony, founded in 1926 by German native Kurt Berger and some of its first performances were in connection with the Tulsa Little Theatre.

That group became the Tulsa Philharmonic in 1948 and lasted until 2002, ceasing operation in the aftermath of an economic downturn that severely impacted donations from large local corporations.

Dr. Frank Letcher, who was on the board of directors of Tulsa Opera, teamed with a group of Philharmonic musicians who founded TSO in 2005. TSO frequently collaborates on presentations by Tulsa Ballet, the Tulsa Oratorio Chorus the Gilcrease and Philbrook Museums and the Oklahoma Aquarium.

Two musical celebrities have served as the Tulsa Philharmonic's conductors. Lionel "Skitch" Henderson was the conductor from 1971 through 1974 and is best known as the *Tonight Show* bandleader when Steve Allen and Johnny Carson hosted the NBC-TV late night talk show. Pianist-composer Peter Nero served as the orchestra's Pops Music maestro from 1983 through 1994.

Signature Symphony

Formally known as The Signature Symphony at Tulsa Community College, it originated in 1978 as a small chamber orchestra called the

Oklahoma Sinfonia. That group later performed concerts featuring classical and lighter pop music arrangements in addition to being a more-or-less house orchestra for guest musicians performing at the Brady Theatre.

The group began its TCC affiliation in 1996 and quick added more musicians and expanded its musical offerings as well as moving to the VanTrease Performing Arts Center located at TCC's campus in southeastern Tulsa.

Dr. Barry Epperly was the orchestra's founding maestro and retired in 2014. Scott Seaton has served since 2022 as the organization's Artistic Director.

One of its most popular events is *Tulsa Sings!* Founded in 2018, this ongoing event gives aspiring singers with Tulsa connections the privilege of being mentored by New York City-based vocalist Scott Coulter and then performing on stage with the Signature Symphony as a featured vocalist.

Chapter Twelve

Hip-Hop, Rap and Reggae

"Sometimes I feel that rap music is almost the key to stopping racism."

Eminem

"I guess hip-hop has been closer to the pulse of the streets than any music we've had in a long time. It's sociology as well as music, which is in keeping with the tradition of black music in America."

Quincy Jones

"In Hawaii, some of the biggest radio stations are reggae. The local bands are heavily influenced by Bob Marley."

Bruno Mars

"The thing about hip-hop today is that it's smart, it's insightful. The way they can communicate a complex message in a very short space is remarkable."

Barack Obama

***

B. Lou and Zias

Former University of Tulsa football players Bishop Louie and Zik Asiegbu used the internet video-sharing service YouTube to launch a career that has drawn more than 3.5 million followers. They were Golden Hurricane teammates in 2014 and 2015. Louie played wide receiver while Aguibu played outside linebacker.

Their original venture of reaction videos to tracks by nationally-known rapper XXXTENTACION and Lil Uzi Vert went viral. In 2018, the duo released an original song "Molly" that featured rapper Stick Up Starr.

Gang51e June

This rising star in the rap world, also known as The Hope, grew up in north Tulsa and was quickly signed to a contract with Atlantic Records. He has worked with rap heavyweights such as Mozzy, No Cap and Kevin Gates and his YouTube videos have drawn over 20 million views.

June started out writing poems and singing in church with his grandmother. Legendary rappers Tupac and Nipsey Hussle were the inspirations for pursuing a career as a rapper. During the Covid pandemic, his hard-hitting lyrics derived from life in Tulsa and in Oklahoma quickly went viral.

June has proven to be more than just a rapper, having directed and edited all of his videos and working as an engineer for aspiring artists in Oklahoma.

Gary "Litefoot" Davis

Davis spent part of his childhood in Tulsa and has evolved from a Native American (Cherokee Nation) rapper-actor into a successful entrepreneur, author and motivational speaker. His best-known movies are *The Indian in the Cupboard* (1995) and *Mortal Kombat Annihilation* (1997) and he appeared on the TV crime drama, *C.S.I. Miami*.

He currently serves as the Executive Director of the Native American Financial Services Association (NAFSA).

Davis founded Red Vinyl Records, authored a 2010 inspirational book *The Medicine of Prayer* and is a highly sought motivational speaker for colleges, business organizations and Native American groups.

Joseph Israel

Born in Tulsa as Joseph Montgomery Fennel, this reggae musician collaborated with legendary performers Matisyahu and Ziggy Marley. His 2007 album *Gone Are the Days* peaked at number 11 on the Billboard Top Reggae album chart.

After moving to Fayetteville, Arkansas during his childhood, he became interested in reggae through his father and uncle who frequently traveled to Jamaica and were fans of reggae idol Bob Marley. He later chose the pseudonym Joseph Israel with the last name reflecting his personal spirituality, formed The Jerusalem Band and frequently toured throughout the midwestern United States.

Israel passed away in 2018 at the age of 40 after a brief battle with cancer.

Jelly Roll

Currently based in Los Angeles, the Tulsa-born rap producer has produced CDs for rap legends such as Snoop Dogg, Method Man, Foxy Brown, Jadakiss and Busta Rhymes. His works are known for solid bass lines along with elements of classic soul and funk music.

As youngsters living in North Tulsa, Jelly Roll and his four brothers formed a group called the Drew Brothers that sang in their home church, and they were later influenced by the sounds of the Gap Band.

Kidgoten (Jaiden Lovett)

As a 15-year-old, this rapper and social media personality was signed to a recording contract with Bentley Records and has collaborated with hip hop artists Xanixjay, Chefuno and AMI$$A.

He attended the Tulsa School of Arts and Sciences, a public charter school, and was the youngest rap artist to be nominated for the Tulsa Music Awards.

Rachel Kiwanuka (aka Rachel K)

Born in Tulsa, this versatile entertainer has been active in music, television and movie acting.

Her mother, Halima Kiwanuka, was a popular singer in Uganda and Rachel recorded with Ugandan R&B star Tom Close. She created her own recording label, No End Entertainment in addition to working in Los Angeles as a comedian and a TV presenter.

One of her most recent projects was as an actress in the 2023 spy thriller movie, *MR-9*, which stars Michael Jai White (*The Dark Knight*).

Lega-C (Danielle McLean)

This rapper, producer, singer-songwriter collaborated with hip-hop and rap stars such as Fergie, Nappy Roots and Akon.

Her 2011 YouTube video entitled "White Girl Raps Fast" drew millions of views and earned the nickname of "Tulsa Twista." Other projects have included remixes of "She Will" by Lil Wayne and Drake plus the Tech N9ne hit "Worldwide Choppers." Her 2015 release "Holes" also became a YouTube sensation.

She was five years old when her family moved to Tulsa to serve as children's pastors at a church in the city's predominantly black sector. The church held Friday night parties to help at-risk children and she performed her first rap number at the age of 10.

In later years, she became a producer for Tulsa-based hip-hop and rap artists.

Johnny Polygon (John Armour)

This hip-hop singer-rapper has released 10 CDs and collaborated with big-name rappers Nas and Kid Cudi.

He broke onto the national scene in 2010 when MTV and VH-1 gave heavy airplay to his music video "The Riot Song" which peaked at number eight on MTV's Top 100 videos that year.

Polygon's family moved to Tulsa from Cleveland, Ohio when he was a youngster and his first exposure to rap and hip-hop came by joining friends that sneaked into Cain's Ballroom.

He attended Booker T. Washington and Central High Schools and the Project 12 Program but failed to graduate from any of those institutions and moved to Los Angeles to pursue a music-related career.

In recent years, Polygon launched a new venture involving music video production and children's literature.

P.D.A (Anthony Jenkins)

The rapper's name stands for Public Display of Afflection; the latter being a mashup of affliction and affection for what he describes as a struggle between hate and love.

Jenkins was chosen three times by *Tulsa People* magazine as being one of the city's most influential people.

His career began singing in school choirs at the age of 11 then performing in off-Broadway musicals such as *Joseph and the Amazing Technicolor Dreamcoat*. Then at the age of 13, Jenkins switched to hip hop and a debut album *Prologue* was released when he was 18 years old.

Josh Sallee

This rapper opened for stars like Big Sean, Mac Miller and Kendrick Lamar and is a rising star in the hip hop world.

Sallee was born in Denver but moved to the Tulsa suburb of Bixby to help care for his grandfather who battled complications from multiple sclerosis. He began posting his music on YouTube and quickly caught the eyes and ears of hip hop executives and promoters.

St. Domonick

This up-and-coming rapper has released three mixtapes which have been described as blends of trap beats, chill wave and soul.

Also going by the moniker "Vuelo" (meaning flight), his lyrics have also reflected a somewhat nerdish love for 1990s pop culture and have even referenced comic book heroes, the 1985 comedy movie *Back to the Future* and the Harry Potter books and movies.

He was a featured performer on the 2020 project *Fire in Little Africa* which dealt with the 1921 Tulsa Race Massacre and featured numerous Oklahoma-based rappers.

Stephen Wiley

Wiley is the founding pastor of the Praise Center Family Church in Tulsa and Muskogee but was credited as being the first Christian rap artist with his releases between 1985 and 1991. Legendary rapper T-Bone has credited Wiley as being the founder of the Christian rap music movement.

Wiley's 1985 debut single was "Bible Break" which was a rap song name checking every book in the Old and New Testaments. It became a hit single on the *Billboard* Gospel chart.

Wiley earned a bachelor's degree from the University of Oklahoma and a doctorate degree from Friends International Christian University in Merced, California.

He currently serves as Director of the Center for Christian Ministry and adjunct professor of religion at Bacone College in Muskogee, Oklahoma, which is 50 miles southeast of Tulsa.

Wiley also travels throughout the United States giving motivational speeches to youth groups.

Chapter Thirteen

Songs Mentioning Tulsa–The Top 10

"*Would I go back to Tulsa? Boy, you know that I would. Well, let me off on Archer and I'll walk down to Greenwood.*"

Bob Wills

"*"Gonna set my watch back to it 'cause you know I've been through it. Living on Tulsa time.*"

Don Williams and Eric Clapton

"*I left my heart in Tulsa on the corner of Easton and Main. On the Cain's Ballroom floor soaking up a bourbon stain. Now I'm going back to see her just as soon as I can...*"

Turnpike Troubadours

"*All around this whole wide world there's one thing that everybody knows. All God's children love the Tulsa Shuffle, and this is how it goes...*"

Steve Ripley and the Tractors

"*I'm going back to Tulsa one more time. I got Home Sweet Oklahoma on my mind.*"

Leon Russell

***

"Tulsa Time" - Don Williams and Eric Clapton

The song was written by Danny Flowers and became a number one country song in 1978 for his bandmate, singer Don Williams. It was the first song on Williams' album *Expressions* and was the top-rated *Billboard* country song in 1979.

Flowers and Williams were in Tulsa attending a music industry trade show organized by their booking agent, Jim Halsey. Flowers wrote the lyrics while sitting in the lobby of the downtown Mayo Hotel and observing people that were coming and going.

Rock superstar Eric Clapton had hit versions of "Tulsa Time" on his 1979 album *Backless* and his 1980 live album *Just One Night*. Clapton's version peaked at number 30 on the 1980 *Billboard* rock chart.

"Home Sweet Oklahoma" - Leon Russell

This was on the 1971 album *Leon Russell and the Shelter People*, which peaked at number 17 on the *Billboard* rock music charts. It was an autobiography about Russell's career and appreciation for his Tulsa roots, wrapped up in a song lasting three minutes and 26 seconds.

"Take Me Back to Tulsa" - Bob Wills and the Texas Playboys

This is arguably the most recognizable country song about the city of Tulsa. Co-authored by Bob Wills and his lead singer, Tommy Duncan, it was a hit for Bob Wills and The Texas Playboys in 1941.

The Rock and Roll Hall of Fame cited the song as one of eight country music numbers on its list of 500 songs that shaped rock and roll.

The song's melody comes from a traditional fiddle tune from that same decade called "Walkin' Georgia Rose"

The basis of the song is a chorus of "Take me back to Tulsa, I'm too young to marry." While the rest of the song doesn't have a central theme, Wills and his band tip their hats to Tulsa with references to two streets north of the downtown district: East Archer Street and North Greenwood Avenue.

The song was recorded in 1941 and debuted in the western-style movie *Take Me Back to Oklahoma* that featured Wills and his band. Over the years, *Take Me Back to Tulsa* has become covered by countless country music singers and groups and evolved into one of the most popular songs in the Western Swing genre.

"24 Hours from Tulsa" – Gene Pitney

Co-written by the legendary songwriting duo of Burt Bacharach and Hal David, this top 10 song in four countries was the first track on Pitney's 1963 album *Blue Gene.*

The song was about a traveling husband breaking the news to his wife that their marriage was over because he fell in love with another woman. The song was also covered by Jay and the Americans, Ian and Sylvia and Dusty Springfield, among others.

"Heart of Rock and Roll" – Huey Lewis and the News

This 1984 number was one of three top six singles from the group's album *Sports.* The band's affection for the city was based on the history of Tulsa Sound musicians as well as concert crowds the year before when they performed at Cain's Ballroom as the featured act and at the Tulsa Assembly Center as the opening act for the band Toto.

"Easton & Main" – Turnpike Troubadours

This musical valentine to Tulsa's historic Cain's Ballroom was on the group's self-titled album that peaked at number three on the *Billboard* U.S. Country Music and Indie Music charts in 2015 and number five on its U.S. Rock Music chart as well. All of that was achieved without assistance from commercial country music radio stations.

The song features a classic country music vibe and fondly recalls nights spent at Cain's, located at the downtown Tulsa intersection of East Easton and North Main. The group also referenced Tulsa in many of their subsequent songs as well.

"Rodeo" – Garth Brooks

This song from Brooks' second album, *No Fences,* was about a cowboy whose passion for a rodeo in Tulsa was stronger than his passion for the woman he loved.

Written by Larry Bastian, the song peaked at number three on the American *Billboard* country charts and reached number one in Canada. *No Fences* was a diamond-selling album (over 10 million copies sold) and four other songs from that album reached the top spot on the country music charts that year.

"The Tulsa Shuffle" – The Tractors

The Tractors were a country-rock band composed of several Tulsa musicians who saluted their musical influences while celebrating Tulsa's role in that industry.

The opening single from the group's 1994 self-titled debut album quickly became a popular line dance number in country music night clubs throughout the United States. The song's shuffle-style beat featured plenty of Dixieland-style brass instruments and lead singer Steve Ripley's sometimes-scatting vocals.

"Baby Likes to Rock It" was on that same album and was the group's biggest hit, peaking at number 11 on the *Billboard* Country Music chart.

"Tulsa" – Elle King

This 2023 song from King's album *Come Get Your Wife* wasn't really about Tulsa but about a woman finally standing up for herself in that city.

In an online interview, King said it was " ... a song about that one girl we all know...if you spell it back to front you gonna know what I mean...it's a song about (women) uniting and not taking s*** from this real P.O.S."

Born as Tanner Elle Schneider, King's parents are former *Saturday Night Live* comedian Rob Schneider and international model London King.

"Tulsa Queen" – Emmylou Harris"

The 1976 ballad from the album *Luxury Liner* was about a woman lamenting the end of a love affair and the train that carried her man away. The album reached the top spot on the *Billboard* Country Music chart.

Chapter Fourteen

Songs Mentioning Tulsa – Others of Note

Trying to list every song that has name-checked Tulsa would be a book unto itself, obviously. For the sake of brevity, here's a list of noteworthy songs mentioning Tulsa, as chosen by the publishing staff of this book.

***

"Blame It on Texas" was on Mark Chestnutt's 1990 platinum-selling album *Too Cold at Home*. The song was about a man dating a Tulsa girl whose father was a millionaire oilman, but he chose to leave her and return to Texas. The song reached number three on the Billboard

Country music chart and was one of four top five singles from that album.

"Blow Up (Black Wall Street) was on the 2021 rap album *Evol Genius 2* by Smitty Spread Love and AG Da Genius. The rap dealt with the 1921 Tulsa Race Massacre in general; the destruction of the historic Black Wall Street section of north Tulsa and the ongoing hardships young people face today.

"Convoy" was a country song-narrative by C.W. McCall (real name William Dale Fries, Jr.) on his album *Black Bear Road*. It came out during the craze about citizen band (CB) radios and told about a truck driver creating a convoy of 18-wheel trucks that went through Tulsa on its journey. The song was the basis for the 1978 action movie *Convoy* that starred Kris Kristofferson, Ali MacGraw and Ernest Borgnine. McCall also namechecked Tulsa in "Audubon" on his 1976 album *Rubber Duck*, which was the CB radio pseudonym for the truck driver in "Convoy."

"Don't Let the Sun Set on You (Tulsa)" was on the 1971 album *The Taker/Tulsa* by outlaw country icon Waylon Jennings. The song was about a man vowing revenge for another man's mistreatment of a female acquaintance. The song was originally a minor hit in 1965 for pop singer Billy Joe Royal. It was written by Wayne Carson Thompson who also wrote the lyrics to rock hits "The Letter," "Neon Rainbow" and "Soul Deep" and co-wrote the Willie Nelson country classic, "Always on My Mind."

"Don't Make Me Come to Tulsa" was the first single on Wade Hayes' 1995 debut album *Old Enough to Know Better*. The song was about a man struggling with an opportunity to rekindle a romantic relationship. The third song on that album was "Old Enough to Know Better" and reached the top of the *Billboard* Country Music chart.

"Finally, It's Christmas" was the title track from Hanson's 2017 holiday album. The festive song mentioned Santa Claus making a direct flight from the North Pole to Tulsa. That album peaked at number three on the 2017 *Billboard* holiday music chart.

"Groupie" from Snoop Dogg's 1996 album *Tha Doggfather* featured guest vocals by The Gap Band's former lead singer Charlie Wilson. That double-platinum album debuted in the top spot on the Billboard R&B charts in both the United States and the United Kingdom.

"Helen's Testimony" was on the 1995 album *The Live Experience* by gospel singer Helen Baylor. The song and spoken word recording had Baylor talking about her childhood in predominantly black north Tulsa and the importance that the church played in her personal and professional lives.

"High on Tulsa Heat" was the title track for Tulsa resident John Moreland's 2015 album which also had "Hang Me in the Tulsa Stars." Both songs were about romantic relationships and challenging events. Moreland also mentioned Tulsa in "Nobody Gives a Damn About Songs Anymore" on his 2013 album *In the Throes*. That was about a songwriter's frustration over serious artists finding a loyal audience while slickly produced and less talented singers become overnight sensations.

"King of Oklahoma" was on the 2023 album *Weathervanes* by alternative country singer Jason Isbell and the 400 Unit. A construction worker was seeing his good life, good wife and good family falling apart after suffering an on-the-job injury and falling into the depths of substance abuse. When he turns to a life of crime at job sites to support his drug addiction, his wife threatens to take their children and go back to her parents who live in Bixby, a southern Tulsa suburb.

"La Venganza de Tulsa" (Revenge in Tulsa) was recorded in 2006 by a folk/Basque oriented quartet in Madrid, Spain that called itself Tulsa. A woman who was down on her luck seeks revenge against a man who held her as a mental and emotional hostage.

"Last Train Home" was on the 2004 album *Hearts in Mind* by Grammy Award-winning singer-songwriter Nanci Griffith. The song was about a person who observed a drunken man trying to make it to Tulsa and attempt to reunite with the woman he loved.

"Livin' in the 918" was a 2023 kids-oriented pop song about Tulsa's local attractions by Symon Hajjar who performs under the name Hot Toast Music Company. Hajjar is a Tulsa-based educator and musician.

"Monroe Suede" was on Ashley Monroe's 2013 album *Like a Rose*. The song is about a teenage girl who stole a pickup truck, was almost arrested in Tulsa and has been running from the law ever since. The album reached number 10 on the *Billboard* Country Music chart.

"Next Time You're in Tulsa" was on the 1966 album *I Love You Drops* by Country Music Hall of Fame star Bill Anderson. The song was about a divorced husband who still loved his ex-wife and their children. *I Love You Drops* would become Anderson's first number one album on the *Billboard* charts.

"Northern Lights" was on the self-titled 1998 album by folk supergroup Cry Cry Cry. The song was about the journey of two people in a stressful relationship and their journey to Tulsa. The album was ranked among the top five most-played albums by folk music radio disc jockeys in 1994 and 1995. Cry Cry Cry was composed of Lucy Kaplansky, Richard Shindell and Dar Williams.

"Prisoner of the Highway" was on the 1994 country album *One More Try for Love* by Ronnie Millsap. The song is about a Tennessee-based truck driver that has an urgent delivery deadline in Tulsa before he can return home. Written by former college and pro football standout-turned-songwriter Mike Reid, the album reached number six on the *Billboard* Country Music chart while the song peaked at number two.

"Rock and Roll Music to the World" was on Jimmy LaFave's 2001 album *Texhoma*. Tulsa is one of several cities that were named in the song as some of his favorite concert locations. LaFave was one of the pioneers of the Red Dirt music scene which was founded in Stillwater, Oklahoma and blended country music with blues and jazz.

"Sweet Dreams Melinda" was on the 2005 album *Shine* by Trey Anastasio, the co-founder and lead singer of the rock band Phish. The song was about a man's wistful recollection of a woman he loved and a flight from Boston to Tulsa. It was Anastasio's first album since Phish's breakup in August of 2004.

"Sweet Louisiana" was on the 1976 album *Saddle Tramp* by Charlie Daniels, who played in a downtown Tulsa bar early in his career with a rock and roll band. The song is about a man who went to Tulsa to compete in a rodeo but wished that he was back home in Louisiana. The album reached number five on the *Billboard* Country Music chart.

"Tampa to Tulsa" was on the 2003 album *Rainy Day Music* by the Jayhawks, a Minnesota-based alt-country/country rock band called the Jayhawks. The song was about a man's journey from Florida back to Tulsa to reunite with a woman he loved.

"Tell Me Something Bad About Tulsa" was on George Strait's 2003 album *Honkytonkville* and reached number 11 on the 2003 *Billboard* Country Music chart. It was about a man wanting to end his love affair with a woman in Tulsa and he asks his friends to help him do what needs to be done.

"The Victims Have Names" is a 2023 song by folk singer Sarah Popejoy. It dealt with the personal and social injustices associated with the 1921 Tulsa Race Massacre.

"Tokyo, Oklahoma" was the quirky title track from John Anderson's 1985 album. The song is about a man in Tulsa having a very long-distance relationship with a woman in Japan. The couple eventually married.

Tom Paxton referenced Tulsa on three of his best-selling folk music albums. The title track from his 1964 album *Ramblin' Boy* was about two long-time friends traveling through the United States and a job offer while visiting Tulsa. "Is This Any Way to Run an Airline?" was on his 1966 album *Outward Bound* and lamented a series of cancelled flights with Tulsa being one of the destinations. "Passing Through Tulsa" was on the 2001 album *Live from Mountain Stage.* That song was a man's lament over a lost love while driving through Tulsa one morning a few hours before dawn. Some of Paxton's best-known songs are "Bottle of Wine," "The Marvelous Toy" and the Porter Wagoner-Dolly Parton duet "The Last Thing on My Mind."

"Tulsa" was on the 2012 album *Destinations* by smooth jazz saxophonist Grady Nichols and was a regional hit. In 2022, Nichols released a music video for the song that shined a spotlight on numerous Tulsa musical venues.

"Tulsa" was the title track from a 2006 CD by alternative country singer Wayne "The Train" Hancock. He was effusive in his praise of Tulsa and its musical heritage through a song described by music critics as a rousing fusion of Western Swing, jazz, hillbilly and honky-tonk country.

"Tulsa" was the 1999 title track from an album by power pop legend and Tulsa native Dwight Twilley. The song, which lasts almost eight minutes, is a valentine to the city he grew up in and features an extended jam. Two other Twilley songs that expressed his affection for his hometown are "Tulsa Town" from the 2011 album *Soundtrack* and "Tulsa Girl" which was the first single on the 2009 album *Rarities, Volume 7*.

"Tulsa County" was a rock song by the Byrds on their 1969 album *Ballad of Easy Rider* album. The song was about a woman in Charleston, South Carolina who gets a letter from a former boyfriend who is living in Tulsa. She goes there to see him, gets her heart broken and travels on to Mexico. For unknown reasons, the song was not included in the 1969 movie *Easy Rider*. In 1970, the song was a modest country hit for Anita Carter; who was a member of the legendary vocal group The Carter Family, a sister-in-law to Johnny Cash and a former wife of Cash's guitar player (and former Tulsa resident) Bob Wootton.

"Tulsa is the Next Austin" was the title track of the 2023 album by alternative country music band Cody Canada and the April Fools. The song was about an aspiring singer stuck in Tulsa while trying to break into the big time.

"Tulsa, Straight Ahead' was written by Jimmy Hall but the 1947 tune could be considered one of the signature songs for Leon McAuliffe, the steel guitar player in Bob Wills' legendary Western Swing band. Hall was a singer-fiddle player in McAuliffe's band, The Cimarron Cowboys. The song was about a musician rejoicing about finally coming home to Tulsa.

"Tulsa Telephone Book" was on Tom T. Hall's 1971 country album *In Search of a Song*. The tongue-in-cheek song was about a one-night stand and a man's attempt to reconnect with the woman he met. The album reached number eight on the *Billboard* Country Music chart and had the second of Hall's seven number one songs "The Year That Clayton Delaney Died."

"Tulsa Texas" was on the 2012 album *All Over the Road* by Easton Corbin. The song was about a cowboy's love for traveling to rodeos instead of settling down with a woman he loved.

"Tulsa Turnaround" was on the 1979 triple-platinum album *Kenny* by Kenny Rogers. The song was about a brief but deeply passionate romantic fling. The album reached number one on the *Billboard* Country Music chart in the United States and Canada and number five on the Top 200 chart for all types of music. Two songs from that album reached the top spot on the Country Music charts and placed in the top five for Adult Contemporary singles: "Coward of the County" and "You Decorated My Life."

"Tulsa's Last Magician" was a 2022 song by Willi Carlisle. It was about a man who turned the magic tricks he did as a child into a professional career but stopped performing as he grew older. The song encourages people with unique skills to bring magic into the lives of others.

"Tulsa, Oklahoma" was on the 2003 album *So Come On* by the Swedish female pop-punk band Shebang. The song was about a woman wanting to return to Tulsa to party with her gal pals.

"Tulsa Sunday" was a brassy, blues-flavored song on Lee Hazlewood's 1972 album *13*. The song was a valentine of sorts to the state of Oklahoma and Hazlewood's hometown of Mannford, which is northwest of Tulsa. One of the lines in the song was waxing eloquent about clear blue skies and then saying, "Don't it make you wanna get high?"

"Tulsa Waltz" was a country instrumental song recorded in 1937 by Jimmie Revard and His Oklahoma Playboys.

"West of Tulsa" was on the 2023 album *Life Lessons* by alternative country singer Wyatt Flores. Following his concert as well as a one-night stand with a female fan, a singer wonders if there's more to life that what he's facing on a daily basis.

"Wild Nights in Tulsa" was on the 1974 album *Windfall* by Rick ("Ricky") Nelson and the Stone Canyon Band. The album was recorded during the transition from pop music to country-rock by the former TV star and teenage heartthrob. Two of that band's members were bass guitarist Randy Meisner, who co-founded The Eagles in 1971, and steel guitarist Tom Brumley, a long-time member of Buck Owens and the Buckaroos.

"W.O.L.D." was on the 1973 album *Short Stories* by Harry Chapin, whose trademark song was the 1974 hit "The Cat's in the Cradle." The song, which sold a million copies in the United States, was about a rock and roll AM radio disc jockey having a mid-life crisis but trying to reconcile with his wife. The DJ's career took him to Tulsa where he worked as a late-night radio talk show host.

"You're the Reason God Made Oklahoma" was a country duet by David Frizzell and Shelly West that appeared on the soundtrack for the 1981 Clint Eastwood action-comedy movie *Any Which Way You Can*. The song was about two separated lovers and opened with the line "There's a full moon over Tulsa, I hope that it's shining on you." The song reached number one on the Billboard Country Music chart and came from the album *Carryin' on the Family Names*. Frizzell was the younger brother of country music star Lefty Frizzell while West was the daughter of singer Dottie West.

Chapter Fifteen
Stage and Screen

"Filmmaking is a chance to live many lifetimes."

Robert Altman

"Theatre gives you wings as an actor."

Randeep Houda

"Cinema is a matter of what's in the frame and what's out."

Martin Scorsese

"I think cinema, movies, and magic have always been closely associated. The very earliest people who made films were magicians."

Francis Ford Coppola

"All the world's a stage."

William Shakespeare

***

Jacqueline "Jackie" Alloway

This alumnus of Will Rogers High School and the University of Tulsa appeared in several shows on and off Broadway. Two of her Broadway appearances were supporting roles in the musical comedies *Fade Out – Fade In* (1964-65) and *George M!* (1968-69).

Fade Out – Fade In featured music by Jule Styne and was about life in New York City and Hollywood during the 1930s and starred Carol Burnett, Jack Cassidy and Tina Louise. *George M!* was about the life and music of Broadway superstar George M. Cohan and starred Joel Gray and Bernadette Peters.

Ralph Blane

Born as Ralph Uriah Hunsecker, this long-time Broken Arrow resident wrote several songs for musicals and movies during the 1940s, two of which earned Academy Award nominations.

Three of his most famous songs, which were co-written with Hugh Martin, were sung by Judy Garland in the 1944 musical *Meet Me in St. Louis*. Those songs were "The Boy Next Door," "The Trolley Song" and the beloved holiday classic "Have Yourself a Merry Little Christmas."

"The Trolley Song" came about when Blane and Martin visited a public library, hoping to find an inspiration for the tune. They found a book with a picture of a trolley and the caption read, "Clang, clang, clang went the trolley." It struck a proverbial chord with them and the song wound up earning an Academy Award nomination.

They also earned another Oscar nomination for "Pass That Peace Pipe" from the 1947 movie *Good News*, which starred June Allyson, Peter Lawford and a very young Mel Torme.

Martin and Blane worked together for 50 years and collaborated with Cole Porter, Irving Berlin and Richard Rogers. They also helped compose the musical score for Mickey Rooney's 1979 Broadway comeback musical *Sugar Babies*. Another of their hits was the football-themed song "Buckle Down, Winsocki" which was in the 1941 Broadway musical *Best Foot Forward* and the 1943 movie by that same name that starred Lucille Ball.

According to ASCAP records, over 500 songs were registered in Blane's name. But in a 2010 autobiography written when he was in his nineties, Martin claimed that except for one song in *Meet Me in St. Louis*, it was he and not Blane that wrote all of the words and music. Martin also blamed himself for a lack of business knowledge in allowing the duo billing to happen.

Blane attended elementary school in Broken Arrow and graduated from Tulsa's Central High School and Northwestern University before moving to New York City to study music. While attending a Broadway musical with his family at the age of 17, Blane was smitten with the presentation and chose to pursue a musical career.

He later became a radio singer for the NBC Radio Network and about that time changed his name to Ralph Blane for easier pronunciation and because it fit more easily on theatre marquees. He moved to Broken Arrow in his later years after retiring from the music industry.

Blane died in 1995. He was inducted into the Songwriters Hall of Fame in 1983 and the Oklahoma Music Hall of Fame in 2011.

Gary Busey

This Nathan Hale High School alumnus made his television debut on a local late-night weekend show then earned an Oscar nomination, worked as Leon Russell's drummer, became renowned for his offbeat nature in reality TV shows, appeared in over 150 movies and TV shows and cheated death three times along the way.

Busey and Gailard Sartain were the stars of *The Uncanny Film Festival and Camp Meeting,* a late Saturday night program that featured comedy skits like those from *Saturday Night Live* between breaks in

B-movies. Busey portrayed Teddy Jack Eddy, a know-it-all who viewed himself as being an American hero.

That show led to Busey, who previously played in a rock band, meeting Leon Russell and playing drums on Russell's album *Will O'The Wisp* and the ensuing national concert tour. Russell later named his son Teddy Jack Russell in appreciation of Busey.

After appearing as a singer's road manager in the 1976 remake of the movie *A Star Is Born,* Busey earned an Academy Award nomination for Best Actor in *The Buddy Holly Story*. Instead of lip-synching the songs as is done in many musical autobiographies, Busey performed Holly's groundbreaking rock-and-roll hits live and critics praised the high level of energy that strategy brought to the movie.

Busey has been of one the busiest actors in the entertainment industry for over 40 years with supporting roles in movies and TV shows, commercial endorsements and even providing character voices in the *Grand Theft Auto* video game series. But four events during the 1980s and 1990s changed Busey's life.

He suffered a traumatic brain injury in a 1988 motorcycle accident because he was not wearing a safety helmet. That incident played a role in the state of California adopting stringent regulations for wearing helmets by motorcycle drivers and passengers. In 1995, Busey nearly died from a cocaine overdose, but he avoided criminal charges by agreeing to undergo substance abuse treatment and counseling and he said that incident marked the beginning of his sobriety.

The following year, Busey announced that he became a Christian and later shared his testimony at large-scale evangelical gatherings. In 1997, a malignant tumor as large as a golf ball was found in a sinus cavity after he experienced several episodes of nosebleeds. A full recovery was made following surgery and radiation treatments.

Busey's unpredictable persona led to a career revival in recent years with appearances on reality TV shows which benefitted several of Busey's charitable causes. His clashes with billionaire (and later American President) Donald Trump on NBC's *Celebrity Apprentice* drew large viewing audiences as did his appearances on the British version of *Celebrity Apprentice* as well as Britain's *Celebrity Big Brother*.

Rodney Carrington

The former Bixby resident has recorded 11 comedy albums, several country music songs and starred in the ABC sitcom *Rodney* which aired from 2004 through 2006 and was generally based on his life.

Entertainment trade magazines have ranked Carrington among the top five stand-up comedians in terms of gross income from live appearances since 2010. All of his shows have been a blend of stand-up comedy and his original songs.

Carrington appeared opposite country music star Toby Keith in the 2008 movie *Beer for My Horses*. His 2009 novelty Christmas song "Camouflage and Christmas Lights" peaked at number 31 on the *Billboard* magazine country music chart.

Kristin Chenoweth

The most famous alumnus of Broken Arrow High School, vocalist/actress Kristin Chenoweth has won a Tony Award for the Broadway musical comedy *You're A Good Man, Charlie Brown*, earned an Emmy Award for the short-lived TV series *Pushing Daisies* and recorded best-selling albums in the musical genres of country, Christian and standards from the 1930s and 1940s.

While Chenoweth often has a speaking voice not unlike the cartoon character Betty Boop, she is a classically trained singer; a *coloratura soprano* who can reach the "F above High C" (F6) note. She earned music-related Bachelor's and Master's degrees from Oklahoma City

University under the guidance of noted vocal instructor Florence Birdwell.

Some of her earliest singing performances came at the Falls Creek summer camp operated by Oklahoma's Southern Baptist churches.

The popular comic strip *Peanuts* was the basis for *You're A Good Man, Charlie Brown* and Chenoweth won a 1999 Tony Award for Best Actress in her portrayal of Sally Brown. Sally was Charlie Brown's sister who loved to sit in a beanbag chair and watch TV, question how life can be unfair and told her troubles to the school building.

Chenoweth originated the role of Glinda the Good Witch in the Broadway musical *Wicked* and would earn a 2004 Tony nomination for her performance. *Wicked* was a prequel to *The Wizard of Oz* that dealt with the relationship between Glinda and her sister who would become The Wicked Witch.

Chenoweth earned another Tony nomination in 2015 for her role in the revival of a 1930s play and movie *On the Twentieth Century*. The screwball comedy has Chenoweth portraying Lily Garland, a somewhat temperamental actress on a luxury train ride from Chicago to New York and her interactions with a down-on-his luck theatre producer.

Pushing Daisies was a fantasy drama series that lasted just two years on ABC but was known for double entendres and quick quips. Chenoweth's Primetime Emmy came for her portrayal of Olive Snook, a waitress at the Pie Hole Restaurant who was devoted to the restaurant's owner, but that owner also possessed a touch that could reanimate dead people.

Chenoweth also made frequent guest appearances on TV shows such as *Glee*, *The West Wing* and *GCB*. She was scheduled to have a recurring role in the CBS drama *The Good Wife* in 2012 but suffered a near-fatal skull fracture along with rib and mouth injuries when struck by a falling piece of lighting equipment on the show's New York City set.

In recent years, she began a program in Broken Arrow to mentor aspiring performers and the theater within the city's new Performing Arts Center was named The Kristin Chenoweth Theater in her honor. She also contributed to the 2014 performances at Carnegie Hall by Broken Arrow High School's orchestra, band and choir. Chenoweth was the guest conductor for the high school group's grand finale, a performance of the theme song from Rogers and Hammerstein's Broadway musical *Oklahoma!*

Chenowith has written two autobiographies and a children's book. Her first autobiography was *A Little Bit Wicked: Life, Love and Faith in Stages* and was published in 2010. The other was *I'm No Philosopher but I Got Thoughts: Mini-Meditations for Saints, Sinners and the Rest of Us* and was published in 2023. Her 2022 children's book was *What Will I Do with My Love Today?*

In the 2022 documentary *Keeper of the Ashes: The Oklahoma Girl Scout Murders* that aired on the Hulu streaming service, Chenoweth revealed that she planned to go to the Girl Scout camp east of Tulsa where three of her childhood friends would be murdered in 1977. But an illness led her parents to cancel her reservation at that camp. No one was ever convicted of the three murders.

Chuck Cissel

This graduate of Tulsa's Booker T. Washington High School is a dancer, singer and choreographer who appeared in the *Hello Dolly* production starring Pearl Bailey and Cab Calloway and was an original member of the Tony Award winning cast of *A Chorus Line.*

Cissel was among the first African American students to graduate from the University of Oklahoma's fine arts school prior to appearing on Broadway. His first record was "Swept Away" which was produced by the choreographer of *A Chorus Line*, Michael Bennett.

"Cisselin' Hot" was a song from his 1980 album *Just for You* that became an international dance hit. That album climbed into the Top 40 on the *Billboard* Black Albums chart.

Cissel later returned to Tulsa and served as the Chief Executive Officer of the Oklahoma Jazz Hall of Fame from 2000 through 2009.

Eric Cornell

This 2002 graduate of Tulsa's Union High School won his first Tony Award in 2019 as co-producer of a revival of the legendary Broadway musical *Oklahoma!*

Teaming with co-producer Jack Sennott and director Daniel Fish, this version of the Rodgers and Hammerstein production stripped away the lavish orchestra and dance numbers and replaced them with bluegrass and country-flavored tunes performed by a seven-piece band onstage. On top of that, outside the box casting helped bring out elements of darkness that existed beneath the sunny exterior created by Rodgers and Hammerstein. Actress Ali Stroker, who lost use of both legs at the age of two in an automobile accident and performs in a wheelchair, made history in 2019 when her performance in that musical as Ado Annie also earned a Tony Award for Best Featured Actress in a Musical.

Cornell also served as executive producer for the 2017 Broadway hit *Anastasia: The Musical*. He attended Emerson College and currently serves as an assistant professor at The Boston Conservatory at Berklee, teaching courses on acting and business-related operations related to the performing arts.

Sam Harris

The Sand Springs native is a renowned singer/actor/director who has appeared in numerous Broadway musicals and was nominated for a Tony Award. He has been a featured soloist with the Boston Pops Orchestra and performed at major venues in London, New York City and Los Angeles.

Harris broke into show business in 1983 as the grand champion of the first *Star Search* TV talent show and his rendition of the classic song "Over the Rainbow" has become his theme song. His first Top 40 single was "Sugar Don't Bite" which was released in 1984. In subsequent years, he appeared in several Broadway musicals, three movies and co-created the TBS sitcom *Down to Earth* which aired from 1984 through 1987.

In 2013, Harris released a memoir entitled *Ham: Slices of a Life*. Among its topics are his life as a gay teenager in Sand Springs, the roller-coaster ride of fame and fortune, dealing with substance abuse issues and parenthood. He later adapted the book into a solo music show *HAM: A Musical Memoir*.

Harris wrote a 2020 novel *The Substance of All Things*. The fictional drama was about Theo Dalton, a six-year-old Oklahoma boy who was left with mangled hands in a car wreck that killed his mother. Dalton learns that his disfigured hands have a miraculous healing ability and his being taken into a world where his own life is threatened while he saves the lives of other people.

A song he wrote in 2010, "My Reclamation," has been featured in campaigns for equality in marriage. Harris and his long-time partner, Danny Jacobsen, have an adopted son.

Kelli O'Hara

This Tulsa-born Broadway performer has become of one Broadway's leading ladies with seven Tony Award nominations and also made her Metropolitan Opera debut in 2014.

O'Hara's performance as the British educator Anna Leonowens in the Lincoln Center Theater's 2015 revival of *The King and I* won the 2015 Tony Award for Best Actress in a Musical.

Among O'Hara's other Broadway credits are roles in *Follies, Dracula, The Pajama Game, Nice Work If You Can Get It, South Pacific, Kiss Me, Kate* and *The Bridges of Madison County.*

She shares a common bond with Broken Arrow native and Broadway star Kristin Chenoweth in that they attended Oklahoma City University and were students of vocal music instructor Florence Birdwell. O'Hara spent most of her childhood in the western Oklahoma town of Elk City.

She is a frequent performer for special events at Carnegie Hall and the Kennedy Center as well as Independence Day concerts carried on public television.

O'Hara's Metropolitan Opera debut came in the 2014 presentation of Franz Lehar's *The Merry Widow*, performing with the renowned soprano Renee Fleming. Her other Met Opera performances have been in Mozart's *Cosi fan tutte* and in Kevin Puts' *The Hours.*

In 2016, she made her solo concert debut at Carnegie Hall and earned an honorary doctorate of human letters from her alma mater, Oklahoma City University.

O'Hara has also appeared in several TV series and earned a Primetime Emmy nomination for a starring role in the 2017 web drama *The Accidental Wolf.*

Mary Kay Place

A graduate of Tulsa's Nathan Hale High School and the University of Tulsa, Mary Kay Place is an Emmy Award-winning actress who has also appeared in numerous movies and placed two songs in the top 10 of the Billboard country music charts during the 1970s.

Place's breakout role was that of aspiring country music singer Loretta Haggers on NBC's soap opera spoof *Mary Hartman, Mary Hartman* which only aired for two seasons (1976 and 1977) but became a cult favorite. She had previously worked for the show's producer, Norman Lear (*All in the Family*), as a production assistant and writer. While Place was on *Mary Hartman, Mary Hartman*, she wrote scripts for the CBS sitcoms *M*A*S*H* and *The Mary Tyler Moore Show*.

Place's 1976 song "Baby Boy" was sung in the Loretta Haggers character and peaked at number three on the *Billboard* country music chart. The following year, she and Willie Nelson recorded their version of the 1970 Charlie Louvin-Melba Montgomery duet "Something to Brag About" and it peaked at number nine on the *Billboard* country chart.

Place's biggest movie role came in *The Big Chill*, a 1983 film that earned three Academy Award nominations with a soundtrack featuring some of the biggest pop and R&B songs from the late 1960s and 1970s. Place portrayed a corporate attorney, Meg Jones, who desperately wanted to have one of her former college classmates be the father of her first child.

In recent years, Place appeared in the movies *Sweet Home Alabama, Private Benjamin,* and *Julie and Julia*. She starred in a 2018 movie *Diane*, a drama about an aging and widowed Baby Boomer dealing with aging issues while clinging to an echo of desires and hopes held in her younger years. Martin Scorsese was the movie's executive director, and the film took top honors at the 2018 Tribeca Film Festival.

Tony Randall

One of the best-known alumni from Tulsa's Central High School, Tony Randall spent six decades appearing on Broadway, in movies and on television. One of his best-known roles was that of neat-freak

Felix Unger in the ABC-TV sitcom based on Neil Simon's successful Broadway play, *The Odd Couple.*

That show, which aired from 1970 through 1975, was based on the lives of two newly divorced journalists who become roommates and their relationship is challenged when they keep making the same mistakes that led to their respective divorces. Randall's Unger was meticulous in everything that he said and did but Oscar Madison, played by Jack Klugman, was a slovenly, brash-talking sportswriter.

Born as Arthur Leonard Rosenberg, Randall spent one year at Northwestern University prior to moving to New York City to try his hand in theatre. He was cast in numerous Broadway productions and once appeared opposite Ethel Barrymore prior to spending four years with the United States Army Signal Corps during World War II.

Randall earned a 1958 Tony Award nomination for his role in the musical comedy *Oh, Captain!* a show that featured a famous dance sketch opposite ballet star Alexandra Danilova. He later founded the National Actors Theatre and reunited with Klugman for a revival of the Broadway hit, *The Sunshine Boys.*

On the radio drama *I Love a Mystery,* Randall portrayed Englishman Reggie York who was part of a trio of soldiers-turned detectives traveling the world fighting crime.

He also had a wide variety of supporting movie roles, including several romantic comedies that starred Doris Day and Rock Hudson as well as playing opposite of sex sirens Marilyn Monroe and Kim Novak.

Randall also played all seven lead characters in the 1964 movie *7 Faces or Dr. Lao* in which a mysterious circus visits a small town in the southwestern United States.

His first major TV series was the 1950s NBC sitcom *Mr. Peepers* in which he portrayed history teacher Harvey Weskit. The TV success

Randall enjoyed with *The Odd Couple* was soured in ensuing years by a couple of unpopular sitcoms and he returned to Broadway, which many considered to be Randall's truest love.

Randall was a frequent guest on TV game shows and late-night talk shows hosted by Johnny Carson and David Letterman. When Randall died in 2004 at the age of 84, his 105 appearances on *The Tonight Show* were the most by any celebrity to that point in time.

Susan Watson

This 1957 Tulsa Central High School alumnus was one of Broadway's brightest stars in the 1960s, earning acclaim for creating the role as Luisa in the 1960 musical *The Fantasticks* and being nominated for a 1966 Tony Award for Best Actress in a Musical for her role in *A Joyful Noise* and co-starred with John Raitt.

As a youth and the daughter of a dance instructor, she became enamored by the music of Rodgers and Hammerstein and Gilbert and Sullivan. Watson performed in local summer stock musical before going to New York City's Juilliard School of Music, the latter being the stepping stone for her Broadway career.

Watson's first Broadway role was as Velma (girlfriend of The Jets gang leader Riff) in the original West End production of *West Side Story* in 1958. In the 1960 musical *The Fantasticks,* she created the role of a young love-struck girl named Luisa. *The Fantasticks* would be performed 17,162 times and was the world's longest-running musical.

Shortly afterwards, Watson portrayed the precocious teenager Kim MacAfee in the original Broadway cast of the musical comedy *Bye Bye Birdie* and co-starred with Dick Van Dyke and Paul Lynde. That show won the 1961 Tony Award for Best Musical and was a 1963 movie that earned two Oscar nominations.

Watson co-starred with the legendary Ruby Keeler in the 1971 re-vival of *No, No Nanette* and with Robert Preston in the 1964 musical *Ben Franklin in Paris*.

She released a 2016 album of 14 jazz and Broadway standards en-titled *The Music Never Ends*.

Kathryn Zaremba

This Broken Arrow native captivated New York City theatre crit-ics as the nine-year-old star of the 1993 off-Broadway musical *Annie Warbucks*. The show was a sequel to the Tony Award-winning Broad-way show *Annie* which evolved from the long-running comic strip "Little Orphan Annie."

While *Annie Warbucks* never found its way to Broadway, Zarem-ba's acting and singing drew high praise in a *New York Times* review. During her early teenage years, she appeared in the final season of the TV sitcom *Full House* as Lisa Leeper and appeared in four episodes of the short-lived sitcom, *The Jeff Foxworthy Show*.

Zaremba retired from acting when she was 13 years old, choosing to study design work and art. She graduated from Broken Arrow High School then attended design and art schools in Kansas City and Washington, D.C.

She owns and operates the Kate Zaremba Company, which special-izes in original art prints, textile design and custom illustrations. She and her pianist husband, Jeremy Ney, live near the Nation's Capital.

Violet (Broadway musical)

A disfigured woman's journey from North Carolina to Tulsa for physical, emotional and spiritual healing was the focal point of *Violet*, a musical that won three awards in 1997 and was nominated for four Tony Awards in 2014. The musical is based on a short story by Doris Betts called *The Ugliest Pilgrim*.

The plot is about a bus ride in the fall of 1964 during the Vietnam War and the civil rights movement. Violet Karl was disfigured by her father in a tragic farm accident involving an axe. She chooses to take a three-day bus ride to Tulsa and meet with a televangelist whom she believes can heal her physical and emotional issues.

In Tennessee, she befriends two soldiers: a black sergeant named Flick and a young white paratrooper named Monty. After the trio traveled through Memphis, the soldiers got off the bus in Fort Smith, Arkansas but asked Violet to keep in touch with them.

After arriving in Tulsa, Violet confronts the televangelist in his chapel and pleads for him to perform a miraculous healing. But when nothing happened, Violet looks to Heaven and her father replaces the televangelist and apologizes for what happened to her. She feels that something about her has changed and presumes that her physical scar is gone.

When the bus stops again in Fort Smith, Monty and Flick are at the bus station waiting to see her. Monty tells her that her scar hasn't changed at all but he asks for her hand in marriage before he's sent into combat in Vietnam. Violet turned him down and Monty left brokenhearted. Flick also tells Violet that her scar is still there but asks her to stay with him. Her healing is fulfilled when she commits to a new life with him.

Violet was an off-Broadway musical in 1997 and won the Drama Critics' Circle Award and the Lucille Lortel Award as that year's best musical. In 2014, Violet was nominated for four Tony Awards: Best Revival of a Musical, Best Actress (Sutton Foster) in a Musical, Best Featured Actor (Joshua Henry as Flick) in a Musical and Best Direction of a Musical.

Chapter Sixteen

Reality TV and Music

"I knew it was time to get off reality TV when someone asked me if I sang as well as I acted."

Ozzy Osbourne

"Modern reality TV sets up these competitive situations to show us real human nature."

Alexander Ludwig

"I humbly apologize for reality television. But reality television is here to stay."

Cilla Black

"'American Bandstand' was the original reality show. I mean, it was an open window to kids dancing and the fashions changed, and the music was there."

Dick Clark

***

Two acts from the Tulsa area achieved fame on *Star Search*, an inter-active talent and reality show that first aired from 1983 through 1995 and then revived for a two-year run in 2003 and 2004. Voting was done by a panel of celebrity judges and a studio audience. Ed McMahon hosted the first version and Arsenio Hall hosted the second version.

While six-figure cash prizes were awarded to the grand champion, there was no guarantee of a radio or TV contract that was common-place in current reality talent shows like Fox's *American Idol* or NBC's *The Voice*.

Here is a summary of Tulsans who appeared on music-themed reality television shows:

Star Search (Syndication and CBS)

Sand Springs native Sam Harris won $100,000 as the 1983 Male Vocalist winner. His performance of "Over the Rainbow" from the *Wizard of Oz* movie classic would become his signature song. He later recorded several CDs, appeared on TV sitcoms and became a standout Broadway and concert performer.

Eight dance students from Tulsa, Broken Arrow and Coweta formed the dance troupe Shockwave that reached the 2003 Dance Competition finals, which were aired by CBS. They performed en-ergetic versions of clogging, which is a type of folk dancing in which a shoe's heel or toe or both strike either the floor or the other foot to create a percussion rhythm.

The members of Shockwave were Sarah Bina, Hannah Gallion, Ashley George, Tristan Keim, Jeff Moore, Jennifer Moore, Hayley Spencer, and Allison Stout.

American Idol (Fox)

David Cook, the 2008 (Season 7) winner, was a singer-songwriter whose journey to fame and fortune took some unusual turns. Cook moved to Tulsa to pursue a music career after graduating in 2006 from the University of Central Missouri. He became the bass guitarist for the Midwest Kings, a band for whom he once opened as a solo act.

Cook went to *American Idol* auditions in Omaha, Nebraska to support his older brother Adam, who had battled brain cancer since 1998 and dreamed of auditioning as well. Adam did not qualify for a Hollywood audition and would pass away in 2009. But David's music caught the ears and eyes of the show's producer and earned that trip to Hollywood.

After his *American Idol* victory, Cook made music history in late May of 2008 with 11 of his songs debuting on the Hot 100 List of *Billboard* magazine. That was the highest number of debut songs by a singer or group since The Beatles put 14 songs on that same list in April of 1964.

That self-titled debut album peaked at number three on the Billboard album chart. His 2011 album *This Loud Morning* peaked at number seven.

Since that time, Cook did not achieve the large-scale success that previous *American Idol* winners or competitors have achieved but he continued to generate new projects and continues touring for national and international appearances.

Melinda Doolittle, a 1995 graduate of Tulsa's Union High School, finished in third place in the 2007 (Season 6) version. Her singing style was described by some critics as a cross between Gladys Knight and Tina Turner. The 2007 *American Idol* winner was Jordin Sparks but during an interview with ABC TV's *Good Morning America* after the competition ended, *Idol* judge Simon Cowell said that he felt Doolittle should have been the winner.

While attending Union, Doolittle also dressed up as the school's mascot for one football season. She later attended Belmont University in Nashville, Tennessee, majoring in music and also portrayed that school's mascot. In recent years, Doolittle has performed with the Boston Pops orchestra, traveled to Africa for charity work and recorded CDs and EPs.

Tulsa hosted one of the earliest solo concerts performed by Carrie Underwood after she won the 2005 (Season 4) *American Idol* competition. The native of Checotah, Oklahoma (about 75 miles south-southeast of Tulsa) who became an international superstar performed at the Expo Square Pavilion on November 19, 2006 on an open date while touring as one of the opening acts for country music star Brad Paisley.

In June 2015, the Guthrie Green in downtown Tulsa was the site of contestant auditions prior to the final season of *American Idol* on Fox TV, which aired in 2016.

The Voice (NBC)

Thirteen of the 22 Oklahoma-based acts appearing on NBC music-related reality show *The Voice* came from the metro Tulsa area. Six of them were mentored by country music superstar and Ada, Oklahoma native Blake Shelton.

Arguably the most successful Tulsa-area performer from that group is Corey Kent White who competed on Season 8 which aired in the spring of 2015.

Performing today as Corey Kent, his first number one song was "Wild as Her" which drew over 250 million streams. The song's video earned a 2023 nomination for Male Breakthrough Video of the Year by the CMT Music Awards.

A graduate of Bixby High School and Oklahoma State University, the aspiring singer-songwriter's musical roots were based in Western

Swing, and he debuted at the age of 11 with a local band called Oklahoma Stomp.

White's debut EP, *Making Noise*, was distributed through digital music outlets and quickly led to his sharing the stage with country music superstars such as Toby Keith, Willie Nelson, Hank Williams Jr. and Luke Bryan.

In 2016, White performed concerts as part of his affiliation with the non-profit Folds of Honor Foundation. More information about the Folds of Honor can be found elsewhere in this book.

Mary Sarah Gross appeared in 2016 and had the longest tenure of any Tulsa-area performer on that show.

Performing as Mary Sarah, the aspiring country singer finished in sixth place in Season 10 in the spring of 2016. She was born in Tulsa but moved with her family to southern Texas as a youngster.

Her versions of country classics performed by Carrie Underwood, Loretta Lynn, Randy Travis and Tammy Wynette, coupled with a soulful cover of Connie Francis' pop ballad "Where the Boys Are" became favorites of the viewers and celebrity judges.

Mary Sarah's 2014 debut album *Bridges* features duets with country legends such as Willie Nelson, Ray Price, Merle Haggard, Vince Gill and Dolly Parton.

Other 2016 performers with Tulsa connections eliminated in the early live performance rounds were country singer Kata Hay from Skiatook, Oral Roberts University alumnus and contemporary Christian singers Brian Nhira from Tulsa and Chelsea Gann from Mounds.

Prior to Mary Sarah's 2016 performance, the longest tenure on The Voice was Corey Kent White reaching the final eight performers in 2015.

Other Tulsa-area performers on *The Voice* were the vocal duo of Alaska and Madi (Alaska Holloway and Madi Metcalf) in 2014 and soloist Adley Stump in 2012. Alaska and Madi are currently based in Nashville but return to the metro Tulsa area frequently to perform at local events. Stump's debut album *Like This* was released in May of 2015 and the Oklahoma State University graduate later worked as an opening act for Zac Brown, Train and Tim McGraw.

The duo Jubal Lee Young and Amanda Preslar had a short run during Season 9 of *The Voice* but their debut was memorable one, indeed. Shortly after their performance and with a little assistance from Blake Shelton, Young dropped to one knee in front of the studio audience and asked a stunned Preslar to marry him. (She said yes)

The couple returned to Tulsa and opened a music school, Preslar Music. She also currently serves on the staff of the Unity Church of Christianity-Midtown in Tulsa.

Paul Pfau appeared in Season 8 in 2015 and was a pop singer whose family lived in Tulsa until he was four years old then they moved to Texas and eventually to western Maryland.

Maye Thomas and Austin Allsup appeared in Season 11 which began in October of 2016. Thomas was eliminated early in the competition while Allsup advanced to the final 10 contestants before being eliminated.

Thomas, a Broken Arrow High School graduate and daughter of a former Muskogee, Oklahoma radio personality, was chosen for a team led by pop singer Miley Cyrus. Thomas cited jazz legend Ella Fitzgerald along with country music and classic rock as being her musical influences. She and her Glenpool native husband, Grant, moved to Nashville in 2013 attempting to further their musical careers.

Allsup, who was on Blake Shelton's team during Season 10, reached the top 10 singers before being eliminated. The son of former Tulsa musician Tommy Allsup is currently based in Texas but came back to Tulsa to recorded an album at The Church Studio which was released in 2024. He was also a featured performer at The Church Studio's annual Carney Fest music festival. Allsup is part of the Red Dirt alt-country music scene and performed alongside artists such as John Mellencamp, Jason Aldean, Stoney Larue and Jason Boland.

Former Tulsan Bransen Ireland competed for Blake Shelton's team in Season 14 which aired in the spring of 2018. He was one of the first singers eliminated in the Battle Rounds. Ireland went on to be an opening act for country stars Lee Brice, Rodney Atkins and Gary Allan.

Kata Hay of Skiatook (real name Kata Huddleston) competed for Christina Aguilera's team during Season 10 which aired in the spring of 2016. She reached the first round of live playoffs before being eliminated.

Whitney Fenimore from Tulsa completed for Adam Levine's team during Season 13 which aired in the fall of 2017. Fenimore reached the semifinals before being eliminated. She married Olympic skeleton bobsledder Kendall Wesenberg in 2022.

Gracee Shriver competed in Season 17 for Blake Shelton's team as a 16-year-old singer. Shriver reached the final 16 singers before being eliminated. Shriver is involved with country music projects in Oklahoma and Tennessee when she's not making new music for digital services.

Kailey Abel from the northeastern Tulsa suburb of Verdigris competed in Season 18 for Blake Shelton's team as a 16-year-old vocalist. She reached the Battle Rounds before being eliminated. Abel later attended Oral Roberts University and was a featured vocalist for ORU Worship's live album *My Offering*.

Natalie Brady, a 2003 Union High School graduate, was chosen for a team led by Maroon 5 singer Adam Levine during Season 15 in 2018 but was eliminated during the Battle Rounds. She credited her father, longtime Tulsa nightclub performer Jack Brady, as being her inspiration for pursuing a musical career. Brady currently lives in Nashville and performs with her band, Natalie Brady and the Night Owls.

Chavon Rodgers, who was on Ariana Grande's team in 2021, participated in the early rounds of Season 21 in the fall of 2021. When Grande's approached Rodgers to give him a hug after being eliminated, he walked past her and a minor controversy arose. Rodgers later said it wasn't intentional and both parties made up after the dustup.

Jenks native Michael B (full name Michael Burns Williams) was chosen by pop singer Niall Horan in the spring of 2023. Michael B reached the quarterfinal round before being eliminated. His mother was a radio news anchor in Tulsa and the family later moved to Los Angeles due to his father's employment with Southwest Airlines.

Chapter Seventeen

Musical Venues

"Live music is where you get the inspiration and creativity."

Paul Rodgers

"There's nothing to compare to live music, there just isn't anything."

Gloria Gaynor

"It is good medicine to go to a concert hall and forget the harshness of what's going on. It can be a very positive thing."

Itzhak Perlman

"Live music is better."

Neil Young

"There's one thing you can't download and that's a live performance. And I know how to put on a show and enjoy performing, and I'll always have that."

Madonna

***

BOK Center

This multipurpose arena has become of one America's most popular concert and sports venues since its opening in 2008. Many internationally known entertainers have lauded the BOK Center's acoustics and amenities.

The BOK Center received the 2016 and 2018 Arena of the Year award from the International Entertainment Buyers Association trade group. The BOK Center beat out internationally known venues such as New York City's Madison Square Garden, London's O2 Arena and the T-Mobile Arena in Las Vegas.

In 2023, *Billboard* magazine ranked the BOK Center 26th in the United States and 36th internationally in its Box score Top Venue report, which measures gross revenues from event ticket sales. The BOK Center grossed almost $29.5 million from 54 events and sold more event tickets than all other venues in its region.

Construction of the new arena was the focal point of the Vision 2025 civic improvement program approved by local voters in 2003 after previous attempts at such an undertaking were soundly rejected. The local sales tax was increased by six-tenths of one cent for 13 years to provide public funding worth $178 million. An additional $18 was raised through private donations. The Tulsa-based Bank of Oklahoma, known locally as BOK, paid $11 million for naming rights to the arena.

The BOK Center contains 17,343 fixed seats with seating capacities of 17,096 for ice hockey, 17,839 for basketball games, 13,644 for concerts or other events that use a stage and 19,199 for concerts held in the round.

Parking and highway access to the BOK Center is very convenient. Surveys by the city of Tulsa show that there are 12,000 parking spaces within a 10-minute walk. For certain events, the city's mass transit system provides shuttle buses to and from remote parking facilities.

The BOK Center is the home arena for the Tulsa Oilers of the East Coast Hockey League (ECHL), the Tulsa Oilers of the Indoor Football League (IFL) and the NBA's Oklahoma City Thunder also plays an annual preseason game there.

It was also the home of the Tulsa Shock of the Women's National Basketball Association (WNBA) from 2010 through 2015 and the Arena Football League's Tulsa Talons in 2010 and 2011.

The BOK Center has also hosted early round games in the NCAA Men's Basketball Championship Tournament, more commonly known as March Madness. Second round games were played there in 2011 with first and second round games played in 2017 and 2019. The Conference USA men's and women's postseason college basketball tournaments were played there in 2010 and 2013.

Recent additions to the arena's sports menu have been the USA Gymnastics Championships and the High School Hoops Showcase, featuring boys and girls teams from Tulsa-area high schools and the Big 12 Conference Wrestling Championship.

Besides concerts and sports, the BOK Center has events connected with the Bassmaster Fishing Championship, nationally-televised professional wrestling events, stand-up comedy shows, rodeos, indoor motorsport races, public speeches and motivational seminars.

Celine Dion, the Grammy Award-winning singer, had agreed sight unseen to perform the BOK Center's inaugural concert. That event quickly sold out but her performance was delayed until February 2009 when throat and vocal cord infections developed. As a result, the legendary rock band The Eagles played in the BOK Center's first concert on September 4, 2008.

Country music superstar Garth Brooks holds the record for the most concert sellouts at the BOK Center. All seven of his performances during January 2015 sold out in a single day. Other music acts to sell out the BOK Center twice are pop singers Taylor Swift, Katy Perry and Sir Paul McCartney along country music stars George Strait and Zach Bryan as well as the contemporary Christian band Casting Crowns.

Metallica holds the BOK Center record for the largest single concert attendance, drawing 19,228 people for its January 28, 2019 performance.

Blue Dome District

This nine-square block area on the eastern edge of downtown Tulsa is known for its nightlife and plethora of locally owned restaurants, a retro-style bowling lounge, 1980s-style arcade and cafes. Eight of the buildings in that area date back to the 1920s.

The Blue Dome District cornerstone and namesake is a one-time Gulf Oil gas station at the southwest corner of East Second Street and South Elgin Avenue, a site that was part of the original path of Route 66 from 1926 through 1932.

Back then, the 24-hour gas station had a full-service attendant that lived in an upstairs apartment and the dome had a much lighter color that became a tourist attraction at night thanks to having hundreds of lights beneath it. Over several decades, the building would be used as a pub and for other ventures.

Cain's Ballroom

Located at 423 North Main on a hill in the northern part of downtown Tulsa, Cain's Ballroom is still going strong after its grand opening a century ago.

Once the mecca of Western Swing music as well as owning a place in rock-and-roll infamy, Cain's has evolved into a highly sought-after venue for musicians from all genres and is listed in the National Register of Historic Places. Since the mid-2000s, Cain's has consistently been ranked by *Pollstar* magazine among the world's top 30 club venues for the highest attendance with a seating capacity of under 3,000.

Many of today's top musicians have made it a point to play at Cain's in various stages of their careers, even though they are capable of selling out much larger venues in the blink of an eye. Some of the top performing acts who have done that include Bob Dylan, Robert Plant, Jack White, Brooks and Dunn, Beck, Buddy Guy, Elvis Costello, Wilco, Loretta Lynn, Alice in Chains, Hanson, Haim, Kings of Leon, Kacey Musgraves, Collective Soul, Blake Shelton, Trisha Yearwood, St. Vincent and One Republic.

As part of its 100th anniversary celebration concerts in 2024, Cain's hosted three major events. Alison Krauss and Robert Plant opened their 2024 tour with a concert at Cain's. The others were a reunion of the 1990s pop band Hanson and the alternative country stars Jason Isbell and the 400 Unit.

Cain's today is a smoke-free business with ample standing room for major concerts but seating is provided for certain special events.

Tate Brady, one of Tulsa's co-founders, originally built the structure in 1924 to serve as a garage. A few years later, he changed it into a nightclub called the Louvre Ballroom where dance lessons cost 10 cents apiece. Madison "Daddy" Cain bought the building in 1930 and after rechristening it as Cain's Dance Academy, dance lessons were still a dime.

During the early 1930s, the leader of a Texas-based band named Bob Wills brought his Texas Playboys band to Tulsa, seeking a new manager and a new venue for their up-tempo music that would be known as Western Swing. That infectious type of music drew its influences from the big bands of that era along with hillbilly, jazz, blues and jitterbug musical styles.

Cain's Ballroom would be the musical headquarters for Bob Wills and The Texas Playboys from 1934 through 1943. The band played a live weekday noon-hour show on Tulsa's KVOO-AM radio as well as playing for dances in the evenings. Because KVOO's 50,000-watt signal reached across most of the United States back then, Cain's drew even more national attention and Wills' popularity soon rivaled that of big band leaders Glenn Miller, Tommy Dorsey and Benny Goodman.

When Bob Wills left for Hollywood in 1943, younger brother Johnnie Lee Wills stepped in with his new band and kept up that schedule through 1958. During ensuing years, a gallery of portraits of country music legends was acquired and still surrounds the dance floor and stage.

Cain's fell upon hard times during the 1960s and early 1970s due to rock music sweeping the nation along with the facility earning an unsavory reputation for drunken brawls and gang fights.

Rock music promoter Larry Shaeffer purchased Cain's in 1977 and turned it into a rock music mecca for nearly two decades. He was a musical visionary who brought up-and-coming acts to play at Cain's just before hitting the big time.

Among those aspiring rockers performing at Cain's were Van Halen, Huey Lewis and the News, Pat Benatar, Talking Heads, INXS, Marilyn Manson, the Police and Metallica as well as pioneers in the New Wave, punk rock and techno fields.

But the most infamous rock concert at Cain's was the January 11, 1978 performance by the British punk rock legends, The Sex Pistols. Lead singer Sid Vicious became so frustrated that he punched a massive hole in a wall in the Green Room. That hole is still there and numerous musicians have paid tribute, of sorts, by placing their fist through that gaping hole whenever they've played at Cain's.

Danny and Mark Finnerty, sons of the late Tulsa sports and entertainment promoter Hugh Finnerty, purchased Cain's from Shaeffer in November of 1999. They continued Shaeffer's tradition of bringing up-and-coming rock bands to Cain's, spotlight such acts as Weezer, String Cheese Incident and Reverend Horton Heat.

Cain's was sold to Tulsa neurosurgeon Jim Rodgers and his wife, Alice, in 2003. Rogers changed the building in a way that gave their new business a shot in the arm. Air conditioning was added and bands that avoided Cain's during the torrid Oklahoma summers came running.

Shortly afterwards, Jim and Alice turned the business, appropriately named as Doc Roc Productions, over to sons Chad and Hunter Rodgers.

Cain's had a unique wooden dance floor that according to an urban legend was built on large springs to make the sensation of dancing the Lindy Hop, swing dancing, ballroom dancing or line dancing even more special. But when a long-overdue replacement of the 83-year-old wooden floor was made in 2007, the Rodgers family found that there were no springs.

Cain's was part of the circumstances that led to rock superstar Eric Clapton spending a night in the Tulsa jail in 1978. Clapton had many friends among Tulsa-area musicians and was invited to perform in a jam session to celebrate Cain's anniversary.

Clapton became intoxicated on a flight from Miami, Florida to Tulsa earlier that day, allegedly got into an altercation with crew members and Tulsa police were alerted to be ready to arrest him. Then Clapton got into another argument with a Tulsa police officer and was taken to the jail's drunk tank.

Tulsa World photographer John Southern snapped a picture of Clapton behind the jail's bars that was quickly picked up by newspapers around the world. What's not widely known is that Southern then contacted the mother of a friend to help Clapton get out of jail.

Church Studio

Renowned during Leon Russell's heyday as his primary recording studio and the 1970s home office for Shelter Records, the nearly 110-year-old stone structure east of downtown Tulsa that once housed a church has become one of America's premier recording studios.

It was placed on the National Register of Historic Places in 2017 due to its significance in American music culture as well as being what some people having loving referred to it as being The Mother Church of the Tulsa Sound.

A not-so-short list of internationally known artists that have recorded there includes Eric Clapton, Tom Petty, J.J. Cale, Jimmy Buffett, Asleep at the Wheel, Stevie Wonder, Kansas, The Gap Band, Roy Clark, Michael Bolton, The Tractors, Rita Coolidge, Willie Nelson, and the Turnpike Troubadours.

Husband and wife co-owners and Tulsa entrepreneurs Ivan Acosta and Teresa Knox completed a massive five-year restoration project in 2022 that enhanced the recording facilities as well as creating a museum, an audio engineering school and event space. Their priorities were to preserve the Leon Russell legacy as well as creating a collaborative space and entertainment network along with the Church Studio foundation to support the advancement of music and related educational programs.

Located on the southwest corner of East Third Street and South Trenton Avenue, the building opened in 1915 as the Grace Methodist Episcopal Church. In subsequent years it housed the First United

Brethren Church (1928-46), the First Evangelical United Brethren Church (1948-61) and the First Church of God (1961-70). The church was originally a brick structure and the current castle-like stone was added during the middle 1950s.

Local musician, record producer and guitar manufacturer Steve Ripley, best known as the lead singer of the country-rock band The Tractors, purchased The Church Studio in 1987 after Russell moved to Nashville to further his music career. He operated the facility for two decades before selling it to Knox and Acosta.

The facility received additional attention in January 2024 when the Turnpike Troubadours recorded a one-hour program that aired on the Sirius XM Outlaw Country music channel.

Bob Dylan Center

More than 6,000 items from the legendary singer-songwriter's 60-year career found a new home in this Tulsa museum in 2022. It is located on the corner of East Archer Street and Martin Luther King Boulevard in the Tulsa Arts District on the northern edge of downtown and within walking distance of the Woody Guthrie Center.

The museum's mission is to enable the public to study Dylan's works and his impact on the world of music and society as a whole.

While the Bob Dylan Center is the primary public venue for the singer-songwriter's archived collection, the center offers additional exhibits and public programs and performances to encourage conversations about creativity in one's life.

The museum displays Dylan's works in much the same manner as the nearby Woody Guthrie Center preserves and celebrates the life and musical legacy of the Oklahoma-born folk singer.

Dylan long considered Guthrie to be his musical inspiration and idol, as evidenced by "Song for Woody" being the 12th song on his self-titled 1962 debut album. Dylan tipped his hat to Guthrie's influence in a statement released in March of 2016 about the archives coming to Tulsa.

The entirety of the Bob Dylan Archives is open only to qualified researchers.

In a 2019 *Tulsa World* article, Dylan was quoted as saying, "I'm glad that my archives, which have been collected all these years, have finally found a home and are to be included with the works of Woody Guthrie and especially alongside all the valuable artifacts from the Native American Nations (in Philbrook Downtown)."

The Helmerich Center for American Research, affiliated with the University of Tulsa and Gilcrease Museum, has a team of curators digitally preserving the items for future display and, more importantly, to serve as an academic resource in the study of American music.

The vast collection of Dylan's recordings, manuscripts, photos, notebooks and other items was purchased by the University of Tulsa and the George Kaiser Family Foundation. The two organizations declined to provide specific financial figures about the transaction. However, a New York Times article said the Dylan collection has been appraised at over $60 million and was purchased by the Tulsa organizations for between $15 and $20 million.

That collection gained additional prestige when Dylan was presented with the 2016 Nobel Prize for Literature, making him the first musician to receive that award. Some of the prior recipients of that award are book-writing legends Samuel Beckett, Toni Morrison and T.S. Eliot.

While he was unable to personally accept the Nobel Prize in December of 2016, punk rock music legend Patti Smith read Dylan's acceptance speech and performed with an orchestral arrangement of his legendary song "A Hard Rain's A-Gonna Fall."

Four of Dylan's nine concerts in Tulsa were staged at the downtown Brady Theater with the most recent one at that venue being an October 23, 2016 performance. Prior to starting his 2004 Never Ending Tour, Dylan and his band rehearsed in a Tulsa warehouse and opened the tour schedule with a performance at Cain's Ballroom. Additional Dylan concerts were in 2005 at Drillers Stadium with Willie Nelson and at the BOK Center in 2012 with Mark Knopfler.

Dylan's first Tulsa concert, at the River Parks Amphitheater on September 4, 1990 was not fondly remembered by the Rock and Roll Hall of Famer. He wasn't happy with the concert's location along the banks of a smelly section of the Arkansas River, nor about bugs flying into his face and mouth throughout the show and certainly not about a *Tulsa World* review claiming his singing was "mush mouth" and not understandable.

That same newspaper reporter, however, gave high praise for Dylan's 1991 concert at the Brady Theater.

Cox Business Center

This multi-purpose arena that once seated 8,900 people was the focal point in a revival of downtown Tulsa during the 1960s. It was known as the Tulsa Assembly Center at its 1964 dedication and as the Tulsa Convention Center and the Maxwell Convention Center prior to its current branding as the Cox Business Center.

Throughout the 1970s, this arena put Tulsa on the A-list for national and international concerts. Among the top musical acts to perform there were the Rolling Stones, Jackson 5 (with a very young Michael Jackson), the Beach Boys, Dave Clark Five, Johnny Cash, ZZ Top, Sammy Davis Jr., Eric Clapton, Tina Turner, Glen Campbell, Led Zeppelin, Leon Russell, Elton John, Jimi Hendrix, Bruce Springsteen, James Brown and Elvis Presley

The return of minor league hockey to Tulsa was a major impetus for the arena's construction and it served as the home of the Central Hockey League's Tulsa Oilers for 34 years.

In 2018, Tulsa voters approved a bond issue which included $55 million to transform it into a facility for hosting trade shows and conventions. Construction was completed in 2020 with the 8,900-seat arena being replaced by a 41,000-square foot banquet hall.

Oklahoma Jazz Hall of Fame

Housed in the former Tulsa Union Depot train station on the northern edge of downtown Tulsa, the Oklahoma Jazz Hall of Fame and the Jazz Depot are closed to the public while the building is being renovated. The new building will feature an acoustic redesigning of the performance hall plus an in-house production facility geared for live music recording and streaming. A rooftop entertainment space is also planned.

The Oklahoma Jazz Hall of Fame honors musicians with Oklahoma connections who performed the blues, gospel, jazz and other forms of music. The organization's Jay McShann Lifetime Achievement Award salutes performers who influenced Oklahoma's musical heritage. Some of the award's diverse winners include Nat King Cole, Bob Wills, Ramsey Lewis, Marilyn Maye and Dave Brubeck.

The 1988 Oklahoma Legislature authorized the organization's creation with a pair of state senators from Tulsa sponsoring the legislation. It moved into the Union Depot in 2007 after formerly being housed in the Greenwood Cultural Center.

The Oklahoma Jazz Hall of Fame leased the Union Depot building from the Tulsa County Industrial Authority. But a 2021 bankruptcy filing, which detailed unpaid property taxes and past-due utility payments, led to new ownership and the current renovation projects.

OKPOP Museum

This Smithsonian-type Museum that will house artifacts and exhibits related to Oklahoma's contributions to popular culture is expected to open in 2024. It is located on the southwestern corner of West Easton and South Main Streets in downtown Tulsa, directly across from the legendary Cain's Ballroom.

The Oklahoma Historical Society will operate the museum and Interactive exhibits will be placed throughout the structure, saluting the achievements of Oklahomans in the performing arts as well as housing a small performance venue.

OHS officials secured significant pledges for gallery presentations from numerous Oklahoma-based celebrities. Among the big-name stars that have backed the venture are Garth Brooks, Kristen Chenoweth, Roy Clark, S.E. Hinton and Jim Halsey and the late Leon Russell. The families of Bob Wills and Chester Gould (*Dick Tracy* comic strip) have endorsed the concept.

Russell's donation of over 4,500 items to the effort has been the largest contribution to date by an Oklahoma-based performer. The native Tulsans contributed 1,300 audio recordings, over 1,000 photographs, a hundred video recordings and concert posters, programs and tickets.

The OKPOP project was conceived in 2007 and a $25 million bond issue to provide partial funding was passed by the Oklahoma Legislature in 2015.

Country music star Blake Shelton joined the OKPOP Foundation in 2023 to serve as the face of the organization's campaign to raise $18 million in private donations to complete the museum.

Sunset Amphitheater

With an opening scheduled for December of 2025, this 12,500-seat outdoor performance venue will be located in southeastern Broken

Arrow immediately north of the city's Events Park and close to the Broken Arrow campus of Northeastern State University.

Notes Live, a national entertainment and hospitality corporation, is building the venue that will host between 40 and 60 concerts each year by nationally known bands and musicians. Notes Live has built similar concert venues in Colorado, Georgia, Tennessee and Texas and announced plans for a similar facility in the Oklahoma City metropolitan area.

The Broken Arrow project will be a public-private partnership between that local government and Notes Live with an estimated construction cost of nearly $29 million. The city's funding, which involves only sales and hotel taxes and not property taxes, will primarily relate to infrastructure improvements.

Live Nation, an organization widely respected in the entertainment industry for managing top-notch facilities and promotion of musical performers, will operate the amphitheater. The venue will have reserved upper and lower bowl seating, a landscaped berm plus luxury fire pit suites along with custom VIP suites that will be inset beneath the berm.

Aside from concerns expressed by a few local residents related to increased traffic and noise in that neighborhood, the project has received an very positive reception from Broken Arrow residents.

Tulsa Arts District

While the Tulsa Arts District is in one of Tulsa's oldest areas, it has been a major player in the recent revitalization of the city's downtown sector. Construction over the last 10 years has nearly doubled that area's condominiums and urban living spaces.

Many of its buildings are two-story red brick structures that were once warehouses but have found new lives since the 1990s as art galleries, retail stores, museums, restaurants, a public park and night clubs.

Reconciliation Way is the main thoroughfare through an area bounded by Denver Avenue on the west, Elgin Avenue on the east, the Interstate 244 highway on the north and railroad tracks on the south.

The BOK Center anchors the southwestern corner of the Tulsa Arts District and the ONEOK Field baseball stadium along with the Greenwood District anchors the eastern end. Also located within that area are the historic Brady Theater and Cain's Ballroom.

The First Friday Art Crawl is a year-round monthly event that draws up to 3,000 people for evening visits to the Tulsa Arts District's various studios, mini-galleries, museums and other businesses. It is held on the first Friday night of each month between 6:00 and 9:00 at participating venues. Many Tulsans incorporate the First Friday Art Crawl into date night activities that can include dinner, drinks, coffee or listening to music at the various restaurants and clubs.

Tulsa Theater

Located on the northwest corner of Reconciliation Way and North Boulder Avenue in downtown Tulsa, the Tulsa Theater has entered its second century as a theatrical and musical venue.

It earned a spot on the National Register of Historical Places in 1979. But for several decades, many residents lovingly called it "The Old Lady on Brady" when much-needed maintenance and updating was not done. Recent remodeling changed the seating capacity to 2,800 and it now has a state-of-the-art lighting and sound system.

Because of its intimate stage and seating design, the Tulsa Theater has hosted some of the top names in the entertainment world. Comedians and humorists such as Will Rogers, Robin Williams, Bill Maher and Garrison Keillor have performed there.

It also hosted legendary performers of the Great American Song-book such as Louis Armstrong, George M. Cohan, Rosemary Clooney, Pat Boone and Tony Bennett.

Rock music legends performing there have included Buddy Holly, U2, Alice Cooper, Chicago, Genesis, Phil Collins, James Brown, Ted Nugent and Motley Crue. Among the country music stars gracing that stage are Willie Nelson, Roy Clark, Glen Campbell, George Jones and Merle Haggard.

Tulsa voters approved a bond issue in 1912 to build the structure and it was known as Tulsa Convention Hall from 1914 through 1952. Back then, it seated about 4,200 people and had 1,300 balcony seats. Local leaders claimed that it was the largest such hall between Houston, Texas and Kansas City, Missouri.

A major renovation of the building's interior in 1930 had an Art Deco theme and turned a once-drab building into a colorful and warm auditorium. Additional remodeling was done in 1952 and the building was renamed as the Tulsa Municipal Theater. It served as Tulsa's primary concert hall until the Performing Arts Center was built as part of the Williams Center development several blocks to the south-southeast. The Tulsa Philharmonic was the facility's primary tenant from the 1940s through the 1970s.

The structure was renamed as The Brady Theater in 1979 because it was located on West Brady Street; a road that had been named in honor of Tulsa business pioneer W. Tate Brady. But after information was discovered about Brady's connection with the racial hate group the Ku Klux Klan, the street was renamed Reconciliation Way in 2018 and the theater was rebranded as the Tulsa Theater in 2019.

Woody Guthrie Center

This downtown Tulsa facility showcases the legacy of the legendary folk singer and author born in Okemah, roughly 70 miles south-southwest of Tulsa. It is in the Brady Arts District at the intersection of East Brady Street and North Boston Avenue.

The 12,000-square-foot interactive museum which opened in 2013 has climate-controlled displays, showcasing the broad scope of Guthrie's music, writings, artwork and political/social beliefs. While the museum is open to the public with paid admission, its archives are only opened to researchers by appointment. Those archives had been the property of the New York-based Woody Guthrie Foundation which was led by Guthrie's daughter, Nora. The Tulsa based George Kaiser Family Foundation purchased the archives in 2011 and unveiled plans for the Woody Guthrie Center to house the material as a celebration of Guthrie's life and impact on American culture.

Much of Guthrie's music was based on his experiences during the Great Depression when he moved from Oklahoma during the Dust Bowl epidemic to seek a new start in California. During that journey alongside migrant farmworkers, he learned about their traditional blues and folk music and incorporated much of it into his own songs.

Among Guthrie's best-known songs are the 1944 folk classic "This Land Is Your Land" and "Oklahoma Hills", a 1945 composition about his childhood and youth. His 1943 autobiography, *Bound for Glory*, served as the basis for the 1976 film by the same name in which Guthrie was portrayed by David Carradine. That movie won Oscars for Best Cinematography and Best Music-Original Song Score and Adaptation.

Guthrie's social beliefs conflicted with Oklahoma's strongly conservative majority, and he was even reviled in some quarters as an alleged supporter of the Communist Party. But the words in Guthrie's songs struck a chord, to coin a phrase, with people who sought equality or a better way of life. Some of the famous singer songwriters who frequently cited Guthrie's influence on their music and viewpoints includes Pete Seeger, Tom Paxton, Bob Dylan, John Mellencamp and Bruce Springsteen.

The Woody Guthrie Center annually presents the Woody Guthrie Prize to a musician whose career achievements and passion for social justice exemplifies the core values of Guthrie's life. The award is presented on a three-year rotation in California, New York City and Oklahoma; the three locations that were pivotal in Guthrie's musical career.

Legendary folk singer and social activist Pete Seeger was the inaugural recipient of the Woody Guthrie Prize in 2014. Other recipients are gospel music legend Mavis Staples, country music singer-songwriter and movie actor Kris Kristofferson, pioneering TV writer-producer Norman Lear, rapper-music producer Chuck D and singer-songwriter-activists John Mellencamp, Joan Baez and Bruce Springsteen.

Big 10 Ballroom

During the era of racial segregation, this former nightclub in north Tulsa was the place to go to see and hear nationally known jazz, soul, and rhythm and blues artists.

The Big 10 Ballroom is located about three blocks east of the intersection of North Peoria Avenue and East Apache Street and three blocks north of Booker T. Washington High School. It opened in 1948 and was built with the original art deco streamlined style. Lonnie Williams, who was one of Tulsa's first African American police officers, owned the building and his wife, Bessie Mae "Boots" Williams, cooked meals for the acts that played there.

The list of musicians who performed there reads like a Who's Who in music history: Count Basie, Ray Charles, Etta James, Fats Domino, B.B. King, Sam and Dave, The Coasters, Jackie Wilson, the original

Temptations, Hank Ballard and the Midnighters, Ella Fitzgerald, Little Richard and James Brown.

Tulsa Sound icons Leon Russell and JJ Cale frequently spoke fondly of visiting the Big 10 Ballroom and how those touring performers influenced their music careers. Even though a rope down the middle aisle separated black people from white people, they said the music is what mattered the most.

After decades of neglect along with being a warehouse for a Tulsa-based beauty supply company plus occupation by homeless people, a local non-profit organization called A Pocket Full of Hope restored the building to provide a place for Tulsa youth interested in the fine arts and performing arts. It has also been used for town hall meetings led by local and national political figures and motivational speakers.

The building's current owners, Lester "Doc" Shaw and his wife, Brenda, were featured on the 2023 HGTV series "Build It Forward" where the network teamed with Lowe's Home Improvement Centers to revitalize and rebuild important facilities in local communities.

Their work led to the opening of "The Little Big 10 Ballroom" which is a smaller performance venue within the main building and features state-of-the-art lighting and sound equipment.

Cimarron Ballroom

From 1950 until the early 1970s, this former movie theater at the corner of West Fourth Street and South Denver Avenue in downtown Tulsa was one of Tulsa's premier venues for concerts and sporting events and dances in addition to having KRMG-AM Radio as a first-floor tenant.

During the Cimarron Ballroom's heyday, it was the musical base for former Bob Wills steel guitarist Leon McAuliffe and his band, The Cimarron Boys. That band primarily played Western Swing music but also dabbled in Big Band and jazz-influenced numbers during concerts on Wednesday and Saturday evenings.

The Cimarron Ballroom also hosted performances by Big Band legends Stan Kenton and Tommy Dorsey, country music stars Jim Reeves, Carl Perkins and Johnny Cash along with social parties, professional wrestling matches and large-scale banquets.

The structure was built during the 1920s for the Tulsa chapter of the Akdar Shrine Temple. The exterior featured tall towers plus an orange and blue façade. The interior held a lavish opera house that seated 1,800 people.

The grand opening on February 1, 1925 was highlighted by a showing of the Flo Ziegfeld musical comedy, *Sally*. The building also housed the Tulsa Civic Orchestra, which later became the Tulsa Philharmonic, starting in 1927.

The Tulsa Shrine vacated the building after declaring bankruptcy during the Great Depression of the 1930s. For a short time during World War II, it was used as Tulsa's induction center for men enlisted to serve in the United States Army.

McAuliffe later rebranded the building as the Cimarron Ballroom and turned it into a dance hall by leveling the floor and, thusly, eliminating the sloped aisles and cementing over the orchestra pit.

County music icon Patsy Cline performed a historic concert at the Cimarron Ballroom on July 27, 1961. It was Cline's first appearance after nearly being killed six weeks earlier in a head-on auto collision in the Nashville suburb of Madison, Tennessee.

Despite dealing with numerous facial cuts, using crutches for a dislocated hip, having to sit on a stool instead of standing at a microphone and running out of breath many times while singing, the sellout crowd of 2,200 people was delighted by Cline's performance.

The recording of that concert turned into the 1997 album *Patsy Cline: Live at the Cimarron Ballroom* and it peaked at number 32 on the *Billboard* Country Music chart.

Cline frequently used local musicians for her backup bands so that night, McAuliffe and his group gladly worked with her. One of McAuliffe's sound engineers recorded the concert and gave the tape to Cline and her husband, Charlie Dick, who took it home and did nothing with it for years.

MCA Records, which owns the Decca Records label used by Cline, eventually acquired that tape and released the commemorative album in 1997.

Interestingly, the album contained three songs that Cline never recorded in a studio: rock and roll classics "Shake, Rattle and Roll" and "Stupid Cupid" plus the big band standard "When My Dreamboat Comes Home."

Tulsa's municipal government eventually acquired the Cimarron Ballroom as part of a massive land grab during an urban renewal program meant to revive the downtown sector through new buildings and businesses.

After being demolished in 1973 and becoming a parking lot, that property has been the site of the Metropolitan Tulsa Transit Authority's central bus station since 1996.

Chapter Eighteen

Musical Events

"Instinct taught me 20 years ago to pace a song or a concert performance. That translates into pacing a story, pleasing a reading audience."

Jimmy Buffett

"A concert is always like a feast day to me."

James Taylor

"I daresay that one good concert justifies a week of satisfaction at home."

Robert Plant

"Live music is the most primal form of energy release you can share with other people besides having sex or taking drugs."

Kurt Cobain

"Live music is proof that there's some things the Internet can't kill. In our lifetime, we're going to see more and more things start to disappear and get gobbled up by the Internet, but live music won't be one of them."

Jon Batiste

***

Bob Wills Birthday Bash

This annual salute to the life and musical legacy of the Western Swing icon is held in March at Cain's Ballroom, where Wills and his band, The Texas Playboys, performed for many years.

Various local, regional and national Western Swing bands are part of the celebration, performing their versions of Wills' biggest hits. There are also special appearances by relatives of Wills or solo artists who have connections to that musical genre.

Carney Fest

A one-day street festival held in mid-April and surrounding the Church Studio made famous by Leon Russell, this family-oriented music festival features an old-school carnival vibe complete with stilt walkers, jugglers and unicyclists.

And in keeping with Russell's focus, music is the highlight of the activities. Numerous local musicians, some of whom worked with Russell in his heyday, are featured performers along with nationally known singers and bands.

The event is named after Russell's popular 1972 album *Carney;* a project that featured elements of vaudeville and a street festival blended with roots rock and psychedelic music. Two of Russell's signature songs appeared on that album. "Tight Rope" was a jaunty circus-like opening cut on the first side and the ballad "This Masquerade" was the fifth cut on the second side.

The Reverend Horton Heat, a psychobilly rock band, was the featured performer at the inaugural Carney Fest in 2003. Mike Campbell, former lead guitarist with Tom Petty and the Heartbreakers was the

2024 featured performer. The first contract signed by Petty's band was with Russell's Shelter Records and the ceremony happened at a diner across the street from the Church Studio.

A portion of the festival's proceeds goes towards the Church Studio Music Foundation, a public charity that offers recording scholarships to qualifying Tulsa-area musicians and provides educational programming for students and music teachers.

Juneteenth Festivals

Juneteenth is a series of events commemorating the formal ending of slavery in the United States. The Tulsa observance is a nearly week-long series of concerts, educational programs, artistic exhibits and charitable activities.

While Abraham Lincoln's Emancipation Proclamation in 1863 freed most of the slaves in the United States, Juneteenth relates to the state of Texas abolishing slavery on June 19, 1865. That was a pivotal event leading to the 13th Amendment to the United States Constitution being ratified that December and slavery becoming illegal in the United States and all its territories.

Mayfest

Formally known as the Tulsa International Mayfest, this four-day celebration of music, art and food in downtown Tulsa has become Oklahoma's largest fine arts festival. Outdoor activities at the free admission event feature four performing arts stages, an interactive children's exhibit, numerous outdoor booths displaying handmade arts and crafts, three indoor art galleries and a wide variety of festival-style food.

Starting in 2015, Tulsa Opera partnered with Mayfest organizers to enhance the performing arts section of the festival and kicked off their commitment with an operatic presentation on a Saturday morning.

Numerous local organizations provide in-kind gifts and cash donations to help defray the festival's expenses. Hundreds of Tulsa-area residents also volunteer their time to assist in the event's various operations.

The 2014 Mayfest drew over 350,000 people and won national honors from the International Festivals and Events Association (IFEA) for its overall operation and professional excellence. Mayfest beat out similar events in cities such as Seattle, Washington; Philadelphia, Pennsylvania; Denver, Colorado; Kansas City, Missouri; and other venues in southern California and in Canada.

The original festival was held in 1973 at the new Civic Center Plaza and staged by the Junior League of Tulsa as a gift to the city. Since it coincided with three major anniversaries (the 75th for the city of Tulsa, the 50th for the Junior League of Tulsa and the 25th for the Tulsa Philharmonic Society) the festival was christened as Jubilee '73.

The featured event was held at the Civic Assembly Center. Singer-actor Sammy Davis Jr. performed his first Tulsa concert alongside conductor Skitch Henderson and the Tulsa Philharmonic Orchestra. After performing his best-selling songs such as "What Kind of Fool Am I?" and "Candy Man" and a stirring rendition of "The Impossible Dream," Davis drew a standing ovation from an estimated crowd of 5,000 people.

The festival's production was turned over to the Arts and Humanities Council of Tulsa and Downtown Tulsa Unlimited the following year, then rebranded in 1978 as Mayfest. Thanks to part of Main Street being converted into a pedestrian mall and the opening of the Williams Center Green, additional space became available for artistic displays and concert stages. The importance of the artistic displays was enhanced with the addition of a jury system.

Mayfest later made changes to its length, location and presenting organization. It expanded to a 10-day festival in 1992 before reverting to its current format.

Organizers moved the event from the Main Mall to the Tulsa Arts District in 1991 hoping to draw more people. It returned to the Main Mall from 1993 through 2018 and has been held in the Tulsa Arts District in 2019.

When DTU ceased operation in 2009, it became an independent festival staged in cooperation with the Arts and Humanities Council of Tulsa.

Mayfest added international music acts to its menu starting in 1980. While that once lured stars as The Mamas and The Papas, Joan Jett, Leon Russell and others, Mayfest has always featured Tulsa-area entertainers and 1992 was no exception.

Taylor, Isaac and Zac Hanson were three homeschooled brothers making their debut at that Mayfest as the vocal group Hanson. Their *a capella* versions of rock-and-roll classics such as "Rockin' Robin," "Splish Splash" and "Johnny B. Goode" drew larger and larger crowds as word of their talent spread. Hanson later became international superstars, and the trio is still a contributor to the independent pop music industry.

And like many similar festivals, Mayfest is no stranger to wild weather or to controversy. Heavy rainstorms and accompanying high winds have wreaked havoc with attendance and exhibits on 10 occasions.

Allegations of a business monopoly by a Mayfest director on behalf of a beer distributor once resulted in court hearings. Borderline risqué artwork on promotional posters along with a seminude sculpture of Statue of Liberty with a provocative title and gesture once drew the wrath of local citizens.

The Hardesty Arts Center operated Mayfest starting in 2020. But when that organization ran into major financial problems in November of 2022 and the event's future was hanging by a thread, the University of Tulsa and the Oklahoma Center for the Humanities purchased Mayfest and provided enhanced financing and operational support. All of that came just in time for Mayfest to celebrate its 50th anniversary.

Rocklahoma

Tulsa's Hard Rock Casino is the headquarters for Rocklahoma, a three-day camping and outdoor hard rock music festival held on the Friday, Saturday and Sunday of the Memorial Day weekend near the city of Pryor which is approximately 35 miles east-northeast of Tulsa.

Rocklahoma's debut in 2007 drew just over 30,000 people per day and its popularity has increased every year through positive word of mouth among fans of heavy metal, alternative metal and hard rock music.

Featured acts perform nightly on a main stage while regional and local acts perform throughout the day and night on three nearby stages.

Among the hard/metal rock superstars that have performed at Rocklahoma are Guns N' Roses, Kid Rock, Motley Crue, Megadeth, Creed, Rob Zombie, Korn, Alice in Chains, Skid Row, Twisted Sister, Poison, Ratt, Faster Pussycat, Lita Ford, Quiet Riot, Warrant, Triumph, Bret Michaels, Sebastian Bach, Anthrax, ZZ Top, Theory of a Deadman, Tesla, Queensryche, Godsmack, Scorpions, Disturbed, 3 Doors Down, Five Finger Death Punch and Chevelle.

Chapter Nineteen

Tulsa's Largest Concerts

"*It was like being in the eye of a hurricane. You'd wake up in a concert and think 'Wow! How did I get here?'*"

John Lennon

"*A concert is not a live rendition of our album. It's a theatrical event.*"

Freddie Mercury

"*I've been told by a lot of people after concerts that they felt the show was just for them. And I try to make it that way.*"

Barbara Mandrell

"*I say what's in my heart and I do it in my concerts.*"

Rita Coolidge

"*A live concert to me is exciting because of all of the electricity that is generated in the crowd and on stage. It's my favorite part of the business...*"

Elvis Presley

***

Largest One-Night Concerts:

Willie Nelson at Tulsa Fairgrounds Speedway, July 3, 1977

Willie Nelson's Fourth of July Picnic is an all-day outdoor concert featuring musical acts from various genres. In previous interviews, Nelson said his Fourth of July Picnic was inspired by the historic 1969 Woodstock rock concert and his passion for using music to bring people together.

But after more than 100 arrests at Nelson's 1976 concert in Gonzales, Texas, promoters moved it to Tulsa's Fairgrounds Speedway (now known as the Fair Meadows Horse Racing Track) for the 1977 performance. Tulsa's concert promoters anticipated a crowd of 15,000 people but were caught off guard when an estimated 60,000 people showed up. Sightseers created massive traffic jams on all roads leading to the Tulsa State Fairgrounds (now known as Expo Square).

Concession stands kept running out of beer, food, ice and water and when the afternoon temperature soared to 102 degrees, things became even more challenging. Nevertheless, the crowd was enthusiastic, and the rowdiness factor was almost non-existent. A highlight was Tulsa music legend Leon Russell joining Nelson near the end of the concert for a rendition of the gospel music classic "Amazing Grace" that had everyone in attendance singing along.

In addition to Nelson and Russell, other featured acts were outlaw country superstars Waylon Jennings and Jessi Colter, western swing band Asleep at the Wheel and the southern rock band Lynard Skynard.

Peter Frampton at Tulsa Fairgrounds Speedway, July 25, 1976

Peter Frampton was riding a tidal wave of success created by his double live album *Frampton Comes Alive!* when he drew an estimated crowd of 35,000 people to the Tulsa Fairgrounds Speedway.

Other performers at that concert were Carlos Santana ("Evil Ways" and "Black Magic Woman") and Gary Wright ("Dream Weaver").

Frampton Comes Alive! was the best-selling album of 1976, according to *Billboard* magazine. It spent eight weeks as the top-selling album in the United States, produced three singles that reached the Top 15 in music surveys, sold over eight million copies and was ranked 41st by *Rolling Stone* magazine on its list of all-time greatest live music albums.

Unbeknownst to Frampton and everyone at that concert, it would play a pivotal role in Tulsa's music history.

Larry Shaeffer was the promoter for that concert and was interested in reviving Cain's Ballroom in downtown Tulsa. Shaeffer took the concert's proceeds and a loan from his father to pay $60,000 and purchased Cain's Ballroom. Shaeffer and his music promotion business, Little Wing Productions, owned Cain's until 1993.

New Kids on the Block at Skelly Stadium, August 28, 1990

The boy band from Boston drew just over 30,000 fans to Skelly Stadium (now H.A. Chapman Stadium) on the University of Tulsa campus.

They became the idols of young women for their hunky looks, precise harmony and in-concert choreography. One of the featured singers was Donnie Wahlberg, who following a brief career with another band, branched out into dramatic acting and producing a TV crime series.

During their popularity in the late 1980s and early 1990s, NKOTB was accused of lip-synching nearly all of their songs during live concerts. As part of the *Tulsa World's* review of their Skelly Stadium concert, one of the band's stagehands confirmed to the reporter that all of the songs that night were indeed lip-synched.

Edgefest '97 at Mohawk Park, September 7, 1997

Nearly 30,000 spectators came to the spacious park in far northeastern Tulsa for an annual concert sponsored by KMYZ-FM, Tulsa's alternative rock radio station.

Featured performers at that event included rap rock legends Limp Bizkit and powerful lead singer Fred Durst; Sugar Ray, which was transitioning from nu metal to power pop with lead singer Mark McGrath, Smashmouth, whose single "All Star" would be featured in the first *Shrek* movie and metal legends Faith No More.

Diversafest 2008 in Downtown Tulsa's Blue Dome District, July 26, 2008

Known as Dfest for short and Oklahoma's Music Conference and Festival legally, this event ran from 2002 through 2009 as an annual event showcasing independent and emerging artists as well as hosting a musical trade show and music industry discussion panels.

This night drew the event's largest attendance (estimated 30,000) for performances at multiple open-air stages in the Blue Dome District, located on streets of the northeastern section of downtown Tulsa. spectators came to the spacious park in far northeastern Tulsa.

Headline performers that night were the rock bands All-American Rejects and Paramore, the hip-hop band (and future *Tonight Show with Jimmy Fallon* house band) The Roots and Zappa Plays Zappa, led by Frank Zappa's son, Dweezil Zappa.

Alice Cooper, Motley Crue and Def Leppard at Chapman Stadium, August 16, 2023

This trio of metal rock favorites, two of which are in the Rock and Roll Hall of Fame, drew just over 25,000 fans to the University of Tulsa football stadium.

It was the first concert at that venue in 33 years and the school's leadership announced plans for additional concerts in the near future. The stage was located in the northern section of the stadium and the artificial turf playing surface was covered by a heavy plastic material to prevent damage.

Concert goers got a major break in terms of August heat. One year earlier, Tulsa's high temperature was 105 degrees. It was 87 degrees when the concert began at 5:45 p.m. and 77 degrees five hours later.

The 75-year-old Cooper (real name Vince Furnier) opened the show with a vintage blend of current songs and biggest hits. All of them were enhanced by props from the shock rock era that made Alice Cooper the object of adoration by fans and the object of scorn by older adults.

Motley Crue featured two metal rock icons: bassist and band co-founder Nikki Sixx and legendary drummer Tommy Lee. Renowned for their elaborate equipment and naughty behavior, the band displayed plenty of both that night. There was an abundance of pyrotechnics and Lee repeatedly urged women in the crowd to flash their breasts.

Def Leppard was among Britain's top heavy metal bands during the 1980s. Lead singer Joe Elliott that night displayed a powerful and passionate singing style that hasn't changed since the band's breakout days of the infancy of the MTV Network.

Edgefest '99 at Mohawk Park, August 28, 1999

An estimated 20,000 spectators attended what would be one of the last concerts in the Edgefest series.

Headline performers included the heavy metal band Slipknot, industrial metal music pioneers Ministry and Kid Rock, the rap rocker who later achieved greater success as a country rock singer.

***

Largest Multiple-Night Concerts:

Garth Brooks at BOK Center, January, 2015 (seven total concerts)

Country music superstar Garth Brooks drew 137,120 people to the BOK Center in January of 2015, selling out all seven of his performances and setting Tulsa's all-time record for multiple concerts by a single musical performer. That broke Tulsa's record for multiple-night concert attendance that he set 18 years earlier at the former home of the Tulsa Drillers baseball team.

Garth Brooks at Drillers Stadium, July 17-21, 1997 (five total concerts)

A total of 80,782 tickets were sold for the five concerts by Brooks at the Expo Square stadium that had a seating capacity of 10,809 for baseball games.

Even a particularly severe pre-concert thunderstorm and related tornado watch couldn't keep fans from turning out in droves and having a good time.

The Drillers Stadium concerts were held three weeks prior to one of the highlights of Brooks' career: a concert in New York City's Central Park that was televised worldwide.

Additional multiple concerts by rock and pop music acts have drawn over 25,000 fans.

Diversafest (Dfest) at Downtown Tulsa Blue Dome District, 2007 through 2009 (two nights of concerts)

Known as Dfest for short, the two-night event featured independent and up-and-coming musical acts as well as hosting educational music industry panels along with a music-related trade show.

The event was the brainchild of Tom Green and his wife Angie Devore-Green. Tom's career in Tulsa music started out as the drummer for an electrorock band called Ultrafix while Angie was the band's lead singer.

About 10 years later, Tom traded his dreadlocks for a spiffy haircut and his dungarees for a suit and tie and the couple quickly became movers and shakers in the independent music scene.

Dfest grew from a total attendance of 150 people in 2002 at a street corner in the southern part of downtown Tulsa into one of the largest music events in the midwestern United States. Financial and other issues led to the event's cancellation in 2010.

Nevertheless, the final three Dfest events drew some of the largest concert crowds in Tulsa history.

Over 70,000 spectators flocked to the multiple-stage event in 2009 to hear featured artists The Black Crowes, Gogol Bordello, Citizen Cope and Dengue Fever.

Just over 60,000 fans came in 2008 for featured artists The Roots, Zappa Plays Zappa, Clutch, Paramore and The All-American Rejects.

Tulsa Sound icon Leon Russell was the featured performer for the 2007 concerts that drew nearly 40,000 fans. Other headlining acts were The Flaming Lips, Shiny Toy Guns, Amos Lee and Tulsa native John Moreland.

Zach Bryan at BOK Center, August 11 and 12, 2023 (two total concerts)

One of the fastest-rising stars in country music during the 2020s, the Oologah native had a musical homecoming that drew 37,000 people during two very hot summer nights.

Bryan made BOK Center history by drawing over 37,000 people for his two concerts; breaking the record set in 2018 by George Strait. Bryan then proceeded to break two other arena records.

The first record was the highest-grossing total food and beverage sales for a single event. On August 11th, Bryan broke the record set in 2022 by country singer Eric Church then proceeded to break his own record the following night.

Then Bryan set a record for the highest-grossing single night of merchandise sales by any artist or event. Bryan broke a record set in 2019 by the iconic metal rock band Metallica then broke his own record the following night.

George Strait at BOK Center, June 1 and 2, 2018 (two total concerts)

The leader of country music's "New Traditionalist" movement since the 1980s drew nearly 36,000 people for two concerts at the BOK Center.

In a nod to Tulsa's history, the concerts were rebranded as the "Strait Down Route 66 Tour."

Strait announced in 2014 that he was retiring from touring the world for concerts, but he chose to make Tulsa one of just eight stops on a schedule that year.

During the concerts that featured more than 30 songs each night, Strait saluted the city and Western Swing icon Bob Wills by singing "Take Me Back to Tulsa."

Paul McCartney at BOK Center, May 29 and 30, 2013 (two total concerts)

One of the most famous members of The Beatles and a legendary singer-composer in his own right, Sir Paul McCartney drew 26,827 people to the BOK Center for concerts on May 29th and 30th of 2013 as part of the arena's fifth anniversary activities.

Through both concerts, McCartney weaved back and forth through songs from his time with the Beatles and then with Wings and his lengthy solo career.

McCartney told the opening night crowd of times when he and his wife, Nancy, journeyed down Route 66 throughout Oklahoma in a well-worn 1980s style Ford Bronco.

Four downtown streets surrounding the BOK Center were temporarily renamed during McCartney's two concerts. South Denver Avenue became "Penny Lane" and West Third Street was "Abbey Road." West First Street became "Blackbird Crossing" while South Frisco Avenue was rebranded as "All Together Crossing."

McCartney had performed a one-night show at the BOK Center in 2009 as part of the arena's first anniversary concert series.

Chapter Twenty

That Happened in Tulsa?

"*I think it's great when stories are dark and strange and weirdly personal.*"

Robin Williams

"*Only two things are infinite; the universe and human stupidity, and I'm not sure about the former.*"

Albert Einstein

"*If stupidity got us into this mess, then why can't it get us out?*"

Will Rogers

"*These stories of people with unusual powers and unusual appearances, who do unusual things, people are always fascinated by them.*"

Stan Lee

"*I never set out to be weird. It was always other people who called me weird.*"

Frank Zappa

***

The Sex Pistols and a Tulsa...drywall

Cain's Ballroom still proudly displays the hole in the wall punched by the fist of the English punk rock group's bass guitar player Sid Vicious (Simon Ritchie) after their January 11, 1978 Tulsa concert.

Band members had endured internal fistfights, emergency hospitalizations and brushes with local police prior to their Tulsa concert. A crowd estimated at 800 people (about half of the venue's capacity) was on hand when the set began. Newspaper stories indicated that number dwindled rapidly after the first few songs.

In a fit of anger after the show ended, Vicious punched a hole the wall of the venue's Green Room and left an autographed 8-by-10 picture. Three days later in San Francisco, the Sex Pistols performed their final concert.

Today, there's a large frame and plaque surrounding the area where Vicious left his mark. Pictures of musicians from other music genres who have performed at Cain's surround that frame.

Ray Charles' band and a Tulsa...restaurant

The R&B legend was riding the crest of success when he performed on August 29, 1962 at the University of Tulsa's Skelly Stadium (now Chapman Stadium). After the concert, however, his band was denied food service at a local restaurant due to the color of their skin.

The concert raised money for the Hurricane Club, the booster organization for the school's football team. Of particular interest was the fact that TU didn't have black football players until 1964.

Just a few months earlier, Charles released what would become one of his iconic albums: *Modern Sounds in Country and Western Music, Volume One.*

A limousine took Charles directly to Tulsa Municipal Airport for a private jet flight to New York City. The band and singers went separately on a bus provided by the University of Tulsa but stopped at The Pines Drive-In, located a mile south of the airport, hoping for a bite to eat.

When the band members entered, the restaurant's white manager ordered them to leave after declaring that black people weren't allowed to eat there. After he called for the police to help him out, several white customers left to show their displeasure with the owner's action.

A few of the band's members then walked across the street to a convenience store to buy cold cuts to hold them over until stopping in Kansas City.

The Eagles and a Tulsa...air conditioning system

The legendary band's performance at the BOK Center's inaugural concert on September 6, 2008 was memorable...in more ways than one.

The band reportedly required the air conditioning at all venues to be turned off 24 hours prior to their first song, claiming starting out in a slightly warm room is helpful to the vocal cords of the singers.

Much to the delight of the 14,000 people in attendance (as well as to the Eagles themselves), the cooler air came on just as the first song ended...and as requested.

The Eagles returned to the BOK Center in February of 2024 as part of their farewell concert tour, known as The Long Goodbye Tour. And the air conditioning was on throughout the concert.

Garth Brooks and a Tulsa...911 emergency response system

Brooks performed five concerts at Drillers Stadium at Tulsa's Expo Square on July 17-21, 1997 and 75,000 total tickets would be available. But back then, the tickets were sold by telephone instead of online. As expected, the number of callers was extremely heavy.

Unfortunately, the heavy call volume knocked Tulsa's 911 telephone system out of operation. During that outage, one Tulsa woman died of a heart attack because her husband was not able to reach 911 operators to summon an ambulance or paramedics.

Faron Young and a Tulsa...dressing room

The smooth-singing country music star with a salty personality was accused of felony indecent exposure at a New Year's Eve concert at the National Guard Armory at Tulsa's Expo Square.

Sharon Stewart, a secretary to the concert's promoter, claimed Young exposed himself to her in the venue's dressing room. But another woman, Mary Ellen Hardwick, said she was present with Stewart and Young at all time and said that Young never exposed himself.

Legal proceedings dragged on for two years because Tennessee Governor Ray Blanton repeatedly refused requests to extradite Young to Oklahoma. The case was dropped in 1976.

Eric Clapton and a Tulsa...airport

The rock guitar icon flew to Tulsa for a 1975 surprise appearance at Cain's Ballroom. But events leading up to that appearance resulted in a trip to the drunk tank of the Tulsa city jail.

Clapton drank far too much alcohol on his commercial flight from Miami to Tulsa. After causing a ruckus on the plane and later throwing his luggage from the second-floor baggage claim to the ticketing area, police arrested him for public intoxication.

John Southern was a *Tulsa World* photographer and avid Clapton fan who heard on the police radio about Clapton's impending jail booking. Southern got into a prime position and snapped a picture of Clapton behind the metal jail bars with a policeman's hand on his right shoulder. That picture would draw international attention the next day.

Clapton paid a $25.00 fine and was released to perform later at Cain's without incident.

Lana Del Rey and a Tulsa...billboard

The pop singer-songwriter born released an album on December 7, 2022 entitled *Did You Know That There's a Tunnel Under Ocean Blvd?* It earned 2023 Grammy Award nominations for Album of the Year and Best Alternative Music Album.

But the only billboard promoting that album anywhere in the United States appeared near one of Tulsa's busiest intersections. And the equally unusual backstory has Tulsa connections.

Del Rey (born Elizabeth Woolridge Grant) dated former Tulsa Police Department Lieutenant Dennis "Sticks" Larkin from September 2019 through March 2020.

She announced the new album and released the first single December 7, 2022. The billboard was located near the intersection of the Broken Arrow Expressway and the South Mingo Road exit; one of Tulsa's busiest rush-hour intersections.

Del Rey added a cryptic Instagram post regarding the billboard, saying: "There's only one and it's in Tulsa. It's personal."

That catch? December 7th is Larkin's birthday.

Larkin spent 25 years with the Tulsa PD before retiring in 2021 then hosted a couple of crime-related reality TV shows. He married Tulsa businesswoman Carey Cadieux in 2022.

...Ocean Blvd didn't win a Grammy.

Frank Sinatra and a Tulsa...cigarette and cocktail

The iconic vocalist delighted the near-capacity crowd at the Mabee Center on the Oral Roberts University campus in March of 1994. But Ol' Blue Eyes committed two major no-nos that would have resulted in the school's students or faculty being kicked off campus for good.

The 13th song in his 16-song set was the Johnny Mercer classic "One for My Baby (And One More for the Road)" Of course, the 78-year-old crooner lit up the requisite cigarette and sipped his cocktail before, during and after the song.

That Tulsa concert was his first after collapsing onstage a couple of weeks earlier in Richmond, Virginia.

Despite his age and signs of physical frailty, there were countless moments when Sinatra's voice sounded as powerful as it did 30 years ago or more.

Peter, Paul and Mary and a Tulsa...gun dealer

Tensions were high throughout the United States as well as in Tulsa following the March 1965 civil rights march in Selma, Alabama where 600 unarmed protestors seeking equal voting rights were assaulted by law enforcement personnel. Pictures of bloodied victims drew outrage throughout the nation.

The legendary folk music trio was performing at the Tulsa Assembly Center shortly after that incident. Their concert was briefly stopped when a sulfur bomb was thrown into the arena's air conditioning system.

The next day, the trio visited a sporting goods in the southern part of Tulsa's affluent Brookside district and Peter Yarrow purchased a pistol for the group's protection. Back then, groups like their didn't have much in the ways of security or an entourage.

Ironically, the man selling the pistol to Yarrow was the father of Tulsa entertainment promoter Jon Terry.

38 Special and a Tulsa...onstage toast

Donnie Van Zant, the southern rock band's co-lead singer, was arrested for violating Tulsa's liquor-by-the-drink laws during a June 16, 1982 concert at the Maxwell Convention Center.

During each concert, Van Zant traditionally raised and sipped from an opened bottle of whiskey as a toast to the local crowd. Back then, Tulsa was a "dry" county so any type of consumption of alcohol in public violated the city's liquor ordinances and could result in jail time and/or fines.

Tulsa police arrested Van Zant after the concert then the other co-lead singer, Don Barnes, got into a heated argument with the cops. Barnes then came up with an idea to create publicity about the event, claiming that he and Van Zant had long hair but if Jackie Gleason or Frank Sinatra did the same things, neither Gleason nor Sinatra would have been arrested.

After a brief time in jail, Van Zant's charges were dismissed. The band returned to Tulsa for concerts in subsequent years.

Travis Scott and a Tulsa...concert setup

The last-minute postponement of the rapper's sold-out February 11, 2019 concert at the BOK Center resulted in s standoff between unruly fans and police officers.

About 90 minutes before the show was to begin, Scott posted a social media message stating that the show would be rescheduled due to technical difficulties involving a roller coaster that was one of the show's major props.

Some frustrated fans rushed the glass doors at the BOK Center, throwing metal guard rails and other items. A few angered ticket holders managed to get inside but Tulsa police repelled the intruders with pepper balls.

No injuries were reported, the concert was rescheduled for a later date and the subsequent appearance went off without a hitch.

Vinnie Dombroski and a Tulsa...sound system

The lead singer of the Detroit rock band Sponge didn't let a little thing like a sound system stand in the way of racking up $5,500 worth of fines when the band performed as part of a package show at the River Parks Amphitheater on July 6, 1997.

During the amphitheater's 30-year existence, members of the River Parks Authority warned every singer and band that using obscene language over its sound system violated a city ordinance and each word, F-bomb or otherwise, resulted in a $500.00 fine.

The other acts that night, The Reverend Horton Heat, Sevendust and the Bloodhound Gang were warned as was Dombroski and Sponge members.

Dombroski proceeded to drop 11 F-bombs on the audience of 5,000 people and was arrested after leaving the stage. The band's manager offered to pay the fines but the charges were quickly dropped.

Jerry Lee Lewis and a Tulsa...donated piano

The rockabilly and country music legend's reputation for tearing up pianos preceded him to a record hop at Tulsa's now defunct Continental Roller Skating Rink. During his heyday, Lewis was known to frequently bang the piano keys with his fists or use his feet to play the keys or jump up and down on the piano case or the bench.

Dick Schmitz, former disc jockey at KAKC, said after a prominent Tulsa music store refused to rent him a piano for the Lewis concert, he turned to a friend who agreed to lend Schmitz a small blond piano. Schmitz took Lewis aside before the Tulsa concert, told him about the rental issues and politely asked him to not harm his friend's piano. Lewis promised to behave but Schmitz had ample reason for skepticism. Much to everyone's surprise, Lewis didn't pull any of his rough and rowdy antics, the concert was a rousing success, and the piano was returned intact to Schmitz's friend.

Henry Rollins and a Tulsa...wannabe pilot

Before becoming a successful comedian, actor and public speaker, Henry Rollins was the front for the California-based alternative metal band Black Flag from 1981 through 1986. His 1996 University of Tulsa appearance not only turned out to be a living nightmare but spawned one of his most successful comedy CDs.

Rollins called his manager after a commercial flight from St. Louis to Tulsa was cancelled and a charter plane would be sent to pick him up. He admittedly gets queasy anytime there's any type of turbulence on a plane flight. Things got very complicated and downright scary after that.

A young Tulsa-based aircraft mechanic and cover band musician named Eric was a long-time fan of Rollins and heard about the situation. Eric took it on himself to fly to St. Louis to handle the job. The problem was Eric was also an unlicensed pilot and never filed a flight plan with the Federal Aviation Administration.

Rollins in his monologues has referred to that small plane as a "one-propeller death machine" and a "go-cart with wings."

Strong headwinds and almost running out of fuel resulted in an emergency landing in the small town of Grove, Oklahoma, located 90 miles northeast of Tulsa. Rollins hitched a ride into Grove then called his manager from a nearby convenience store, hoping to get a car to take him to his performance at TU.

Clad in a black jacket and black fatigue pants, Rollins looked totally out of place in Grove. Then three police cars wheeled into the parking lot and Rollins was on the phone with his manager then was face-to-face with officers pointing a gun at him.

Turned out there had been a liquor store robbery in an adjacent county and police thought Rollins matched the suspect's description. When the liquor store's owner arrived and said Rollins didn't do it, he was finally able to get a ride to Tulsa much to the dismal of the local cops.

Those misadventures provided the material for the 1999 CD *Eric the Pilot* in which Rollins spent almost an hour recalling the events of that fateful night.

Enrico Caruso and a Tulsa...carriage ride

An urban legend states that the ghost of the internationally renowned opera star of the early 20th century haunts the Tulsa Theater, allegedly for contracting a fatal respiratory illness during a 1920 concert in Tulsa.

Caruso was curious to see the oil fields along the Arkansas River bank and a heavy rainstorm came up while he was out walking. He performed that night but came down with a serious respiratory illness a few weeks later.

Caruso's manager later blamed the Tulsa events for the singer's death and said he wouldn't be surprised if his spirit returned to the downtown Tulsa venue that led to his death. Paranormal researchers have claimed their audio equipment has picked up Electronic Voice Phenomena (EVP) of Caruso's voice at an otherwise deserted Tulsa Theater.

But one of his sons, Enrico Caruso Jr., wrote in a biography that the singer likely died from complications arising from an on-stage injury. While performing in the opera *Samson and Delilah*, a falling pillar struck Caruso over the left kidney and not on the chest as many have claimed. He passed away in Naples, Italy on August 2, 1921 at the age of 48 due to peritonitis (inflammation of the abdominal wall) arising from a subphrenic abscess (infected fluid between the diaphragm, liver and spleen).

Chapter Twenty-One

Music Radio Personalities

"*R*adio continues to be the very best advertising music perform-ers have. No one who ever grabbed a Grammy got there with-out radio."

Gordon Smith

"*A good radio show will captivate you, and it's active listening. It's not in the background.*"

Rush Limbaugh

"*Initially, I wanted to be on the radio, when I saw a radio broadcast done by Gary Moore and Jimmy Durante in an old theater in New York. I said, 'That is what I want.' I was 13. I got my first check in radio when I was 17 and I have been doing it ever since.*"

Dick Clark

"*If the beat gets to the audience and the message touches them, you've got a hit.*"

Casey Kasem

***

Frank Berry

Oklahoma's first black disc jockey profoundly influenced the founding fathers of the Tulsa Sound by playing rhythm and blues music four nights a week on his midnight to 6:00 a.m. radio show on KAKC-AM (970). Longtime Tulsa historians have often said that more than half of the show's listeners were white.

Berry never actually spun the records but worked as an announcer and salesman. He played gospel spirituals on Friday nights and worked for four other Tulsa area radio stations prior to his death in 1992 at the age of 83.

In a 2003 *Tulsa World* interview, Leon Russell said that he was 12 or 13 years old when he got hooked on Berry's show and his music selections.

"He played blues all night. It was an unusual show," Russell recalled. "Of course, in the South, there were a lot of stations that had that blues format but it was kind of a bonus in Tulsa."

Berry was a mild-mannered individual but his playing sometimes raunchy songs often outraged the parents of local teenagers. And as could be expected, those teenagers couldn't get enough of it. Local singer "Jumpin' Jackie" Dunham was one of them.

"Your parents didn't like for you to listen to Frank Berry because it was sex music, you know," Dunham told the *Tulsa World* in 2003, citing the controversial songs "Sexy Ways" and "Annie Had a Baby" by Hank Ballard and the Midnighters.

"All the people I ran around with listened to him, though, you had a radio hidden by your bed," Dunham added.

Danny Dark

Daniel Melville Croskery attended Tulsa's Central High School and used his work as a local disc jockey to build his career as one of the most sought after announcers for television commercials and network programming.

His family moved from Oklahoma City to Tulsa during his youth and he adopted the air name of Danny Dark while working at KOME-AM and KAKC-AM, two of Tulsa's pioneer rock radio stations. After leaving Tulsa he worked at stations in Cleveland, Miami, New Orleans and St. Louis before landing a job as a nighttime deejay at KLAC-AM in Los Angeles.

Some of the most recognizable lines from Dark's TV commercials were for Raid bug spray ("Raid...Kills...Bugs...Dead"), Budweiser beer ("This Bud's for You") and StarKist Tuna ("Sorry, Charlie.")

Other major clients that utilized Dark's distinctive voice in advertisements included Chevrolet, AT&T, K-Mart, Dreyer's ice cream, Keebler cookies, Armor-All authomotive products and Whitman's candy.

Many pop culture lovers remember Dark as the voice of Clark Kent/Superman for 12 years in the animated TV series *Super Friends*. He also did voice-over work for TV shows and documentaries shown on the History Channel.

Charlie Derek

Before starting his four-decade journey around the United States as a successful broadcaster, Charlie Derek spent the first 16 years of his four-decade broadcasting career in Tulsa, working for three rock stations (KAKC-AM, KELI-AM and KMOD-FM), a country station

(KVOO-AM) and a seven-year stint with Tulsa's top Adult Contemporary station (KRAV-FM).

After stops in Florida and the Dallas-Fort Worth Metroplex, Derek currently works as the morning drive personality on WRHM-FM (Interstate 107), a country music station in Rock Hill, South Carolina.

Rockin' John Henry

Billing himself as "Tulsa's Oldest Teenager," his Saturday Bandstand show aired for 25 years on Saturday mornings on four radio stations in Tulsa.

Saturday Bandstand carried the format that originated with Dick Clark's American Bandstand on ABC Television and featured rock and roll hits from popular artists of the 1950s and 1960s along with interviews with musicians from that era.

While Henry didn't care much for CDs, he had a personal collection of over 3,000 vinyl LP albums or 45 RPM or 78 RPM singles. He frequently shared with his listeners unique stories about the song or the performers. He grew up in Sapulpa, a southwestern Tulsa suburb, and frequently said that the first time he heard Buddy Holly singing, it was a turning point in his life.

Henry was an accomplished lead guitarist in his own right and was easily recognized by a thick mane of white hair, black sunglasses and booming voice while playing guitar with a flair and passion. He opened for or played alongside rock legends such as Del Shannon, Fabian, Ricky Nelson, Little Anthony and the Imperials and Gary U.S. Bonds.

Henry also fronted a local nostalgia act called The Bop Cats that performed for private parties and civic events in the Oklahoma-Kansas-Missouri area. Prior to his death in 2004, he was inducted into the Rockabilly Music Hall of Fame.

The spirit of Saturday Bandstand continues today, thanks to Tulsa-area disc jockey Gary Rofkahr on the "Hillcat Sock Hop" which is carried on KRSC-FM Radio (91.3) from 9:00 a.m. until 12 noon on Saturdays. The station is owned by Rogers State University in Claremore.

Rofkhar was admittedly an avid fan of Henry's radio show but his own show never sought to be a copycat of that particular program. Instead, Rofkhar frequently states that his mission is to "keep the roots of rock and roll alive for the next generation." He also makes a point to feature early-day songs by Tulsa Sound veterans such as Leon Russell or David Gates.

Going by "Rockin' Gary," his show blends the top 10 songs on the Billboard music chart for a specific week from the 1950s or 1960s. And one of the show's most popular features is something unheard of in modern radio but a staple of that industry in the 1950s and 1960s: calling the radio station and asking the DJ to play a song and dedicate the song to someone and then hearing that DJ saying it and playing it.

Johnny Martin

Dubbed by local listeners as the King of Tulsa's Late Night Radio, this smooth-talking aficionado of the Big Band era was heard on KRMG-AM from 1963 through 1978.

Martin's musical preferences were obvious: Frank Sinatra, Ella Fitzgerald, Count Basie, Jo Stafford, Johnny Ray or Tommy Dorsey. And he had unique nicknames for some of them. Sinatra was "the skinny kid from Hoboken" and Basie was "the kid from Red Bank, New Jersey." Marilyn Maye was the "big redhead from Kansas City" while Peggy Lee was "my favorite blond" and Stan Kenton and His Orchestra was "the big band from Balboa."

He worked in a darkened control room, a carryover from his pre-radio days working as a musician in local piano bar-style establishments.

His style of intimate conversation plus a knack for pace and timing created a mood of Martin and the listener being the only people in the room. And there was no place that Martin would rather be.

Martin's show ended in June of 1978 and he passed away in 1980 from complications related to emphysema and cancer.

Billy Parker

The anchor of Tulsa's country music radio scene since 1971 was a four-time honoree as the Country Music Disc Jockey of the Year. And his support for country music artists through the years drew praise from a member of country music royalty, Dolly Parton.

Parker's greatest radio fame came from his overnight "Big Rigger Show" on KVOO-AM (1170); a weeknight program geared towards truck drivers that aired from midnight until 5:00 a.m. Central time. Aided by the station's powerful 50,000-watt signal, Parker's show drew listeners from the Rio Grande River valley in southwest Texas to the Canadian Rocky Mountains and points beyond.

And after Parker literally saw the light by becoming the station's Program Director and moving to daytime shifts, his reputation continued to grow in the country music industry. And it didn't matter if the singer or band was a newcomer from the Carolinas or Texas or Ohio or California or if it was George Strait or Garth Brooks, every one of them got the same courtesy and friendship and fair shake from Parker when it came to getting a helping hand.

Parker won the Nashville-based Country Music Association (CMA) Disc Jockey of the Year award in 1977. Then he won the same award from the Los Angeles-based Academy of Country Music (ACM) in 1977, 1978 and 1984.

After beginning a singing career at the age of 14, Parker became the leader of the Texas Troubadours; the backup band for country music legend Ernest Tubb. Parker later left the touring life and returned to

Tulsa for family reasons and to revive a radio career that previously took him to Oklahoma City and Wichita, Kansas.

Parker recorded 20 songs that reached the *Billboard* Top 100 Country chart between 1976 and 1989. The highest-ranked song on that United States chart was "(Who's Gonna Sing) The Last Country Song?"; a 1982 duet with Texas honky-tonk legend Darrell McCall that peaked at number 41. His 1988 song "You Are My Angel" peaked at number 10 on the *Billboard* Canadian Top 100 Country chart. A 1990 album entitled Billy Parker and Friends featured duets with legendary singers such as Webb Pierce, Jack Greene, Cal Smith and Ernest Tubb.

In Parker's 2021 autobiography *Thanks-Thanks A Lot,* Parton wrote that "Billy Parker will always be one of the greats." Duane Allen, lead singer of the Oak Ridge Boys, said of Parker: "He helped break all of our songs and the Midwest followed."

Phil Stone and Brent Douglas

Over a 27-year span, these KMOD-FM co-hosts had the most listened-to morning show on any rock and roll station in Tulsa history.

Phil Stone (real name: Phillip Riddle) and Brent Douglas (real name: Brent Douglas) were a throwback to the heyday of comedians Bud Abbott and Lou Costello with Stone playing Abbott's straight man role with Douglas getting the laughs.

Their comedy never reached the obscene level or dove into the depths of personal humiliation and degradation that many current radio personalities try to pass off as being acceptable, much less humorous. With that said, Phil and Brent weren't the least bit shy about tiptoeing right up to a line that shouldn't be crossed and leaning over that line as far as possible.

Their partnership began during the 1980s when Douglas was working as a pharmacist for a national supermarket chain and frequently listened to Stone's show on KMOD-FM. Douglas periodically called in with comments and impromptu routines that left Stone laughing uncontrollably on the air. So Stone invited him to come to the studio and they began adlibbing between records and commercials and the rest became Tulsa radio history.

But their most popular routines involved Douglas portraying a rustic redneck named Roy D. Mercer. On Fridays, Stone called Mercer to get tips on where to go fishing that weekend. When Mercer wasn't cracking Stone up with his off-beat comments, he would be moaning and groaning about his personal life as well.

On Thursdays, Mercer played a practical joke on an unsuspecting person in a format straight from the 1960s TV show *Candid Camera*. Close friends of the soon-to-be victim would provide background information about that person's life or work. Then Mercer would call the victim at work with an unusual sounding complaint. Mercer would get the other person riled up and ready for a fight then the two would let the victim in on the joke, who set him up and a good laugh was had by all.

Those skits became so popular that 16 CDs were created and distributed by major recording companies such as Capitol Records and Virgin Records.

Their final show aired on October 27, 2012 as the station's management wanted to change direction and lure a younger listening audience.

Forty days later, Stone died at the age of 57 due to undetected heart problems. Douglas has since made occasional appearances in the Roy D. Mercer persona but has essentially retired from the radio industry.

Don Wallace

Prior to becoming a pioneer for outdoor TV sports programming, Don Wallace was the first disc jockey to play rock and roll music in

Tulsa. Wallace worked at KRMG, KTUL and KOME Radio in Tulsa but his career took off after following in the footsteps of New York City's rock and roll radio pioneer Alan Freed.

Sometimes he hosted as many as three different rock music programs each weekday and he became a hero to Tulsa-area teenagers. That popularity led Wallace to host teen dances at Tulsa's VFW Hall and many local musicians used those events to help build their careers. Among the aspiring local musicians at Wallace's dances were J.J. Cale and David Gates.

Wallace moved to Oklahoma City in 1958 and kept winning rave reviews as one of America's top radio personalities. But his love of outdoor sports in general and fishing in particular led to the creation of *The Wallace Wildlife Show*. That nationally-syndicated show lasted 23 years with Wallace, a self-taught photographer, handling nearly all of the duties related to video production as well as the advertising sales.

Dave Weston

This morning drive personality on KXOJ-FM (94.1) has been the guiding force for one of America's top-ranked Contemporary Christian Music radio stations.

A former Marine Corps sergeant and graduate of Wheaton College in Illinois, Weston worked briefly in Huntsville, Texas and Fayetteville, Arkansas before launching his lengthy radio career in Tulsa.

Weston also works as the program director for a soft rock station which is part of KXOJ-FM's ownership group and has done voiceover work for commercials, Christian-themed movies and served as the public address announcer for Oral Roberts University basketball games.

Epilogue

The legendary rhythm and blues singer Etta James once said, "I wanna show that gospel, country, blues, rhythm and blues, jazz, rock and roll are all just really one thing. Those are the American music and that is the American culture."

Those words from a member of the Rock and Roll and Blues Halls of Fame so aptly describe every facet of Tulsa's musical heritage; a heritage that is vibrant, exciting and growing even today.

And a 1956 performance by James at the Big 10 Ballroom in the predominantly black section of north Tulsa would also shape the future of another legendary figure in rock and roll.

One afternoon, a 13-year-old white girl found an unlocked staircase at the back of the Big 10 Ballroom. She walked right up those stairs into the building and proceeded to sit next to the stage where James was doing a sound check prior to that night's concert.

A surprised James told the alarmed nightclub staff that everything was okay then she took time out from her rehearsal to visit with that teenage girl about music.

The rawness and brassy attitude and the passion in James' singing style were things the teenager later said would be the most profound influences in her own career.

Fast forward to 1969. James was in a closed recording session, but she spotted a woman in a corner of the studio that wearing an unusual hat and a large puffy overcoat.

James asked another person who was that woman and why is she in this closed recording session. The other person whispered that woman's name to James and added that she is a big star.

When James overhead that woman talking to someone, she remembered that it was that 13-year-old girl she met in Tulsa back in 1956.

Who was that teenage admirer in Tulsa? Janis Joplin.

And as Sonny Bono once wrote, the beat goes on.

Selected Bibliography

T he author conducted extensive research through all of these sources in an attempt to ensure that the information contained in this book is as complete and accurate as possible.

The author assumes no responsibility for omissions, errors, inaccuracies or any other type of inconsistency. If there appears to be a slight against any individual or organization, it is completely unintentional.

Books

Clapton, Eric. *Clapton: The Autobiography.* 1st ed., Broadway Books, 2008,

Janovitz, Bill. *Leon Russell: The Master of Space and Time's Journey Through Rock & Roll History.* 2nd ed., Hachette Books. 2023.

Keys, Bobby and Ditenhafer, Bill. *Every Night's a Saturday Night: The Rock 'n' Roll Life of Legendary Sax Man Bobby Keys.* 2nd ed., Counterpoint Press, 2012.

Tichi, Cecilia. *Reading Country Music: Steel Guitars, Opry Stars and Honky-Tonk Bars.* 2nd ed., Duke University Press, 1998.

Wooley, John. *From the Blue Devils to Red Dirt: The Colors of Oklahoma Music.* 1st ed., HAWK Publishing Group. 2006.

Zane, Warren. *Petty: The Biography.* 1st ed., St. Martin's Publishing Group. 2015.

Internet Sites

A Pocket Full of Hope: apocketfullofhope.com

Alaska and Madi: www.alaskaandmadi.com

AllMusic: www.allmusic.com

AM Music: www.amsounds.com

American Songwriter: www.americansongwriter.com

Andres Franco: www.andres-franco.com

Association of Independent Music Producers: www.aimp.org

Binky Records: www.binkyrecords.com

Blue Dome District: www.bluedometulsa.com

Bob Wills and His Texas Playboys: www.texasplayboys.net

Brandon Jenkins: www.brandonjenkins.com

Carl Radle: www.carlradle.com

Carman Licciardello: www.carman.org

Center of the Universe Festival: www.centeroftheuniversefestival.com

Charlie Daniels Band: www.charliedaniels.com

Church Studio: www.thechurchstudio.com

Country Fan Cast: www.countryfancast.com

Country Music Hall of Fame: www.countrymusichalloffame.org

Country Now: www.countrynow.com

Daily Oklahoman: www.newsok.com

Dwight Twilley: www.dwighttwilley.com

Elvis Presley History Blog: www.elvis-history-blog.com

Emmy Awards: www.emmyawards.tv

Encyclopedia.com: www.encyclopedia.com

Encyclopedia of Arkansas History and Culture: www.encycloped iaofarkansas.net

Eric Clapton: www.ericclapton.com

Eric Cornell Productions: www.ericcornellproductions.com

Feenotes: www.feenotes.com

Forbes Magazine: www.forbes.com

Forgotten Artists: www.engine145.com.

Garden City Telegram: www.gctelegram.com

Genius Lyrics and Songs: www.genius.com

Google Books: https://books.google.com

Greater Tulsa Reporter: www.gtrnews.com

Guitar World: www.guitarworld.com

Huffington Post: www.huffingtonpost.com

John Wooley: www.johnwooley.com

Joplin Globe: www.joplinglobe.com

Kaitlin Butts: www.kaitlinbutts.com

Kim Manning: www.kimmanning.com

KOSU-FM: www.kosu.com

KXBL-FM: www.bigcountry995.com

Last.FM: www.last.fm

Leon Russell: www.leonrussellrecords.com

Los Angeles Times: www.latimes.com

Marcella Detroit: www.marcelladetroit.com

Modern Drummer: www.moderndrummer.com

Muscogee (Creek) Nation: www.muscogeenation-nsn.gov

Nashville Tennessean: www.tennessean.com

National Public Radio: www.npr.org

New York Times: www.nytimes.com

OKPop Museum: www.okpop.org

Oklahoma Center for Poets and Writers: www.poetsandwritears.okstate.edu

Oklahoma Historical Society: www.okhistory.org

Oklahoma Magazine: www.okmag.com

Oklahoma Press Association: www.okpress.com

Oklahoma Today Magazine: ww.oklahomatoday.com

Patsy Cline Tribute: www.patsyclinetribute.com

Phil Driscoll: www.phildriscoll.com

Rap Industry: www.rapindustry.com

Recording Industry Association of America: www.riaa.com

Red Dirt Rangers: www.reddirtrangers.com

Relix Magazine: www.relix.com

Rockabilly Hall of Fame: www.rockabillyhall.com

Rocklahoma: www.rocklahoma.com

Rolling Stone Magazine: www.rollingstone.com

Sarah Popejoy Jackson: www.sarahpopejoy.com

Spin Magazine: www.spin.com

Steve Pryor Band: www.stevepryorband.net

The Boot: www.theboot.com

The Church Studio: www.thechurchstudio.com

The Morning Call: www.mcall.com

Time Magazine: www.time.com

Tuck and Patti: www.tuckandpatti.com

Tulsa Historical Society: www.tulsahistory.org

Tulsa International Mayfest: www.tulsamayfest.org

Tulsa Oktoberfest: www.tulsaoktoberfest.org

Tulsa People Magazine: www.tulsapeople.com

Tulsa Preservation Commission: www.tulsapreservationcommission.org

Tulsa Signature Symphony: www.signaturesymphony.org

Tulsa Spotlight Theatre: www.spotlighttheatre.org

Tulsa State Fair: www.tulsastatefair.com

Tulsa TV Memories: www.tulsatvmemories.com

Tulsa Voice: www.tulsavoice.com

Tulsa World: www.tulsaworld.com

Union Public Schools: www.unionps.org

US News and World Report: www.usnews.com

USA Today: www.usatoday.com

Variety Magazine: www.variety.com

Voices of Oklahoma: www.voicesofoklahoma.com

Windy City Times: www.windycitytimes.com

Woody Guthrie Center: www.woodyguthriecenter.org.

Newspaper and Magazine Articles

Agha, Lama. "Okie Rapper Josh Sallee Reflects on Rocky Path to New Album." *Daily Oklahoman*. July 8, 2016. Accessed July 12, 2023. www.oklahoman.com.

Anicetti, Brittany. "Shout Out: International Spotlight." *Oklahoma Magazine*. May 2015. Accessed May 13, 2015. www.okmag.com.

Arnett, David. "Alsuma: The Town That Disappeared from Southeast Tulsa." *GTR Newspapers*, March 30, 2007. Accessed December 23, 2014. www.gtrnews.com.

Associated Press. "Grammy-Winning Trumpeter Phil Driscoll Convicted in Tax Case." *USA Today*, June 8, 2006. Accessed July 23, 2014. www.usatoday.com.

Barnard, Matt. "From Ruins to Tulsa Icon: The Story Behind the Famous Outsiders House" *Tulsa World*, April 17, 2022. Accessed July 27, 2023. www.tulsaworld.com.

Betts, Stephen L. "25 Things You May Not Know About County Icon Willie Nelson." *The Boot*, April 30, 2012. Accessed January 4, 2015. www.theboot.com.

Betts, Stephen L. "Legendary Fiddle Player Johnny Gimble Dead at 88." *Rolling Stone*, May 11, 2015. Accessed May 13, 2015. www.rollingstone.com.

Bienstock, Richard. "Freak Juice's Tori Ruffin Talks High-Profile Gigs with Prince and Morris Day and Backing Eddie Murphy in *Coming to America*." *Guitar World*, February 22, 2021. Accessed July 31, 2023. www.guitarworld.com.

Brewer, Graham Lee. "New Bob Wills Recording is Out on Vinyl." *Daily Oklahoman*, May 26, 2015. Accessed May 27, 2015. www.newsok.com.

Brown, Lane. "The Inquisition: Rufus Wainwright." *Spin Magazine*, June 20, 2007. Accessed June 2, 2014. www.spin.com.

Chancellor, Jennifer. "Rock Icon Paul McCartney Pulls Out All the Stops." *Tulsa World*, May 30, 2013. Accessed August 2, 2023. www.billboard.com.

Chancellor, Jennifer. "Rod Stewart Talks 'American Songbook Vol. V,' Songwriting" *Billboard*, October 2, 2010. Accessed December 30, 2016. www.billboard.com.

Chancellor, Jennifer. "Magic Maestros: A Couple Works All the Angles to Get State's Music in the Spotlight.'" *Tulsa World*, March 9, 2008. Accessed September 14, 2023. www.tulsaworld.com.

Chancellor, Jennifer. "Prodigal Son: Dave Terry Took Aqueduct to Seattle to Produce 'Quirk Pop.'" *Tulsa World*, October 5, 2007. Accessed February 23, 2019. www.tulsaworld.com.

Conner, Thomas. "N.O.T.A Back Pushing Punk.'" *Tulsa World*, September 27, 1996. Accessed February 13, 2019. www.tulsaworld.com.

Crutchmer, Josh. "Turnpike Troubadours Talk Anticipated New Comeback Album and Real Reason Behind the Breakup.'" *Rolling Stone,* May 3, 2023. Accessed June 4, 2023. www.rollingstone.com.

Donahue, Ann. "Bob Dylan Puts Philosophy to Music at BOK Center" *Tulsa World*, November 3, 2012. Accessed May 9, 2016. www.tulsaworld.com.

Dowling, Marcus K. "Kaitlin Butts' Authentic Country Stylings, Dramatic Flair, Offer Mainstream Stardom" *Nashville Tennessean*, April 9, 2023. Accessed September 21, 2023.. www.tennessean.com.

Elliott, Matt, "Underwood Brings It Home," *Tulsa World*, November 20, 2006. Accessed February 7, 2014. www.tulsaworld.com.

Fletcher, Lydia, "Historic Music Venue Revived by Tulsa Remodeler on HGTV's 'Build It Forward,'" *Tulsa World*, June 24, 2023. Accessed July 7, 2023. www.tulsaworld.com.

Foley, Hugh W. Jr.. *Oklahoma Music Guide: Biographics,* New Forums Press, Inc. 2013. Accessed January 26, 2019. www.books.google.com.

Freeman, Jon. "Kaitlin Butts' 'What Else Can She Do' Upends Nashville Expectations and Peers Into the Darkness.'" *Rolling Stone,* April 15, 2022. Accessed September 22, 2023. www.rollingstone.com.

Gammon, Josh. "Travis Scott Concert: Police Want to ID People Who Caused Damage at BOK Center.'" KOKI Television. November 23, 2019. Accessed August 24, 2023. www.fox23.com.

Geier, Thom. "St. Vincent's Annie Clark to Make Directorial Debut with Horror Anthology Film 'XX'". April 12, 2016. Accessed May 3, 2016. www.thewrap.com.

Gibson Gilroy, Laureen. "New Kids on the Block." *Tulsa World*, August 28, 1990. Accessed May 12, 2016. www.tulsaworld.com.

Glionna, John M. "The Beat Goes On: Musician Tries to Begin His Life Again After Debilitating Bicycle Crash." *Los Angeles Times*, January 22, 1995. Accessed July 2, 2014. www.articles.latimes.com.

Goodwin Jr, Ed. "Ray Charles Band Refused Service." Oklahoma Eagle, August 30, 1962. Accessed July 27, 2023. www.oklahomaeagle.com.

Grace, Gordon. "The Year in Oklahoma Music." *Daily Oklahoman*, December 23, 2013. Accessed February 11, 2019. www.newsok.com.

Gwartney, Kirk. "Coming Home: The Woody Guthrie Center Opens in Tulsa." *NPR All Things Considered*, May 20, 2013. Accessed December 29, 2013. www.npr.org.

Hadsall, Joe. "Gypsy Journey: Session with Musical Idol led Ron Radford in Pursuit of Flamenco Music." *Joplin Globe*, January 17, 2014. Accessed July 30, 2014. www.joplinglobe.com.

Haisten, Bill. "Still Fine at 40: Built in 1972, ORU's Mabee Center Remains an Effective Venue Today." *Tulsa World*, December 21, 2012. Accessed November 17, 2014. www.tulsaworld.com.

Hall, Michael. "Trigger: The Life of a Guitar." *Texas Monthly*, December 2012. Accessed February 3, 2015. www.texasmonthly.com.

Harkins, Paighten. "A Spot for OKPOP." *Tulsa World*, December 15, 2016. Accessed December 17, 2016. www.tulsaworld.com.

Haring, Bob. "Large, Lovely and Long Gone." *Tulsa People*, March 2012. Accessed February 24, 2019. www.tulsapeople.com.

Hawkinson, Tamara Logsdon. "'The Poster Boy of Rock." *This Land*, May 26, 2012. Accessed February 13, 2019. www.thislandpress.com.

Hart, Sarah. "'Star' Quality: Dance Team to Perform on Star Search April 9 in Los Angeles." *Tulsa World*, March 29, 2003. Accessed June 21, 2014. www.tulsaworld.com.

Hodge, Will. "How JD McPherson Blew Up Christmas Album Clichés on New 'Socks'" *Rolling Stone*, December 3, 2018. Accessed February 13, 2019. www.rollingstone.com.

Hunt, Steve. "Rising Country Musician Kaitlin Butts is a Union Alumna." *Tulsa People*. August 2021 edition. Accessed September 15, 2023. www.tulsapeople.com.

Jackson, Debbie. "Throwback Tulsa: Storms, Hanson – Must Be Mayfest." *Tulsa World*, May 18, 2014. Accessed August 9, 2014. www.tulsaworld.com.

Jones, Preston. "Take Us Back to Tulsa: The Tulsa Sound Part Two." *Oklahoma Today*. August 2020 edition. Accessed April 6, 2023. www.oklahomatoday.com.

Kauffman, Gil. "Lana Del Rey Gets Last, Biggest Word With Billboard in Ex's Hometown Promoting Upcoming Album." Billboard. December 22, 2022. Accessed November 17, 2023. www.billboard.com.

Kinder, Kevin. "Tribute and Benefit Planned to Remember the Life of Joseph Israel." *Fayetteville Flyer*, April 12, 2018. Accessed February 22, 2019. www.fayettevilleflyer.com

Kreps, Daniel. "Nobel Prize Member Calls Bob Dylan's Silence 'Impolite and Arrogant." *Rolling Stone*, October 22, 2016. Accessed October 23, 2016. www.rollingstone.com.

Kuykendall, Lindsey Neal. "Take Me Back to Tulsa. *"Tulsa People*, September 2013. www.tulsapeople.com. Accessed July 18, 2014.

Lauter, Jesse. "Rolling Away the Stone: A Tribute to the Majesty of Leon Russell." *Relix Magazine*, November 16, 2016. www.relix.com. Accessed December 3, 2016.

Lester, Terrell. "On the Street." *Tulsa World*, January 18, 1998. www.tulsaworld.com. Accessed November 24, 2016.

Little, Tonya. "What Is Red Dirt Music Anyway? (Part One: A History and The Farm)." *The History of Red Dirt,* May 2, 2017. www.littleokieland.com. Accessed February 27, 2019.

Logsdon, Guy. "Guthrie, Leon Jerry "Jack."" *The Encyclopedia of Oklahoma History and Culture.* May 31, 2009. Accessed September 28, 2023. www.okhistory.org.

McDonnell, Brandy. "Charlie Daniels and Wife Hazel to Celebrate 50th Wedding Anniversary at Saturday's Oklahoma State Fair Show." *Daily Oklahoman,* September 19, 2014. Accessed January 18, 2015. www.newsok.com.

Middleton, Nicole Marshall. "What Is Tulsa's Center of the Universe?" *Tulsa World,* July 23, 2014. Accessed August 5, 2014. www.tulsaworld.com.

Milam, Cathy. "Bob Dylan" *Tulsa World,* October 31, 1991. Accessed May 19, 2016. www.tulsaworld.com.

Montague, Joe. "Marcella Detroit Interview" *Riveting Riffs Magazine,* October 4, 2017. Accessed July 10, 2023. www.rivetingriffs.com.

Moser, John J. "Singer Ivy Levan Tells Those Who Try to Categorize Her: 'Kiss My Biscuit.'" *The Morning Call,* July 1, 2015. Accessed July 13, 2023. www.mcall.com.

Nunn, Jerry. "Ivy Levan Talks 'Biscuit', Bisexuality.'" *Windy City Times,* August 11, 2015. Accessed July 13, 2023. www.windycitytimes.com.

O'Connell, Madeleine. "Elle King Exposes the New Meaning of 'Tulsa' in Latest Release" *Country Now,* January 8, 2023. Accessed July 12, 2023. www.countrynow.com.

Phillips, Faith. "Bob Dylan Sets Brady Ablaze" *Tulsa World,* October 26, 2009. Accessed May 13, 2016. www.tulsaworld.com.

Shade, Damion. "Paying Homage." *Tulsa Voice*, December 8, 2017. Accessed February 28, 2019. www.tulsavoice.com.

Shade, Karen. "Bringing Back the Big 10'" *Tulsa World*, August 17, 2008. Accessed February 2, 2019. www.tulsaworld.com.

Sherrow, Rita. "Bixby Singer Shares Stories from 'Voice.'" *Tulsa World*, March 5, 2015. Accessed March 9, 2015. www.tulsaworld.com.

Sherrow, Rita. "Tulsa-Born Musician Joins 'Voice.'" *Tulsa World*, March 11, 2015. Accessed March 14, 2015. www.tulsaworld.com.

Sisario, Ben. "Bob Dylan's Secret Archive.'" *New York Times*, March 2, 2016. Accessed March 4, 2016. www.nytimes.com.

Sisario, Ben. "Bob Dylan Wins Nobel Prize, Redefining Boundaries of Literature.'" *New York Times*, October 13, 2016. Accessed October 20, 2016. www.nytimes.com.

Smith, Michael. "29 Memorable Words: Ayn Robbins is Tulsa's Knockout Songwriter for the 'Rocky' Movies." *Tulsa World*, November 30, 2018. Accessed January 27, 2019. www.tulsaworld.com.

Spangler, Todd. "Garth Brooks Inks Exclusive Streaming Deal with Amazon Music." *Variety*, October 19, 2016. Accessed October 22, 2016. www.variety.com.

Stanley, Tim. "Longtime Tulsa Musician Made Rock 'N' Roll History: Buddy Bruce 1930-2014." *Tulsa World*, August 13, 2014. Accessed September 14, 2014. www.tulsaworld.com.

Stanley, Tim. "Rites Held for Guy Logsdon, Former TU Library Director, Woody Guthrie Scholar." *Tulsa World*, February 15, 2018. Accessed February 13, 2019. www.tulsaworld.com.

Stanley, Tim. "New TIF District to Fund Infrastructure for Broken Arrow Amphitheater Project." *Tulsa World*, January 20, 2024. Accessed January 21, 2024. www.tulsaworld.com.

Sullivan, James. "Longtime Eric Clapton Band Member Dick Sims Dies." *Rolling Stone*, December 12, 2011. Accessed July 5, 2014. www.rollingstone.com.

Thomas, Nick. "The Music Never Ends for Broadway Actress Susan Watson." *The Spectrum*, March 2, 2017. Accessed January 31, 2019. www.thespectrum.com.

Thompson, Tichi. "Ryan Tedder Talks OneRepublic and Why He's Leaning Into TV and Movies" Forbes, January 13, 2019. Accessed February 23, 2019. www.forbes.com.

Tramel, Jimmie. "Charlie Wilson of The Gap Band to be Honored with Star on Hollywood Walk of Fame.'" *Tulsa World*, January 25, 2024. Accessed January 25, 2024. www.tulsaworld.com.

Tramel, Jimmie. "Live Nation Selected as Operator of Planned Broken Arrow Amphitheater.'" *Tulsa World*, January 25, 2024. Accessed January 25, 2024. www.tulsaworld.com.

Tramel, Jimmie. "Robert Plant, Alison Krauss Concert Among Centennial Shows Announced at Cain's Ballroom.'" *Tulsa World*, January 24, 2024. Accessed January 24, 2024. www.tulsaworld.com.

Tramel, Jimmie. "Tulsa Music Artist Dwight Twilley Dies." *Tulsa World*, October 18, 2023. Accessed October 19, 2023. www.tulsaworld.com.

Tramel, Jimmie. "Surging Country Music Artist Corey Kent Draws Attention to Bixby, Tulsa." *Tulsa World*, April 9, 2023. Accessed July 1, 2023. www.tulsaworld.com.

Tramel, Jimmie. "Album is Next Chapter of Tulsan Casey Van Beek's Storied Life in Music." *Tulsa World*, March 15, 2020. Accessed July 19, 2023. www.tulsaworld.com.

Tramel, Jimmie. "Tulsa's Bob Dylan Center Expected to Open in 2021." *Tulsa World*, July 26, 2019. Accessed July 29, 2019. www.tulsaworld.com.

Tramel, Jimmie. "Fresh Breeze: Posthumous JJ Cale Album Showcases Previously Unreleased Material." *Tulsa World*, February 24, 2019. Accessed February 25, 2019. www.tulsaworld.com.

Tramel, Jimmie. "Batter Up." *Tulsa World*, September 12, 2018. Accessed February 22, 2019. www.tulsaworld.com.

Tramel, Jimmie. "Hometown Favorite: Five Reasons to Root for Tulsa's Natalie Brady on 'The Voice.'" *Tulsa World*, October 15, 2018. Accessed February 10, 2019. www.tulsaworld.com.

Tramel, Jimmie. "LANY's Paul Klein Talks About Tulsa Roots Before Brady Show." *Tulsa World*, May 10, 2018. Accessed February 15, 2019. www.tulsaworld.com.

Tramel, Jimmie. "Jack White (he said he has a home here) Explains Why He Loves Tulsa." *Tulsa World*, August 10, 2018. Accessed February 22, 2019. www.tulsaworld.com.

Tramel, Jimmie. "Musical Genius: Tommy Allsup's Storied Career Went Far Beyond His Part in 'The Day the Music Died.'" *Tulsa World*, January 8, 2017. Accessed January 9, 2017. www.tulsaworld.com.

Tramel, Jimmie. "Austin Allsup Eliminated on 'The Voice'." *Tulsa World*, December 2, 2016. Accessed December 4, 2016. www.tulsaworld.com.

Tramel, Jimmie. "Archie Goodwin Worthy of Hall of Fame Honor." *Tulsa World*, March 23, 2015. Accessed March 26, 2015. www.tulsaworld.com.

Triplett, Gene. "Rock Comic Hosts State Visit Calmer." *Daily Oklahoman*, February 21, 2003. Accessed November 21, 2023. www.oklahoman.com.

Twitchell, Allen. "Area Hit Right Note with Mantooth." *Garden City Telegram*, March 1, 1999. Accessed November 27, 2016. www.frankmantooth.com.

Watson, Julie Wenger, "'Like Deftones Meets Miles Davis': Tulsa's Tori Ruffin Gets Freaky." *NPR Music*, May 5, 2021, Accessed August 2, 2023. www.npr.org.

Watts, James D. Jr., "Mayfest Back on Track for 50th Anniversary Arts Festival Under TU's Leadership." *Tulsa World*, February 2, 2023, Accessed July 2, 2023. www.tulsaworld.com.

Watts, James D. Jr., "Tony Award-Winning Oklahomans making *Oklahoma!* Come to Life." *Tulsa World*, June 10, 2019, Accessed July 5, 2019. www.tulsaworld.com.

Watts, James D. Jr., "Brady Theater to Change Its Name to Tulsa Theater Next Year." *Tulsa World*, December 6, 2018, Accessed February 10, 2019. www.tulsaworld.com.

Watts, James D. Jr., "Teresa Miller Ready to Turn a New Page." *Tulsa World*, May 17, 2015, Accessed May 19, 2015. www.tulsaworld.com.

Watts, James D. Jr., "Frank Sinatra Review." *Tulsa World*, March 25, 1994, Accessed May 28, 2023. www.tulsaworld.com.

Wilson, John S. "Lee Wiley Dead, Jazz Singer 60." *New York Times*, December 12, 1975. Accessed February 12, 2019. www.nytimes.com.

Wofford, Jerry. "Doolittle: Doing a Lot with Life. "*Tulsa World*, December 24, 2013. Accessed January 1, 2014. www.tulsaworld.com.

Wofford, Jerry. "Tulsa's Blues Roots Explored Ahead of Blues Challenge, Festivals." *Tulsa World*, August 13, 2014. Accessed August 15, 2014. www.tulsaworld.com.

Wofford, Jerry. "Tulsa Musician Steve Pryor Dies After Motorcycle Crash." *Tulsa World*, May 8, 2016. Accessed May 12, 2016. www.tulsaworld.com.

Wofford, Jerry. "Broken Arrow Native Maye Thomas Says 'The Voice' Run is a Dream Come True." *Tulsa World*, October 8, 2016. Accessed October 10, 2016. www.tulsaworld.com.

Wofford, Jerry. "Illuminating Woody's Life." *Tulsa World*, October 19, 2016. Accessed October 21, 2016. www.tulsaworld.com.

Wong, Joe. "Catching Up With…John Convertino." *Modern Drummer Magazine*, December 2015. Accessed January 29, 2019. www.moderndrummer.com.

Wooley, John. "Going Back to T-Town: A New Book Explores a History-Making Oklahoma Bandleader." *Oklahoma Magazine*, June 1, 2023. Accessed July 29, 2023. www.okmag.com.

Wooley, John. "Tulsa Sound Musician Jim Karstein Dies." *Tulsa World*, May 8, 2022. Accessed April 6, 2023. www.tulsaworld.com.

Wooley, John. "A Punk Music History." *Oklahoma Magazine*, July 19, 2018. Accessed February 13, 2019. www.okmag.com.

Wooley, John. "Rock of Ages: Birth of the Beat." *Tulsa World*, December 28, 2003. Accessed July 5, 2014. www.tulsaworld.com.

Wooley, John. "Back Where He Belongs." *Tulsa World*, June 15, 2005. Accessed November 27, 2016. www.tulsaworld.com.

Wooley, John. "Gordon Shryock: Grammy Winner Is Home to Stay." *Tulsa World*, February 26, 1989. Accessed February 16, 2019. www.tulsaworld.com.

World Scene Writers. "Words and Music." *Tulsa World*, April 24, 2005. Accessed June 30, 2015. www.tulsaworld.com.

Zylstra, Sarah Eekhoff. "After Cancer Resurrects Career, Christian Music Star Cured in Time for Tour." *Christianity Today*, February 14, 2014. Accessed July 26, 2014. www.christianitytoday.com.

"Eric Clapton and Friends Unite to Honor JJ Cale Legacy in New Release." *Eric Clapton.com*. April 30, 2014. Accessed July 5, 2014. www.ericclapton.com.

"When the Count Came to Tulsa." *TulsaGal.net*, March 29, 2010. Accessed April 6, 2014. www.tulsagal.net.

"Hysteria at Elvis's '56 Tulsa Show Like Tossing Christians to Lions." *Elvis Presley History Blog*. Accessed July 29, 2014. www.elvis-history-blog.com.

About the Author

Elven Lindblad is the founder an author of the Books About Tulsa project; a program that describes the people and events that have made Tulsa, Oklahoma one of America's truly unique cities.

Lindblad has over 50 years of professional experience in print and electronic journalism and information research. His services are frequently used by local, national and international sports communication outlets. He skills have also been utilized in such diverse industries as health care services, private education, background screening and financial operations.

Lindblad is a member of the Tulsa Historical Society and lives in Broken Arrow, Oklahoma, which is Tulsa's largest suburb.

Contact the author by email at booksabouttulsa@gmail.com

Also By Elven Lindblad

Tulsa Baseball History: 2024 Edition

Coming Soon
The 2024 A to Z Guide to Tulsa

www.ingramcontent.com/pod-product-compliance
Lightning Source LLC
Chambersburg PA
CBHW072210150726
48002CB00005B/1750